As the Paint Dries

The History of the Art Association of Harrisburg

Carrie Wissler-Thomas
with Michael Barton

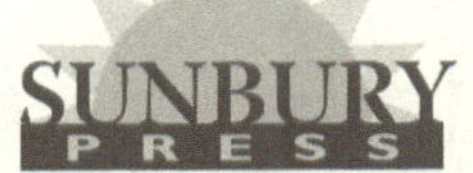

Mechanicsburg, Pennsylvania USA

Published by Sunbury Press, Inc.
Mechanicsburg, Pennsylvania

www.sunburypress.com

For information about special discounts for bulk purchases, please contact Sunbury Press Orders Dept. at (855) 338-8359 or orders@sunburypress.com.

To request one of our authors for speaking engagements or book signings, please contact Sunbury Press Publicity Dept. at publicity@sunburypress.com.

ISBN: 978-1-62006-500-6 (trade paperback)

Library of Congress Control Number: 2014956264

FIRST SUNBURY PRESS PAPERBACK EDITION: February 2020

Product of the United States of America
0 1 1 2 3 5 8 13 21 34 55

Set in Bookman Old Style
Designed by Lawrence Knorr
Cover by Lawrence Knorr
Edited by Michael Barton and Amanda Shrawder

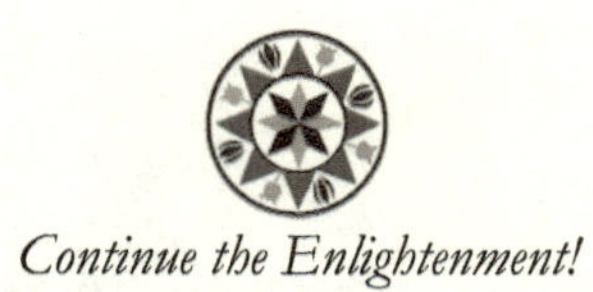

Continue the Enlightenment!

DEDICATION

This history of The Art Association of Harrisburg is dedicated to all the many people who have made this organization what it is today:

The men & women who founded The Art Association in the 1920s

The artists who created The Art Association Studio

Edward C. Michener, who master-minded the merger of the Studio and AAH in 1954

All the artists who have exhibited in AAH shows over the decades

All the dedicated instructors and their enthusiastic students

All the committed Board Members over the past 88 years

Charles Stoup and Richard LeBlanc, who orchestrated the Capital Campaigns to Preserve the Historic Governor Findlay Mansion in 1985 and 2007

Charles Schulz, the first full-time Executive Director, who brought AAH into the Modern Era

All the hardworking AAH staff, past and present, who keep the doors open and the wheels turning daily

Paul Beers, whose generous bequest several years ago made it possible to "Catch Up"

And last but not least, my husband Scott K. Thomas, whose behind-the-scenes support over the past 42 years has enabled me to dedicate myself to the AAH mission.

I ALSO EXTEND A SPECIAL THANK-YOU TO DR. MICHAEL BARTON, MENTOR AND EDITOR OF THIS LABOUR OF LOVE.

Carrie Wissler-Thomas

Table of Contents

INTRODUCTION

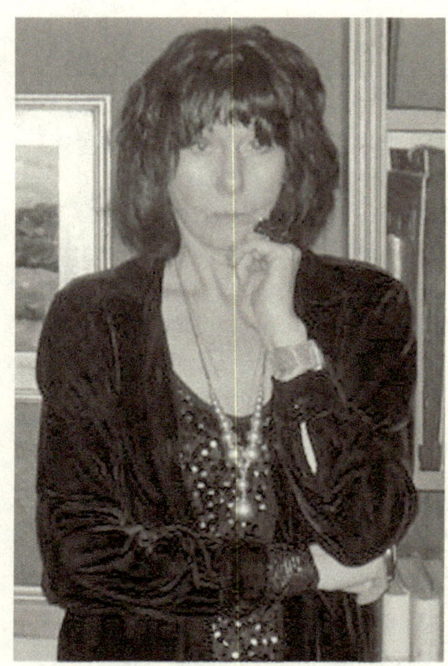
Carrie Wissler-Thomas, AAH President/author

The Art Association of Harrisburg has been a force for cultural excellence in the central Pennsylvania region ever since its founding in 1926. It was the creation of Gertrude Howard Olmsted McCormick and her colleagues, inspired by a lecture by Homer St. Gaudens in 1924 at the Civic Club.

My life became entwined with The Art Association in 1972, shortly after my husband and I moved to Harrisburg the night of our wedding, March 3, 1972. We lived in a one-bedroom apartment in East Park Gardens, and I clearly remember one Sunday morning gazing at *The Patriot News* features section, entranced by all the photos of people in costume, preparing for The Bal Masque. I said to Scott, "Someday I want to be part of that group!" Little did I know that one day I would be in charge of the Bal Masque.

The die was cast when I called AAH to inquire how to join in order to exhibit my paintings. I became an Artist Member, and I began entering my oil paintings into the Membership Exhibitions. The ladies of the Board soon enlisted me as a volunteer to serve tea and punch during the Sunday receptions. Apparently they approved of my tea and punch-pouring skills, and later the President of the Board, Mary McInroy Sheffer, invited me to help with the Bal Masque, soliciting patrons. Although I knew absolutely no one, as a new Harrisburg resident and AAH member, she helped me, and put my name on the Bal committee in the program.

By that time, 1976, my husband, toddler son Dylan, and I were living in a small house in Paxtang. Mary Sheffer very kindly gave my little son and me rides to AAH committee meetings since I didn't have a car then. The Bal theme that year was the USA Bi-

Centennial, and Scott and I attended as characters from Michener's "Centennial." The Board discovered that I was a copywriter as well as an artist, so they invited me to join the governing body as publicity chairman. I've been writing all the press releases ever since. (My having been Editor of the weekly Hood College newspaper gave me a great background, not to mention my being a copywriter at a radio station and doing freelance work.)

The Bal Masque theme in 1977 was "Anything Goes," and I was determined to appear as my historic alter-ego Mary, Queen of Scots. I first met Charles Schulz that summer when I mentioned to his mother at church that I needed someone to create my costume. She put me in touch with Charles, who did indeed create my fabulous 16th-century costume, perfect in every detail. We became fast friends in the process, and I recommended him in 1979 to the Board as the person to hire as the first full-time Executive Director of The Art Association. I was Vice President of the Board in 1979, with artist David F. Lenker as President.

Then in 1980, I was elected President of the AAH Board. With Charles Schulz as my Executive Director, we made history! There had not been regular gallery hours at AAH prior to 1980, since there had only been part-time Studio Directors. Charles engaged the services of individuals from the Federally-funded Senior Employment Agency so that we could have stated gallery hours, with receptionists at the desk. This enabled him to go out to attend meetings, and made the running of the organization far more efficient. The fact that most of the senior employees were less than qualified for office work just made for interesting anecdotes, but that's for another chapter!

Charles made the annual Juried Exhibition international through accepting slide entries instead of the actual artwork, and he and I brought Charles "Li" Hidley onto the AAH faculty, opening the exhibitions to the excitement of Expressionism. We brought a great many artists to the Board, such as Charles Hickok and Bob Bissett. But money was dreadfully tight, and the decision was made to recruit more business people to the Board. Artists on the Board made for exciting exhibitions, but not for bringing in funds. Dr. David Bronstein, Morris Schwab and Charles Stoup all joined the Board, and by the time my fourth term as Board President ended in 1984, things were turning around financially.

Elsie Swenson joined the Board and under her guidance, with advice from decorator Mary Knackstedt, the AAH Sales Gallery was established, with Shari Brandt hired as part-time Sales

Gallery Manager. Charles left as Executive Director in 1985, and Linda Horowitz was hired, with me heavily involved as Exhibitions Chair. Linda left after only a few months, and after a challenging application and interview process, the Board hired me in April 1986, as Executive Director and Sales Gallery Manager, with the two positions combined.

Charlie Stoup was Board Chair when I was hired, and he admonished me sternly, "You'll have to prove yourself with all these businessmen on the Board. They know you were a 'flower girl.'" (He meant "flower child," referring, I suppose, to my having been known as a rather "free spirit" in college and a Vietnam War protestor.) At any rate, the Board eventually changed my official title to "President," and here I remain, still at the helm after 28 years—34 years if one counts from 1980, when I was elected Board President. I am the "bridge" between the Art Association of Mrs. McCormick and Mary Sheffer, and the modern era of today. So it's my task, and pleasure, to compile this history. The Art Association of Harrisburg has touched thousands of lives of art lovers during its 88 years' existence. Hopefully this volume will tell the story of how the organization has evolved and thrived since 1926.

HOW THE ART ASSOCIATION CAME ABOUT: 1921-1926

The minutes of the Harrisburg Civic Club from March 21, 1921, record that Mrs. Mabel Crouse Jones was elected President, with Mrs. William Jennings as one of three vice presidents. In the May 11, 1921, minutes it was noted that Miss Letitia Brady was appointed as head of the "Art" committee. By the October 15, 1921, meeting President Jones had died, and Mrs. Jennings was "in the chair." At the November 21 meeting, the President "reported the personnel of the Art Committee," as follows:

Miss Letitia Brady, Chairman
Mrs. Martha Cox Colt, Vice Chairman
Mrs. Ralph Baker, Secretary
Mrs. William Bailey
Mrs. John Y. Boyd
Mrs. Frank Payne
Mrs. Bailey Brandt
Mrs. James Chamberlain
Mrs. Farley Gannett
Mrs. Frank Robbuur—Steelton
Mrs. W. F.R. Murrie—Hershey
Mrs. John E. Snyder
Mrs. William Penrose Moore
Mrs. Samuel Fleming

All this prominence of the Art Committee in the Civic Club's minutes in 1921 certainly reflects a strong interest among members in the arts. On December 18, Miss Brady, Chairman of the Art Committee, "promised an exhibition of oil paintings early in the New Year," and indeed at the January 16, 1922, meeting she reported that "the exhibit of forty paintings would be ready February 11 and would be at the Club House for three weeks."

At the February 11, 1922, meeting, in the absence of the Chairman, Mrs. Chamberlain "told of the plans of the committee for entertaining the nurses of the city at the Art Exhibit, for free Sunday afternoons, and for free afternoons for school children and the general public, and spoke with regret of the fact that only about fifty club members had attended." Unfortunately, no mention was made of the artists who had created the exhibited oil paintings.

In the minutes of the May 15 "annual social meeting of the Civic Club," Mrs. Marlin Olmsted was listed as the new president of the Club, Mrs. Jennings having announced that she would only serve one term. At the same meeting, Letitia Brady was re-appointed Chairman of the Art Committee. At the February 15, 1923, meeting Miss Brady announced a lecture was to be given by Henry Irvine Bailey on March 27, which would be free to members. At the March 19 meeting she informed members that Mr. Bailey would be speaking on "Citizen ship in the World of the Arts."

At the annual social meeting of the Club on May 21, 1923, Miss Letitia Brady was again appointed Chair of the Art Committee, ditto at the May 18, 1924, meeting.

Unfortunately, the minutes of May 18, 1924, do not mention the imminent visit to Harrisburg of Homer St. Gaudens, son of the famous sculptor Augustus St. Gaudens, which later reports state took place in May. Homer St. Gaudens (1880-1958) was the only child of Augustus and Augusta Homer Saint-Gaudens. After attending Harvard College, he became a writer, art critic, theatrical manager, and after 1921, director of the art museum of the Carnegie Institute.

However, thanks to an article that appeared in *The Patriot* on May 22, 1924, we know exactly what Homer St. Gaudens spoke about at the dinner. On May 21, an article in *The Patriot* told that "HOMER ST.GAUDENS TO ARRIVE TODAY – Mrs. William Elder Bailey of Front and South Streets, to Entertain Director of Art During His Stay." The May 21 article stated that St. Gaudens will "speak on the interest of developing a community art movement, following a dinner, given in his honor at the Civic Club by Mrs. Marlin E. Olmsted, president of the club, and the art committee of the Civic Club."

The May 22 article went into great detail, announcing, "ART ASSOCIATION IS PROPOSED FOR CITY; TO NAME COMMITTEE – Plan Is Endorsed at Dinner Meeting at Civic Club Addressed by Homer St. Gaudens, of Carnegie Institute."

"A committee of seven will be appointed soon by the Civic Club to submit plans for the organization of a Harrisburg Art Association. Mrs. Marlin E. Olmsted, president of the Civic Club, will be a member of the committee, ex-officio. Of the other six members of the committee, three are to be members of the Civic Club, and three of the community at large.

The Patriot, May 22, 1934

ART ASSOCIATION IS PROPOSED FOR CITY; TO NAME COMMITTEE

Plan Is Endorsed at Dinner Meeting at Civic Club Addressed by Homer St. Gaudens, of Carnegie Institute

A committe of seven will be appointed soon by the Civic Club to submit plans for the organization of a Harrisburg Art Association.

Mrs. Marlin E Olmsted, president of the Civic Club, will be a member of the committee, ex-officio. Of the other six members of the committee, three are to be members of the Civic Club, and three of the community at large.

The decision to establish an art association followed a talk given by Homer St. Gaudens, art director of the Carnegie Institute, Pittsburgh, at a dinner at the Civic Club last night.

The project was enthusiastically endorsed by those at the dinner.

Mr. St. Gaudens spoke briefly of the three stages in the life of a nation: the first, when trade and industrial activity predominates; the second, when there is a demand for higher education, and the third, a time of leisure, when there is a well-balanced desire for the higher things of life mingled with the industrial activities.

"Harrisburg is entering upon the third stage, Mr. St. Gaudens said, "we are responsible that the desire for the finer things of life will be put into the heart of the man of the street."

He then suggested in a very sensible, business-like way how this desire might be created: by having exhibits of the really worth while works of arts that almost any museum would be glad to lend upon the assurance that they will be returned safely, by having public lectures by artists of note and by purchasing a few pictures as a nucleus for a permanent art institution.

The large auditorium of the club upstairs, where the dinner was held, and the lounge downstairs were artistically decorated with tulips, iris, dogwood, lilacs and delicate spirea or bridal wreath.

Hosts for the Evening

The tables were arranged in three long rows with the speakers' table forming a cross bar at the head. The flowers mingled with the soft glow of candles formed a charming picture. About eighty-five guests were present.

The hosts for the evening were: Mrs. Marlin E. Olmsted, president of the Civic Club, and the members of the art committee; Miss Letitia G. Brady, chairman; Mrs. James I. Chamberlain, secretary; Mrs. William E. Bailey, Mrs. Farley Gannett, Mrs. Frank A. Robbins, Jr., Mrs. J. W. Parker, Mrs. Lesley McCreath, Mrs. D. Bailey Brandt, Mrs. Lyman D. Gilbert, Mrs. John Y. Boyd, Mrs. C. Valentine Kirby and Mrs. Guy Colt.

Mrs. William E. Bailey was chairman of the decorating committee.

Those who attended the dinner were: Mrs. Marlin E. Olmsted, Mr. and Mrs. William Elder Bailey, Mrs. Gifford Pinchot, Mr. and Mrs. Farley Gannett, Mr. and Mrs. Lesley McCreath, Mrs. Bailey Brandt, Dr. C. Valentine Kirby, Mrs. Francis N. Maxfield, Dr. and Mrs. William E. Wright, Mr. and Mrs. William Jennings, Miss Fanny Eby, Bishop and Mrs. James Henry Darlington, Mr. and Mrs. E. Z. Wallower, Mrs. Herman Astrich, Mr. and Mrs. John E. Fox, Miss Letitia G. Brady, Miss Anna Brady, Mrs. James I. Chamberlain, Mrs. Harvey Smith, Dr. and Mrs. Charles A. Miner, Miss Caroline Pearson, Miss Mary Pearson, Vance C. McCormick, Dr. John J. Moffitt, Mr. and Mrs. J. Horace McFarland, Mrs. Edwin S. Herman, Dr. and Mrs. C. H. Garwood, Miss Mary Jennings, Dr. and Mrs. F. E. Downes, Dr. and Mrs. Carson Coover, Mr. and Mrs. Walter E. Severance, Mr. and Mrs. Walter Spofford, Miss Anne U. Wert, Mrs. Henry Gross, Miss Rachel Pollock, Mr. and Mrs. A. H. Stackpole, Miss Minna McLeod Beck, Mrs. Guy Colt, Miss Sara Wierman, Mr. and Mrs. Paul Johnston, Dr. George Becht, Daniel C. Herr, Mr. and Mrs. V. Hummel Berghaus, Jr., Mrs. Douglas Ramsay, Miss Sue Seiler, Mrs. George Kunkel, Miss Helen Wallace, Mr. and Mrs. William Pearson, Mr. and Mrs. Herbert Thomas, Dr. and Mrs. C. Waldo Cherry, Mr. and Mrs. Berne Evans, Miss Alice R. Eaton, Mr. and Mrs. Ralph Baker, Mr. and Mrs. R. Gillispie, Miss MacDonald, Miss Nancy Etter, Mrs. John Oenslager, Miss Annette Bailey and Miss Dorothy Cox.

"The decision to establish an art association followed a talk given by Homer St. Gaudens, art director of the Carnegie Institute, Pittsburgh, at a dinner at the Civic Club last night. The project was enthusiastically endorsed by those at the dinner. Mr. St. Gaudens spoke briefly of the three stages in the life of a nation: the first, when trade and industrial activity predominates; the second, when there is a demand for higher education, and the third, a time of leisure, when there is a well-balanced desire for the higher things of life mingled with the industrial activities.

'Harrisburg is entering upon the third stage,' Mr. St. Gaudens said. 'We are responsible that the desire for the finer things of life will be put into the heart of the man of

The Patriot
Nov. 14, 1924

ART ASSOCIATION PLANNED AT DINNER

Mrs. Olmsted Will Name Committee on Constitution to Be Adopted for Organization Here

The members of the Art Association committee of Harrisburg met last evening at a dinner given by Mrs. Marlin E. Olmsted, chairman of the committee, at her home, 105 North Front street, and discussed informally the formation of a permanent organization.

Everyone was very enthusiastic about putting the organization upon a permanent basis. The constitutions and by-laws of five other art associations were gone over in the discussions to help get a nucleus for the association to be organized in Harrisburg.

Mrs. Olmsted was empowered to appoint a committee upon a constitution for the Art Association of Harrisburg. They will meet again in the near future when the constitution will be voted upon and officers elected.

the street.' He then suggested, in a very sensible, business-like way, how this desire might be created: by having exhibits of the really worthwhile works of arts that almost any museum would be glad to lend upon the assurance that they will be returned safely, by having public lectures by artists of note, and by purchasing a few pictures as a nucleus for a permanent art institution.

"The large auditorium of the club upstairs, where the dinner was held, and the lounge downstairs were artistically decorated with tulips, iris, dogwood, lilacs and delicate spirea or bridal wreath."

The article went on for several more lengthy paragraphs, describing how the tables were arranged, who the evening's hosts were, and then the names of all the 85 guests in attendance.

In an article in *The Patriot* on November 14, 1924, the headline stated, "ART ASSOCIATION PLANNED AT DINNER," with the subtitle "Mrs. Olmsted Will Name Committee on Constitution to Be Adopted for Organization Here." The article read, "The members of the Art Association committee of Harrisburg met last evening at a dinner given by Mrs. Marlin E. Olmsted, chairman of the committee, at her home, 105 North Front Street, and discussed informally the formation of a permanent organization.

"Everyone was very enthusiastic about putting the organization upon a permanent basis. The constitutions and by-laws of five other art associations were gone over in the discussions to help get a nucleus for the association to be organized in Harrisburg.

"Mrs. Olmsted was empowered to appoint a committee upon a constitution for the Art Association of Harrisburg, They will meet again in the near future when the constitution will be voted upon and the officers elected."

Subsequently, at the November 17 meeting of the Civic Club, Mrs. McCreath, of the Art Committee, reported on "the visit of Mr. Homer St. Gaudens, in May. His helpful talk on Art and its practical application to the life of a community brought about the appointment of an Art Committee, with Mrs. Olmsted as temporary chairman. The name of the Art Institute of Harrisburg was decided upon and the legal end of drafting a constitution was placed in the hands of Mr. A. Carson Stamm."

In an article in *The Patriot* on December 30, 1924, the title stated, "ART COMMITTEE WILL HOLD MEETING TODAY."

The article read, "The Art Association Committee will meet at the home of Mrs. Marlin E. Olmsted, 105 North Front Street, today at 4:30 o'clock. Homer St. Gaudens, art director of Carnegie Institute, of Pittsburgh, who spoke at the dinner at the Civic Club last May when the association was organized, will attend the meeting this afternoon.

"The charter and by-laws of the association will be discussed. The committee is: Paul Johnston, Vance C. McCormick, Miss Mary Pearson, Mrs. John Y. Boyd, J. Horace McFarland, E. J. Stackpole, Jr., Frank A. Robbins, Jr., C. Valentine Kirby, Mrs. John W. Reily, Mrs. Marlin E. Olmsted, Judge John E. Fox, Mrs. Lyman D. Gilbert, E. Z. Wallower, Mrs. William E. Bailey, Miss Letitia Brady, A. Carson Stamm, Mrs. Lesley McCreath, Mrs. James I. Chamberlain, Dr. John J. Moffitt and Miss Caroline Weiss."

Then on December 31, 1924, *The Patriot* ran another article, indicating how important the news of an art association's founding was to the community. "ART ASSOCIATION IS FORMED

HERE... By-Laws Are Approved by Committee and Application Will Be Made for Charter for Organization."

The article stated, "At a meeting of the committee of the Art Association, at the home of Mrs. Marlin E. Olmsted, yesterday afternoon, the Art Association of Harrisburg was formed.

"The by-laws and charter as prepared by A. Carson Stamm and Paul Johnston were read in sections, approved and accepted. Mr. Stamm, the chairman of the committee for the charter, and Mr. Johnston were authorized to apply for the charter.

"Homer St. Gaudens, art director of the Carnegie Institute, of Pittsburgh, who spoke at the dinner at the Civic Club last May when the association was first organized, was present at the meeting yesterday and made several suggestions.

"After the charter is received, officers will be elected, until then the temporary committee, of which Mrs. Olmsted is chairman, will remain in charge."

The above-listed committee members were acknowledged in closing.

In the Civic Club's minutes from the March 16, 1925, meeting, Mrs. Olmsted was not present, and Mrs. Harvey Smith, First Vice President, chaired the meeting. In the slate of officers presented for election at the upcoming April meeting, Mrs. Smith was named as the nominee for President. One can only assume that Mrs. Olmsted was otherwise occupied with the founding of the fledgling Art Association, and with her marriage to Vance McCormick. At the April 20, 1925, annual meeting of the Civic Club she appears in the minutes as Mrs. Vance C. McCormick, new Chairman of the club's Municipal Department.

Apparently Mrs. McCormick did give what she called an annual report "valedictory in nature" at the April 20 meeting. She told the club, "My report for this year is in the nature of a valedictory, since after three years of the most interesting work I have ever done I am passing again into the ranks, and giving over the office which you entrusted to me into most capable hands. Your new President and many of the nominees have worked with me over all the problems that have come up during these three years and I feel the greatest confidence in turning over the Club to them; and I beg for the whole ticket the same loyal support you have given me, and you will be rewarded by seeing the Club go ahead in usefulness and interest.

"I have to report during the year several items of new work. You will all remember our little houses furnished and planted through the cooperation of all departments and visited by hundreds of people in Better Homes Week in May; and during the same month the Art Committee's dinner to Mr. Homer St. Gaudens to discuss the formation of an Art Association for Harrisburg. In the Fall there were more meetings of this committee, one of which Mr. St. Gaudens attended and gave the most valuable advice. The Art Association is in process of being legally started under an able committee of men and women."

Mrs. McCormick closed with stating, "Again I want to express to you my grateful thanks for your delightfully friendly spirit, and your unfailing good humour and patience with my strange parliamentary methods. It has been one of the greatest pleasures of my life to serve as your president."

The next mention of The Art Association in the Civic Club minutes appeared on January 18, 1926, when "Mrs. Chamberlain announced that the Art Association of Harrisburg which had its beginning in the Civic Club several years ago is now a chartered organization. It expects to bring an exhibit to Harrisburg, of a collection of paintings by Sir John Lavery. The collection, forty six in number, consists of portraits, interiors and landscapes; and will be free to the public."

Indeed, the *Evening News* had announced on January 5, 1926, "STATE CHARTER FOR ART BODY." The article continued, "Application made a month ago by the Art Association of Harrisburg for a State charter was granted yesterday by the Dauphin County Court. The association was organized by a number of men and women for the purpose of developing an art center and gallery in the city and with the view to interesting the general public in art and to giving art instruction to those desiring it.

"The association, under its charter, can create an art gallery, can accept and administer gifts to such an art centre and can sponsor lectures on art. Application for the charter was made by Miss Letitia G. Brady, Mrs. Fay Alger Bailey, Vance C. McCormick, Mrs. Jean Bosler Chamberlain and Paul Johnston. Trustees of the Association are: Miss Brady, Mrs. Bailey, Mr. McCormick, Mrs. Chamberlain, Mr. Johnston, Judge John E. Fox, Mrs. Eleanor Herr Boyd, Mrs. Gabriella C. Gilbert, Henderson Gilbert, Mrs. Belle W. Jennings, E. Valentine Kirby, Mrs. Gertrude McCormick, Henry McCormick, Jr., Mrs. Margaret B. McCreath, J. Horace McFarland, John J. Moffitt, Warwick M. Ogelsby, Miss Mary Pearson, Mrs. Helen Boas Reily, Frank A. Robbins, E. J. Stackpole, Jr., A. C. Stamm, Mrs. Gertrude H. Tracy, E. Z. Wallower, Miss M. Carrie Weiss."

These were all stars in the firmament of 1926 Harrisburg society. Many of their names appeared on the boards of other civic

ART ASSOCIATION ELECTS OFFICERS

Plans Discussed for Exhibitions and Lectures—Committees Will Be Announced Soon

At a meeting of the trustees of the Art Association of Harrisburg yesterday afternoon, Mrs. Vance C. McCormick was elected president.

The other officers are: Vice-presidents, Mrs. William Elder Bailey and J. Horace McFarland; secretary, A. Carson Stamm, and treasurer, Warwick M. Ogelsby.

The meeting was held at the home of Mr. and Mrs. McCormick, 105 North Front street, and was the first since the granting of the charter.

Plans were discussed for exhibitions and lectures. The officers and trustees will meet shortly, the date to be announced by the president, for the appointment of committees.

* * *

organizations and businesses. They were civic-minded people, culturally aware, and founded the Art Association of Harrisburg with the highest principles and aspirations.

Another *Patriot* article from February 4, 1926, said, "ART ASSOCIATION ELECTS OFFICER Plans Discussed for Exhibitions and Lectures – Committees Will Be Announced Soon." The article stated, "At a meeting of the trustees of the Art Association of Harrisburg yesterday afternoon, Mrs. Vance C. McCormick was elected president. The other officers are: Vice-presidents, Mrs. William Elder Bailey and J. Horace McFarland; secretary, A. Carson Stamm, and treasurer, Warwick M. Ogelsby. The meeting was held at the home of Mr. and Mrs. McCormick, 105 North Front Street, and was the first since the granting of the charter. Plans were discussed for exhibitions and lectures. The officers and trustees will meet shortly, the date to be announced by the president, for the appointment of committees."

In the April 19, 1926, minutes Mrs. Chamberlain reported for the Art Committee, in the absence of Miss Brady, the chairman. "She told of the Art Association of Harrisburg, which had its beginning in the Art Committee of the Civic Club when Homer St. Gaudens came to address a group of people. Later an independent organization was formed and chartered. When the Art Association made its bow to Harrisburg, with an exhibit of paintings by Sir John Lavery, free to the public, the Art Committee of the Civic

Club cooperated to make the exhibit a success, and as a contribution to the cause, donated the use of the Assembly Hall."

The Art Association of Harrisburg was up and running, an independent organization determined to fulfill its mission as stated in the Articles of Incorporation on February 3, 1926: "The purpose of this corporation is the encouragement and development of an interest in the arts by establishing and maintaining in the city of Harrisburg a place where public exhibitions of pictures and statuary and other objects of art may be held, by providing lectures and instruction on art in its various branches for the benefit of the people of Harrisburg and vicinity, and by promoting in every appropriate way the study and enjoyment of the arts, and for that purpose, when necessary or convenient, to acquire by purchase, gift, devise or otherwise lands and real property and to construct and maintain building thereon and dispose of the same, to receive and dispose of gifts of bequests of moneys, works of art or other articles of use or value, and to do all things necessary or incident to the above mentioned purpose."

The Art Association was founded by civic and community leaders, not by artists, and these people began to bring in exhibits of world-renown for the edification and enjoyment of the people of Harrisburg, commencing with a stunning collection of oil paintings by Sir John Lavery, which will be discussed in detail in the "Exhibitions" section of this history.

AAH EXHIBITIONS THROUGH THE EARLY YEARS: 1926-1954

FRIDAY, FEBRUARY 26

LAVERY PAINTING EXHIBIT OPEN AT 11 THIS MORNING

Dr. C. Valentine Kirby Describes English Artist as "Primarily a Portrait Painter" in Describing Work at Pre-Viewing

GROUP OF PICTURES VALUED AT $100,000

Host to Be at Civic Club Each Day to Answer Questions—Mrs. Harvey F. Smith to Be in Charge Today

"The paintings of Sir John Lavery have something in them that shows he paints for the love of painting and not because he had to," is the way Dr. C. Valentine Kirby, director of art in the State Department of Education, described the paintings of Sir John in a short talk at the pre-viewing of the Lavery exhibit in the Civic Club last evening.

Sir John is a portrait painter primarily, Doctor Kirby said, and in his interiors and outdoor scenes he usually has a figure which seems to fit into the surroundings exactly and belong there.

"He subordinates all else to the soul of the person in the portrait, and breathes life into his people that is expressive of their character," Doctor Kirby said.

The paintings of Sir John, about fifty in the entire exhibit, were brought here by the Art Association of Harrisburg. Their value approximates $100,000; many of them are valued at $10,000, and not any are less than $1000.

The exhibit will be open to the public this morning at 11 o'clock. Every day during the week until the close of the exhibit, March 7, the club room where the exhibit is being held will be open from 11 a. m. to 1 p. m., and from 2 p. m. to 10.30 p. m. On Sunday it will be open from 2 p. m. to 10.30 p. m.

There will be no charge for admission. A host will be in charge each day to answer questions. Mrs. Harvey F. Smith will be hostess today.

As has been noted in the section of this book on the early origins of The Art Association of Harrisburg, Homer St.Gaudens, director of the Carnegie Institute of Pittsburgh, was instrumental in the creation of the organization. Even after the charter had been accepted and the Articles of Incorporation finalized, Mr. St. Gaudens retained his abiding interest in the wellbeing of AAH. It was he in February of 1926 who arranged for a major show of paintings by Sir John Lavery, R.A., of England, as the first exhibition to be presented under the AAH auspices.

According to an article in *The Patriot* dated February 15, 1926, Harrisburg was chosen instead of Palm Beach as one of the few cities for exhibition of Lavery's paintings. Apparently, the AAH exhibition committee, chaired by Mrs. Lyman Gilbert of 203 N. Front St. had met to discuss the exhibition, with Homer St. Gaudens planning to arrive the next day to confer with the committee on the location for the show. St. Gaudens had planned the exhibition's circuit, with it originally including only Boston, New York, Pittsburgh and Palm Beach. It seems that the "difficulty of transportation has made it impossible to take the collection of paintings to Palm Beach, and Harrisburg was chosen instead."

The article explained that Sir John and Lady Lavery had been spending time in America, traveling with the collection of 46

TO SHOW LAVERY PAINTINGS HERE

Upwards of fifty paintings of Sir John Lavery will be brought to this city by the Art Association of Harrisburg and will be shown about February 24, it was decided at a meeting yesterday afternoon at the home of Mrs. Vance C. McCormick, 105 North Front street.

The collection is regarded on account of its size and quality as one of the most unusual one-man collections ever exhibited in America. It comes to this country under the patronage of Homer St. Gaudens, of Pittsburgh, and is shown only in such large cities as New York, Washington, Pittsburgh and Chicago. The Sir John collection includes portraits of some of the most distinguished personages of the British Isles who have loaned the pictures for exhibition purposes.

Sir John Lavery is a member of the Royal Academies of London, Edinburgh, Dublin, Rome, Milan and Stockholm; of the Society of French Artists, Beaux Arts Society of Paris, Society of Spanish Artists in Madrid and of the Secessions of Berlin, Vienna and Munich. He has been knighted by the King of England, by the King of Italy and by the King of the Belgians, and has been awarded the degree of doctor of laws by Queen's University, Belfast. He is represented by paintings in the permanent collections of thirty-eight public galleries and museums throughout the world.

A selection of a gallery for its exhibition will be made later.

portraits, interiors, and landscapes selected by the artist himself. An *Evening News* article from February 11 had called the paintings one of "the most unusual one-man collections ever exhibited in America." Sir John Lavery was a member of the Royal Academies of London, Edinburgh, Dublin, Rome, Milan and Stockholm; of the Society of French Artists, Beaux Arts Society of Paris, Society of Spanish Artists in Madrid and of the Secessions of Berlin, Vienna and Munich. The article extolled the fact that Lavery had been knighted by the King of England, by the King of Italy and by the King of the Belgians, and had been awarded the degree of doctor of laws by Queen's University, Belfast. At that time, Lavery was represented by paintings in the permanent collections of 38 public galleries and museums throughout the world. Obviously, having this collection come to Harrisburg as the premier exhibition of the new Art Association was a real coup, and a testament to the value Homer St. Gaudens placed on the organization he had worked so diligently to create.

The Patriot and *The Evening News* enthused over the exhibition, running excited articles as the paintings began to arrive. On February 25, 1926, *The Patriot* announced the arrival of two additional paintings and stated that the Lavery exhibit would open at the Civic Club at 11 AM on February 26 for a ten-day run. The two paintings that arrived were "The Silver Dress," a portrait of Lady Curzon, and "The Red Hammock," a portrait of Lady Hazel Lavery reclining in a hammock. The article explained that for each day of the ten days of the exhibition there would be a hostess on duty at the Civic Club to answer questions. The hours each day would be 11 AM to 1 PM, and 2 PM to 10 PM during the week, and 2 PM to 10 PM on Sunday. One hundred and fifty people were expected to attend the pre-showing, with "each trustee of the Art Association given the privilege of inviting 5 guests."

It was noted that the club's lecture room had been transformed into a "real art gallery," with electric light reflectors installed over each painting to "give just the proper amount of light to bring out the rich colourings of the pictures."

On February 26, *The Patriot* noted that Dr. C. Valentine Kirby described Lavery as "primarily a portrait painter" when he spoke about the collection at the show's preview the evening before. The collection of paintings was valued at $100,000, an astonishing sum for 1926. Dr. Kirby explained, "The paintings of Sir John Lavery have something in them that shows he paints for the love of painting and not because he had to. Dr. Valentine was the director of art in the State Department of Education, and had been invited to give his informed comments to the elite group assembled at the Civic Club for the show's "pre-showing." Dr. Valentine further said that in Lavery's interiors and outdoor scenes, the artist almost always included a figure "which seems to fit into the surroundings exactly and belong there."

Dr. Valentine said that Lavery "subordinates all else to the soul of the person in the portrait, and breathes life into his people that is expressive of their character. "

From all the newspaper accounts, the Lavery exhibition was by far the most exciting cultural event to come to Harrisburg within recent memory. It was literally the first visual arts exhibition of international reputation to appear in the city. On February 27, 1926, George T. Maxwell wrote a lengthy review of the show in *The Patriot*, extolling Lavery's "colour mastery" and "versatility" as evidenced in the collection, going into great detail about several of the paintings. There were several portraits of Lady Hazel Lavery and the Viscountess Curzon, as well as two large views of the House of Lords and House of Commons, and one of the Royal Family. Besides the portraits were interior studies, such as "Argyll House," depicting the hall of a large home looking into a flower-filled garden.

Lavery's painting of his wife Hazel gazing out his studio window at the first daylight air raid over London in 1917 was part of the collection on view, along with outdoor studies with figures, such as " The Putting Green, North Berwick."

The March 1, 1926, *The Patriot* announced that 800 visitors had viewed the Lavery show, and on March 2, another article extolled the fact that "The Civic Club this week is the mecca for thousands of art lovers, teachers, educators, seekers-after-knowledge, scoffers and the just plain curious, but the interesting thing about the exhibition is that all who see come away delighted." The Lavery exhibition was a real coup for the fledgling

MARCH 1, 1926

800 VISITORS AT ART EXHIBIT

Showing of Sir John Lavery's Paintings Attracts Many

Over 800 residents of Harrisburg and vicinity have visited the exhibit of Sir John Lavery's paintings at the Civic Club in the first three days of the showing, under the auspices of the Harrisburg Art Association. Of these 500 were registered in the visitor's book yesterday. The exhibit committee has ordered an additional 1,000 copies of the catalog of paintings as the first supply is almost exhausted.

Mrs. John Oenslager, Mrs. Belle Brady Graham and Mrs. Philip T. Meredith are hostesses to-day.

Art Association, in every respect, with the March 10 *Patriot* stating that over 5000 people had attended the show!

Then on February 11, 1927, *The Evening News* announced the startling news that "Lavery Presents 2 of His Paintings as the Nucleus for Art Museum Here." The painter offered two of his paintings to The Art Association, and they were accepted after a special meeting of the board of trustees at the home of then AAH President Vance C. McCormick. The trustees had employed the advice of Frank Jewett Mather, Jr., Director of the Museum of Historic Art at Princeton University, before accepting Lavery's generous offer. This was in accordance with the AAH By-Laws, which stated, "Gifts of objects of art may be accepted only by a two-thirds vote of the entire board of trustees, and upon the approval of a critic recommended by the director of one of the three leading art museums, and chosen by the trustees of this association."

The article explained that the trustees had further complied with the By-Laws by consulting three "well known art experts," namely, Homer St. Gaudens of Carnegie Institute (who had been instrumental in both AAH's founding and the acquisition of the Lavery exhibition of 1926), Mr. Minnegerode, Director of the Corcoran Art Gallery, Washington, and Mr. Whiting, director of the Cleveland Art Museum. It was these three who had recommended Mr. Mather as the expert advisor on "art objects submitted to the association."

Mr. Mather was subsequently "invited to come to Harrisburg to view the two Lavery pictures and give his judgment on their acquisition as a gift for the permanent museum which has been proposed as the goal of the Art Association of Harrisburg." The article went on to state that ever since Sir John Lavery had exhibited for the Art Association in February of 1926, he had "ever since expressed a peculiar and constant interest in the growth of the local association." Lavery "requested the acceptance of his work as a gift from him, making a nucleus for the gallery that is projected for the future."

The paintings were unanimously accepted—"The Viscountess Wimbourne, Wimbourne House, London," and "A Lady in Black" thereby became the first paintings in the Art Association's collection. According to the *Evening News* article, the two paintings would be on view at the coming exhibition of works by great American illustrators, to be held the next week in the lecture room of the Harrisburg Public Library. After the exhibition, the paintings were expected to be shown in the library proper, "pending the acquisition of a permanent art gallery for Harrisburg." (Which did not occur until 1964...)

The exhibition of 51 works by great American illustrators debuted at the Harrisburg Public Library, showcasing works by such luminaries as N. C. Wyeth, Jessie Wilcox Smith, Elizabeth Shippen Green, Maxfield Parrish, Thornton Oakley, and others, according to *The Evening News* of February 19, 1927.

The Art Association had transformed the lecture room of the Library into a gallery, with soft grey walls, electric lights placed to bring out the "beautiful colourings and rich shadings of portrait, landscape, and illustration." The walls were covered with monk's cloth, and benches were placed in the centers of the room for visitors' ease of viewing. This, the second exhibition presented by AAH, was also a resounding success. On February 23, *The Patriot* stated that over 400 school children took advantage of the holiday of Washington's Birthday to visit the exhibition. The children expressed their delight with the illustrations and "one little fellow said wistfully" that he wished "we could have that picture of Robin Hood in our school," referring to the illustration of "Robin Hood and Little John" by Frank E. Schoonover.

There were even children's books on a table in the exhibition, containing many of the illustrations on view on the walls, and the children of a Miss Harrington's school even voted for their favorite pictures. Although Wilcox-Smith's "Heidi" and "Mid-Ocean" by Frederick Waugh received top votes, one little girl voted for Sir John Lavery's "Wimbourne House" as her favorite!

In April 1927, the First Annual Exhibit of Local Artists was presented by the Art Association in the basement gallery of the

Harrisburg Public Library. An April 14 *Patriot* article explained that the Art Association was sponsoring the exhibit as "part of its program of fostering all worthy art effort." The article continued, "It is not to be expected that all the work to be shown by local artists is the direct result of the awakening or reawakening of popular interest in art. This community has many talented artists who have acquired standing in their fields and whose experience has been broad and tested." This April 1927, exhibition was the first of the AAH Juried Exhibitions, now in 2014 in its 86th year. Apparently, there were over 500 applications made by artists who entered the show.

Among the accepted artists who exhibited were many who went on to be important in future AAH activities, including Ira Deen, Walt Huber, Janet Gannett, C. Valentine Kirby, and Martha Cox Colt. In an article in *The Patriot* on April 14, 1927, it was noted that, "The fact that already five hundred applications have been made by exhibitors indicates with delightful surprise the widespread interest in art, some of it unquestionably due to the stimulation which has been given by the Art Association. The exhibit by local artists will be a further stimulation to the community, extending still farther the circle of interest and awakening the love of beautiful things which is latent in every normal human being."

The first fall exhibition presented by AAH was a collection of paintings by Provincetown artist Gerrit A. Beneker, shown once again in the Art Gallery of the Harrisburg Public Library, from October 18 through 24. *Patriot* writer Marian Inglewood wrote on October 19 that a crowd attended the opening of the show, noting that the artist painted "the working world," and made the commonplace beautiful. He found beauty in the mills of the Hydraulic Steel Company in Cleveland, Ohio, portraying both the machines and the men who worked them. On October 20, *The Patriot* reported that 3135 people had attended the Beneker exhibition.

The Beneker exhibition was followed by "The First Exhibit of Bird and Animal Paintings" in the Library, from December 9 through 19. Seventeen artists from places such as Washington, DC, British Columbia, Boston, New Jersey as well as Harrisburg displayed 108 pieces of art. The exhibition was complemented by a lecture on birds by Dr. George Miksch Sutton, State Ornithologist, on December 12. According to *The Patriot's* article on January 4, 1928, the exhibition had been a memorial to artist Louis Agassiz Fuertes, who had been killed in a grade crossing accident the previous summer when his car was struck by a train.

Apparently, Fuertes' paintings had been rescued from his burning car after the tragic accident, and eight bird paintings by him were included in the AAH show in December.

Then, from January 21 through 30, AAH presented a "Loan Exhibition of Paintings, Portraits, Bronzes and Rare Glass and Furniture" at the Assembly Room of the Civic Club of Harrisburg, borrowed from some of the City's leading families. Included were a Corot painting loaned by Mrs. Henry R. McCormick, a William Merritt Chase painting from Mr. Jackson H. Boyd, and two Lavery portraits from Mrs. Vance C. McCormick. There were also two paintings by James McNeill Whistler lent by Mrs. Lyman Gilbert.

From February 13-18, an exhibition of the Art Department of the Harrisburg Public Schools was presented in the Library, followed by a collection of "Winter Subjects" by The Guild of Boston Artists, members of the summer colony at Ogunquite, Maine. The February 24 *Patriot* article explained that the collection was "sent out by the American Federation of Arts, Washington."

The Second Annual Exhibition of Local Artists was presented in the Library in October, filled with familiar scenes of the area by Ira Deen, Jean Sangree Fahrney, Martha Cox Colt, and others. The October 23 *Patriot* article noted that the fine architectural drawings by Gertrude Olmsted Nauman created quite a stir, evincing comments among several admirers that "a woman could draw like that"!

Ira Deen received the first prize in the exhibition—$25. *The Patriot* called Deen "the foremost landscape painter in the city." He had seven entries in the exhibition.

From December 3 to 10, an exhibition of "Modern Art, " loaned by The Dudensing Galleries of New York, was presented in the Library's Art Gallery. Twenty-four artists showed 69 works, including paintings, woodcuts, lithographs, wood engravings and etchings. Prices in the catalogue ranged from $10 to $1000. This first exhibition of "modernist art" apparently elicited varied comments as to "the excellence, the eccentricity or the meaning of the pictures," wrote Sally Harris in the Harrisburg *Telegraph* on December 11. However, she said "all visitors unite in commending the Art Association for its spirit and enterprise in bringing the Dudensing exhibit to Harrisburg."

Then from January 14 through 23, 1929, an exhibition of portrait silhouettes cut by The Baroness Maydell, caricatures in wax modeled by Luis Hidalgo, and a collection of paintings "sent out" by The American Federation of Arts was featured at the

Library's Art Gallery. A total of 68 works comprised the exhibition, which was viewed by 2800 visitors.

This varied show was followed by the Second Annual Exhibition of the Art Department of the Harrisburg Public Schools, January 28 through February 2, 1929. A William Penn student named Reuel Sides was awarded a prize of $10 for his "decorative map of the Spanish Main."

An exhibition of Book and Magazine Illustrations, lent by Curtis Publishing Company, a Collection of Oil Paintings by John J. Dixon, and a Collection of Decorative Illustrations by Henry Pitz were shown in the Library from February 18 through 28.

An impressive international exhibition followed, from May 8-18, showcasing six paintings loaned by the Carnegie Institute of Pittsburgh, paintings by Francois Gos of Switzerland, and prints by Elizabeth Keith of Scotland. Ms. Keith, although Scottish, depicted Chinese, Korean and Philippine subjects in her works. An article in *The Patriot* on May 14 noted that her painting of the gate to a city in Korea was sold from the show.

The Third Annual Exhibition of Works by Local Artists was presented from October 22 through 30, 1929, with 134 works by 46 on view. The familiar names of Walt Huber, Ira Deen and Janet Gannett appear, as does the young student Reuel Sides, who entered a portrait. An "Exhibition of Contemporary American Paintings" followed from November 6-15, loaned by the William MacBeth Galleries of New York, as well as "Water Colour Studies of Far East" by Miss Georgina Yeatman, 62 works in all.

January 10-30, 1930, were the dates for an exhibition of paintings loaned by The Art Centre of New York City, with works by Gordon Mallet McCouch, Anna Neagoe, and Christadora House, 61 total. An editorial appearing in *The Evening News* on January 11, 1930, observed, "The showing in the Public Library gains importance from the fact that under ordinary conditions it could be seen only in New York. It is brought here and presented to the public's view wholly as a service to the arts. That is the Art Association's program, has been from its organization several years ago. The response of the public has been gratifying. The people have evidenced an appreciation that indicates much, especially among the school children in the art classes."

An exhibition of "Handwrought Jewelry and Enamels" by Frank Gardner Hale, watercolours by Helen Van Der Weyden, Prints and etchings from the Philadelphia Print Club, and Watercolours by Deane Keller was presented from February 12 through 17.

Then, a very ambitious "Sculpture-in-the-Open-Air" exhibition was shown in the Civic Club Garden, in cooperation with The State Art Commission, The Park Commission, Berryhill Nursery Company, The Civic Club, and Pennsylvania Power & Light Company. The exhibit was brought to Harrisburg through the Art Alliance of Philadelphia, and consisted of 28 sculptures, one priced as high as $15,000. *The Evening News* proclaimed on June 16, 1930, "Good taste has gone into the exhibits and their arrangement. Under the gleaming sun, the dull gray of an overcast sky or in the ruddy rays of the spotlight, here is a picture worth even a strenuous effort to see. The outdoor statuary exhibit broadens still more the program, which the Art Association is following. It shows art in a new setting. Art indoors is beautiful but so also is art outdoors. That is bound to be the verdict of the public."

Acknowledgments on the back of the exhibition catalogue for their assistance and cooperation were made to J. Horace McFarland Company, Garden Club of Harrisburg, Earl Johnston, Walt Huber, James Lutz, Jr. and Members of Exhibition Committee of Art Association. This impressive collection of outdoor sculptures remained on view June 14 through 23.

The Fourth Annual Exhibition of Works by Local Artists appeared in the Auditorium of the Municipal Building, Walnut and Aberdeen Streets, from October 22 through November 1, with 177 works on view. The familiar names of Martha Cox Colt, Ira Deen, Janet Gannett, and Walt Huber were in the catalogue, along with 53 other artists. For the first time, Nick Ruggieri was mentioned as an exhibiting artist, as well as Alden Turner. (Ralph Cope Wible's name was also included... He died tragically in the 1980's when a small plane crashed into his New Cumberland house.) Walt Huber received the first prize of $20.

The Municipal Building was the site of the next exhibition as well, from December 2 through 12, which consisted of arts and crafts loaned by The American Federation of Arts—"Facsimiles of Water Colours of French Peasant Costumes, with Samples of Paysanne Silks Showing Adaptation, and Water Colours of Soviet Russia." "Mexican Applied Arts, Handmade Pottery-Handmade Jewelry" were loaned by the Art Centre of New York City. "Handwrought Silver and Copper, Weaving – Pottery" were loaned by The Society of Arts and Crafts, Detroit, Michigan. Book-binding was loaned by John F. Grabau of Buffalo, NY, and Handwoven Work was loaned by Mrs. Edward E.Lee of Pittsburgh. It is amazing that collections of this magnitude were procured and shipped here for display, even more so when one realizes the exhibitions were usually of only one week's duration!

From March 7 through 17, an exhibition of "American Paintings" was shown at the Municipal Building, loaned by the American Federation of Arts of Washington, DC. There were 30 works assembled through the cooperation of the Museum of New Mexico, depicting Navajos and other Southwest themes. The remaining pieces in the exhibition of 64 works were by members of the North Shore Arts Association.

An exhibition of "Pan-American Paintings," loaned by the Baltimore Museum of Art, was on view April 13-23 at the Municipal Building with 67 works by artists from Canada, Argentina, Bolivia, Brazil, Costa Rica, Cuba, Ecuador, Guatemala, Paraguay, Uruguay and Peru.

May 1-11, an exhibition of "Old Masters," loaned by Van Dieman Galleries of New York was presented at the Municipal Building, along with the Albertina Collection of Facsimile Drawings by Old Masters loaned by American Federation of Arts of Washington, DC. The Old Masters collection included works from the 15th through the 18th centuries, including reproductions of Hans Holbein's portrait drawings from the court of King Henry VIII. The American Federation of Arts reproductions were from the Italian, Flemish, Dutch, German and French Schools.

On June 8, 1931, *The Evening News* reported that an article had been published the day before in *The Philadelphia Public Ledger*, giving "much credit" to the Art Association of Harrisburg for the development of its annual exhibition, and "to the art committee of the Harrisburg Civic Club, which was largely instrumental in organizing the association." The review had said, "The gospel of art has been preached with such effectiveness in American cities that few towns have not developed either their own museums or their aspirations for such. The latter procedure is now shaping in Harrisburg, where for some years exhibitions have been shown through interest of the Art Committee of the Civic Club, an enthusiastic body that has since developed the Art Association of Harrisburg." The review had outlined the Association's major exhibitions since its founding in 1926, and praised it for its accomplishments, even though the Association "has neither building nor museum of its own."

The Fifth Annual Exhibition of Works by Local Artists transpired at the Municipal Building in late October, Nick Ruggieri's "Greens of Yesterday" eliciting much attention, according to an article by Earl S. Johnston in the October 27 *Evening News*. Then, December 8-18, an "Exhibition of Oil

Paintings and Water Colours," loaned by the American Federation of Arts, as well as a watercolour collection from the Art Alliance of Philadelphia went on view at the Municipal Building. The 168 works were termed the "finest in years," by reviewer Earl S. Johnston in *The Patriot* on December 9.

February 5-15, a loan exhibition of small bronze sculptures, oils and watercolours from Ferargil Galleries, The American Group, and Milch Galleries of New York, was shown in the Municipal Building, along with paintings and textiles by Ruth Reeves, "collected by Art Centre, New York City. There was even a portrait of Sir John Lavery by an artist named Gleb Derujinsky. In all, there were 124 varied works in the show.

Contemporary Italian paintings, loaned by the Baltimore Museum of Art, were shown April 16-26, 1932, again at the Municipal Building's "Art Galleries," followed by "The Native Element in Contemporary American Painting," gathered from all regions of the US and circulated by the American Federation of Arts in Washington, and shown in the Assembly Room of the Civic Club from January 19-29, 1933.

From February 21-28, 1933, The Civic Club was again the site of the exhibition, which consisted of works by Arthur B. Davies and loaned by The American Federation of Arts. The collection, albeit by one artist, included oils, watercolours, drawings, etchings, drypoints, aquatints, lithographs, and... rugs!

April 22-May 1 were the dates for the Sixth Annual Exhibition of Local Talent, also in the Civic Club's Assembly Room, and featuring 105 works in oils, watercolours, pastels, "black and white," and sculpture. Ira Deen, Walt Huber, Alden Turner, Nick Ruggieri, Martha Cox Colt, Janet Gannett and Ralph Wible all were listed in the catalogue as usual, along with many new names.

Another outdoor sculpture exhibition graced the Civic Club Gardens from October 4 through 18, 1933, and June 18-28, 1934, the Seventh Annual Exhibition of Local Talent came to the Civic Club, with 82 works. Edward C. Michener's name appears for the first time, as the first prize-winner with his oil painting titled "Jimmy." A memorial exhibition of Geri Melchers' oils, watercolours, drawings and etchings was presented by AAH at the State Museum.

Also at the State Museum, AAH presented a stunning exhibition of the paintings of the famous Robert Henri in 1936, followed by an impressive show of works by 24 artists "published in the index of 20th century artists." The works were by such artists as George Bellows, Winslow Homer, Edward Hopper,

Augustus St. Gaudens, and James McNeill Whistler, the exhibition being presented by the National College Art Association. Exhibitions continued to be presented at the State Museum for several years, apparently the Civic Club having been outgrown. The annual shows by local artists were also shown in the State Museum.

Famous artists, whose works were shown during the 1940's at the State Museum under AAH auspices, included John Singer Sargent, Mary Cassatt, James McNeill Whistler, and Thomas Eakins. It would seem a daunting task to bring art exhibitions of this calibre to Harrisburg, and some light was shed on that aspect with a series of letters to and from the Philadelphia Museum of Art, dated April and May 1940. On May 1, 1940, Henri Marceau, Assistant Director of the Museum, wrote to Mrs. Frank Payne of the Art Association that he was enclosing a bill "from the Fidelity twentieth Century Storage Warehouse Company in the amount of $56.25, which covers the cost of trucking the pictures we have lent to the Harrisburg Art Association." He also enclosed "the fine arts policy covering the pictures while in transit both ways and while on exhibition, as well as the bill for this in the amount of $82.01."

In the Board meeting minutes of these years, the Treasurers' Reports list the various expenses associated with shipping in museum-calibre exhibitions as well. This indicates the logistics involved in bringing exhibitions of high value to display here in Harrisburg.

Interestingly enough, all the news clippings from these years indicate the public interest was still high in these top-quality exhibitions, with several thousand attendees noted for each. Throughout the 1930's, most of the founders of AAH continued to serve on the Board and to organize the exhibitions. Vance McCormick served as the second President of the organization until his resignation on March 29, 1937, when Mrs. Lesley McCreath was elected to replace him.

During this period, the Studio, founded and run by artists rather than community leaders, was beginning to flourish. At the AAH Annual Meeting on November 7, 1940, Edward Michener of the Studio reported that the Studio was in a "self-sustaining condition with an average attendance of approximately 55 members." He urged members of the Art Association to visit the Studio, and discussion ensued as to how the Studio should be officially named, to avoid confusion with the Art Association itself.

The minutes from 1940 on, however, begin to show a trend: money to bring in museum shows seems to have become scarce for the organization, and the original Board members began to die off. Exhibitions of local artists seem to have become the order of the day. According to the minutes of the annual meeting of November 5, 1942, held in the offices of Vance McCormick, "a long list of resignations was read." It was then moved by Mrs. Gilbert, seconded by Miss Brady, that "we continue the Art Association in a pleasant way without pressing members for dues." Mrs. McCormick then suggested "the Art Association continue even without exhibits, so that a reserve can be built up for the future." This was a startling departure from the heady enthusiasm of the early years with their outstanding exhibitions shipped in from major museums.

The next indication of a shift in status appears in the minutes of the annual meeting from November 4, 1943, in which Mrs. Gilbert reported "the art interest of Harrisburg is dependent upon the Studio group." This was borne out by Ed Michener's report on the success of a Russian exhibit, and that of the "Local Exhibition"—"the finest we have ever had, with 52 exhibitors and scarcely enough room for the entries." At this juncture, the parent organization was continuing to contribute "the usual allotment to the Studio."

At the Trustees meeting on November 1, 1945, Dr. Valentine Kirby said "he eschews Loan Exhibits because of the responsibility and added that he was gratified to see how much really good art belonged to Harrisburg people." It was noted that the next exhibit was "entirely a local one." The minutes also recorded that the AAH Membership Committee was working with the Studio Committee to increase the enrollment, and went on to describe the various classes being offered. The Studio Treasurer reported a balance of $999.77! The two groups were definitely working in tandem at this point, and the exhibitions had morphed into solely local ones.

At the Trustees Meeting on November 7, 1946, President Mrs. McCreath expressed the "deep loss to the Art Association caused by the death of Mr. Vance McCormick, one of the four original incorporators of the Association and a past president." The Trustees entered a tribute to Vance McCormick in the minutes, expressing their "appreciation of his invaluable service."

"Because of his understanding that as a civic development art is of great importance to a community, he gave the Art Association not only generous financial aid but in addition his unfailing interest and his leadership as President."

Then on November 6, 1947, a similar tribute was entered into the record at the death of Dr. Valentine Kirby. The old guard was passing into Valhalla. The minutes recorded that day note that "In the report of the Exhibition Committee, Mr. Michener said that it had not been advisable to look about for new exhibits to present, because of the lack of adequate and suitable space in which to show them."

The loss of Dr. J. Horace McFarland was lamented in a report on November 4, 1948. Then, in the Annual Meeting report from November 3, 1949, President Mrs. Lyman Gilbert "called attention to the fact that the Association is now twenty-five years old, that it has had a history of bringing beautiful and important exhibitions to Harrisburg but that at present the emphasis is on encouraging the work of local artists and the art studio." The report from the November 2, 1950, Trustees meeting applauded the annual exhibition of local artists, which had been held at the YWCA, and an Outdoor Exhibition held in Capitol Park in October.

At the Annual Meeting on November 6, 1952, all officers agreed to re-election "for one more year, or until a re-organization could be studied and a report submitted at the 1953 annual meeting." More discussion ensued concerning re-organization, and the President Mrs. William Earnest named Ed Michener as "chairman of a committee to study a re-organization plan and present the findings in a report to be considered and acted upon at a future meeting." The scene was being set for the merger of the Studio and the parent organization.

On November 12, 1953, the Annual Meeting was held at the home of President Earnest, 3101 North Front Street. The minutes state, "It was one of the most important meetings in the history of the Association dealing principally with a plan for re-organization." At the meeting, the President tendered her resignation and the meeting was turned over to Ed Michener, who then submitted his report on re-organization. The committee members who had formulated the plan for the consolidation of the Art Association and the Art Association Studio were Russell Charles, E. Z. Wallower, Mrs. L. A. Burkholder, Wilbur Nisley, Nick Ruggieri, Richard Walker, and Mrs. Richard Boyd.

The committee proposed that "in view of the fact that the Charter issued by the Commonwealth of Pennsylvania to the Art Association, was broad enough to encompass all activities in the field of art that might be engaged in by either of the two existing art organizations, that the structure of the Association be retained, and that the Studio as a separate entity by dissolved. It was further proposed that in compliance with the expressed desire of many of the present Board members, including the Secretary, to retire from active participation in the Association, that they be designated as 'Honorary Trustees' in recognition of their service in time, thought, effort and money which they have rendered over the past number of years."

This plan was accepted unanimously by the Board, and a new Board of Trustees was elected, including Charles, Wallower, Nisley, Burkholder, Ruggieri, Mrs. Richard Walker, Ed Michener, Dr. Samuel Fluke, Walt Huber, Mrs. Robert Miller, E. A. Town, Dr. David Johnston, John Stapf, James Johnson, Harley Swift, Frank Foose, Jr., William Ludwig, Dr. Ralph Stone, Ephriam Brenner, Harold Buchter, William Jones, Edwin Green, Mrs. John Cowden, Mrs. Farley Gannett, and Franklin Moore. The era of the civic leaders at the helm had ended, and the local artists were now in charge.

The minutes went on to state that the above-mentioned duly-elected Trustees were instructed to elect a smaller number of "Directors" at a subsequent meeting, and that "the actual management of the organization will be vested in this Board of Directors, who will in turn elect their own officers." Ed Michener was named President Pro Tem until the Directors would have chosen their active officers for the new Association.

At the Trustees Meeting of February 5, 1954, held at the Penn Harris Hotel, rather than at a president's Front Street residence, Ed Michener explained that the purpose of the re-organized Board "is to bring the Studio and the Art Association together as a working unit." New by-laws were presented, and the new organization's officers were elected: Nick Ruggieri as President, Michener as Vice President, Mrs. Burkholder as Treasurer, and Mrs. Walker as Secretary.

An era had ended. Exhibitions to be presented by the new organization would reflect the change.

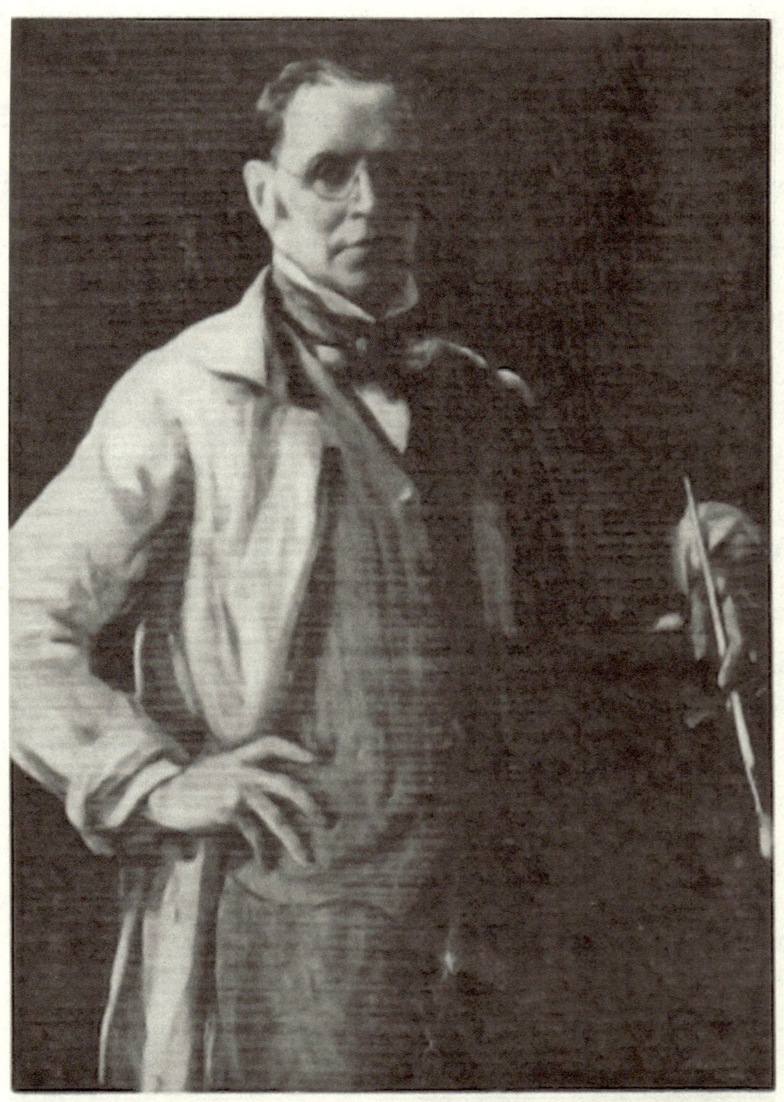

Sir John Lavery, painter

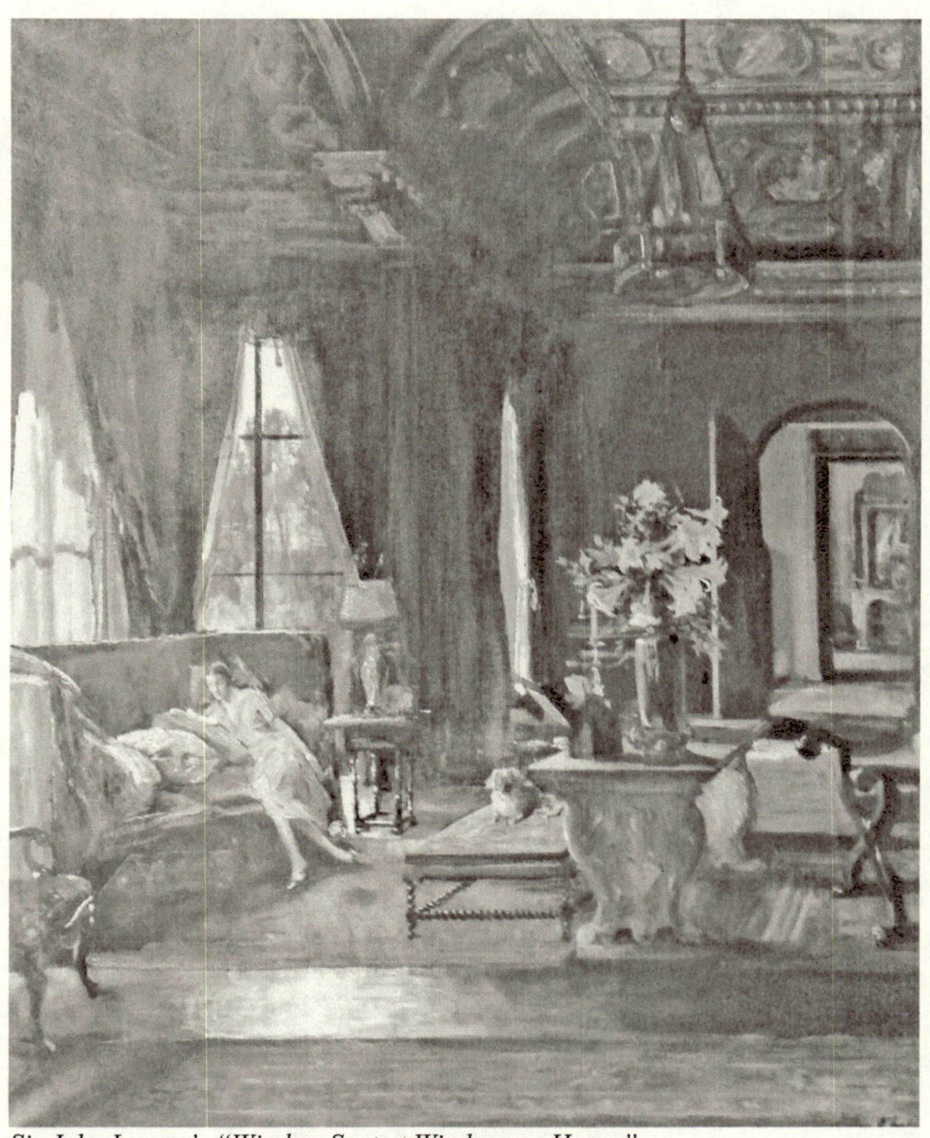

Sir John Lavery's "Window Seat at Wimbourne House"

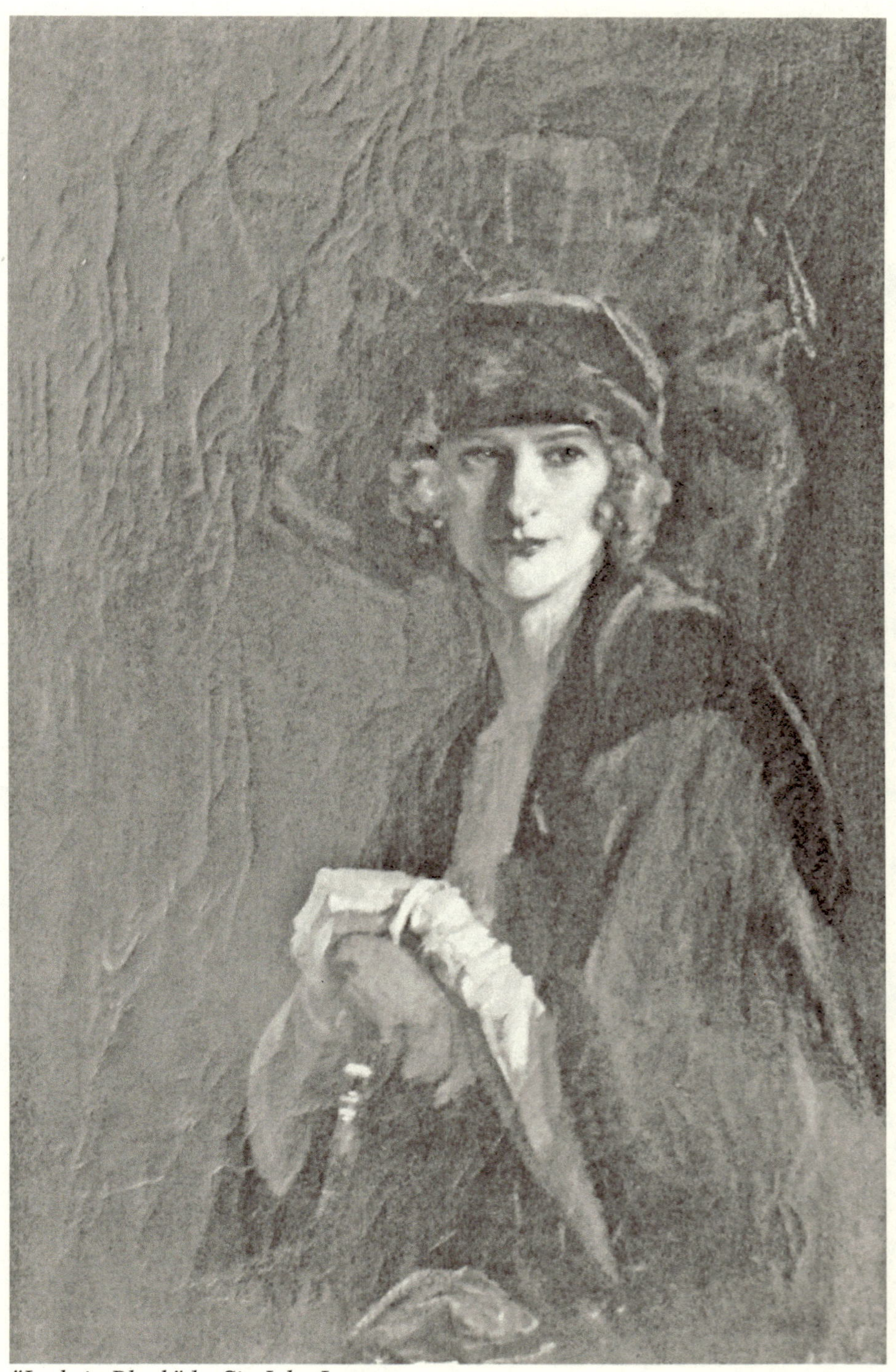

"Lady in Black" by Sir John Lavery

.TRIOT, HARRISBURG, PENNA., THURSDAY, JANUARY 17, 1929

EVENTS OF CITY

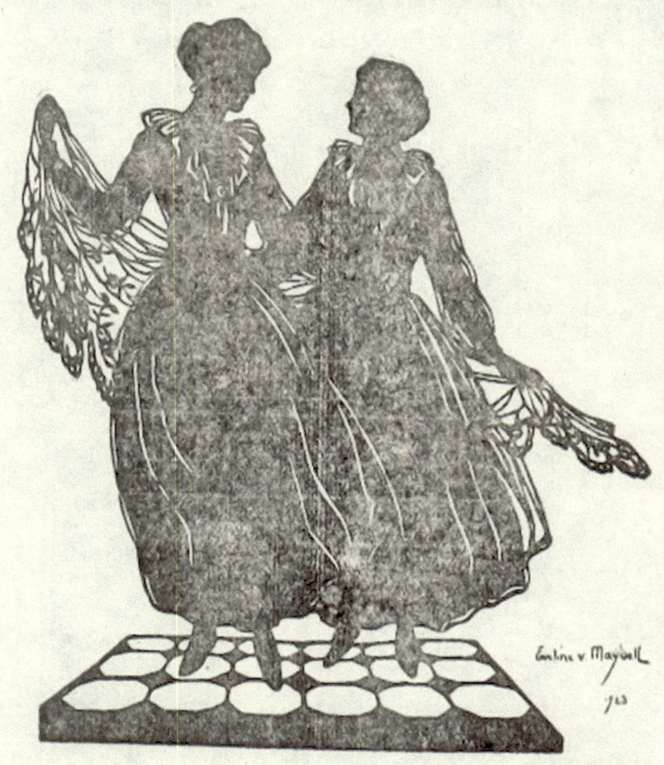

"TWO SISTERS"

This silhouette cut is one of a group by Baroness Maydell on exhibition at the Harrisburg Public Library as a part of the exhibit presented by the Art Association of Harrisburg.

SILHOUETTES IN EXHIBIT POPULAR

"Two Sisters" by Eveline Maybell, silhouette, 1929

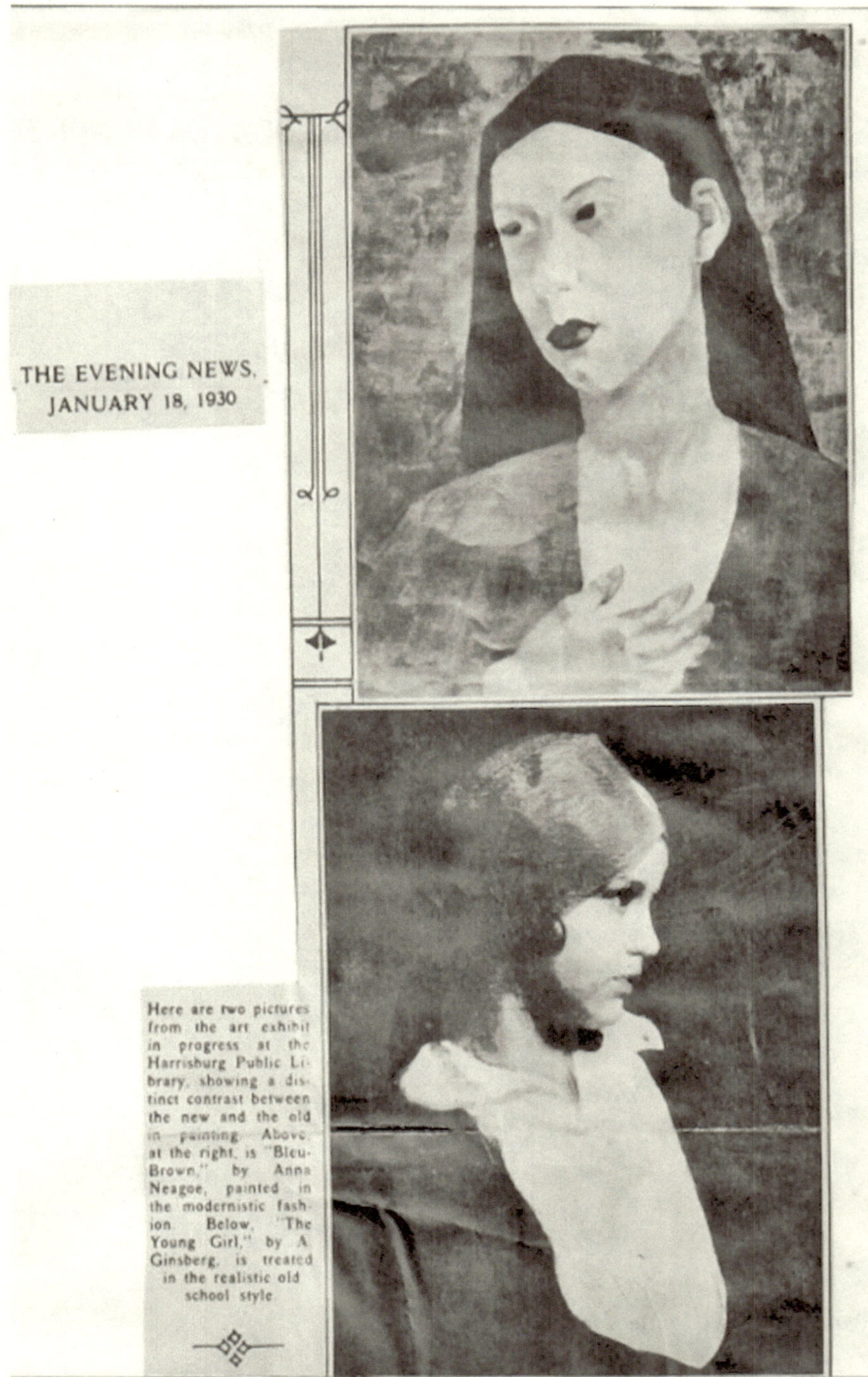

THE EVENING NEWS,
JANUARY 18, 1930

Here are two pictures from the art exhibit in progress at the Harrisburg Public Library, showing a distinct contrast between the new and the old in painting. Above, at the right, is "Bleu-Brown," by Anna Neagoe, painted in the modernistic fashion. Below, "The Young Girl," by A. Ginsberg, is treated in the realistic old school style

1930 clipping of two contrasting portraits

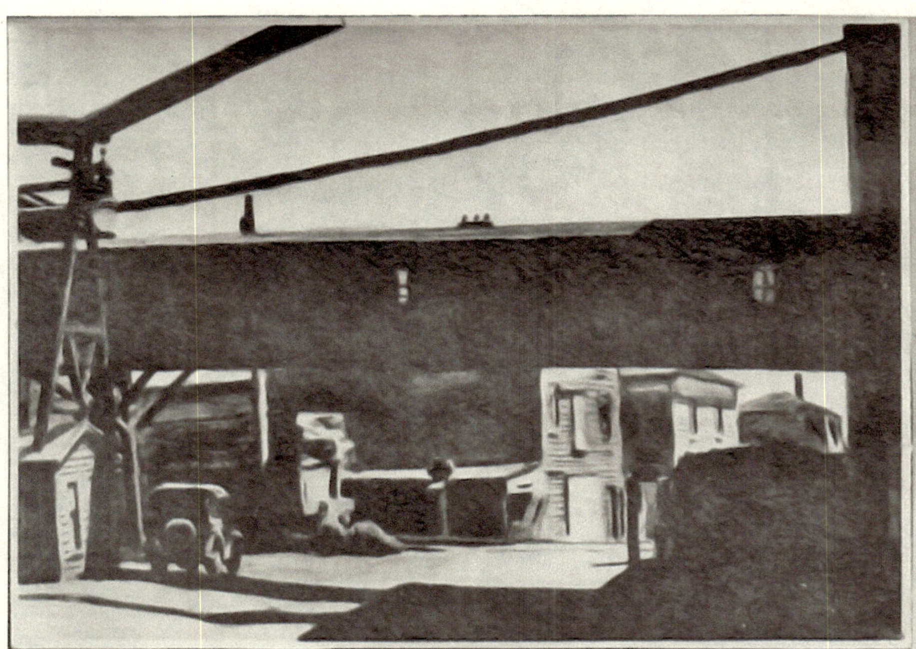

"Box Factory, Gloucester, 1928," from the New York Museum of Modern Art, is by Edward Hopper, born in 1882. His works are characterized by rich toned color and lines with an emphasized architectonic note.

Clipping of "Box Factory" painting by Edward Hopper

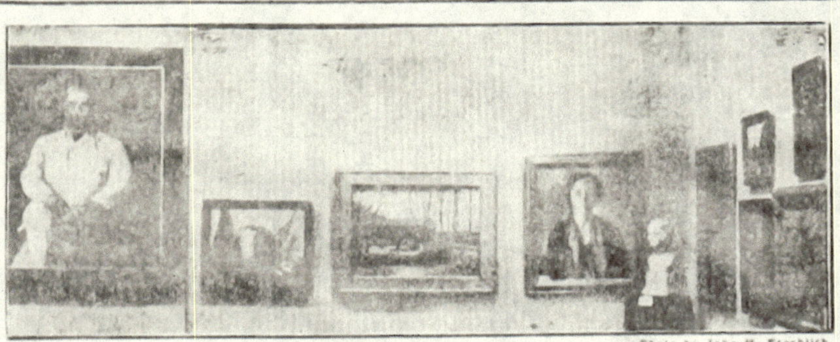

THE PATRIOT, HARRISBURG, PENNA., FRIDAY, APRIL 29, 1927

L NEWS OF CAPITAL CITY

—Photo by John H. Froehlich

CORNER IN THE ART EXHIBIT

A group of oil paintings and one of the busts, all work of local artists, being exhibited in the gallery of the Public Library. The gallery is open from 9 a. m. to 9 p. m.

Clipping of 1927 first show by local artists

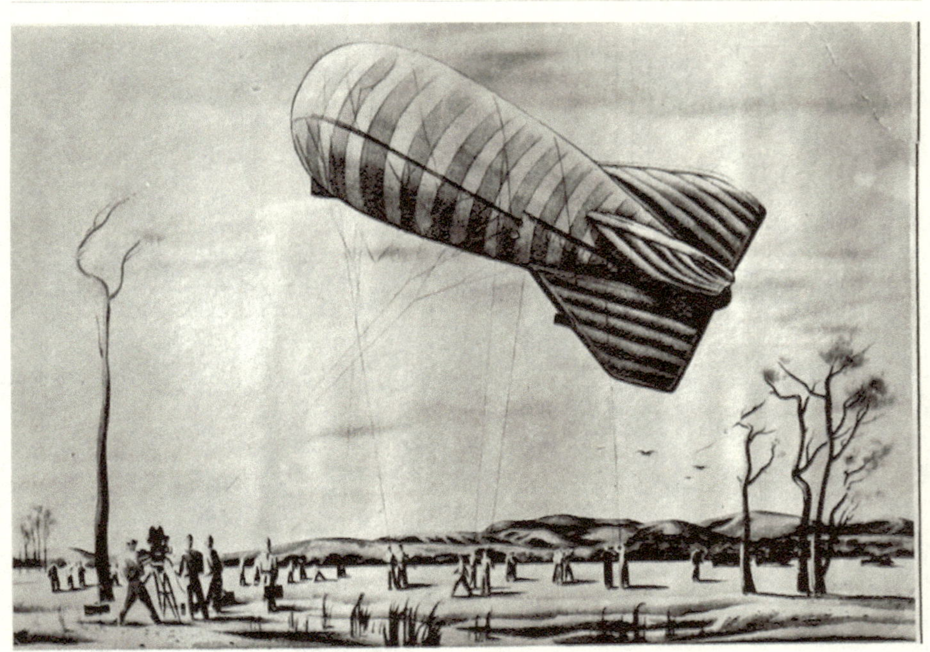

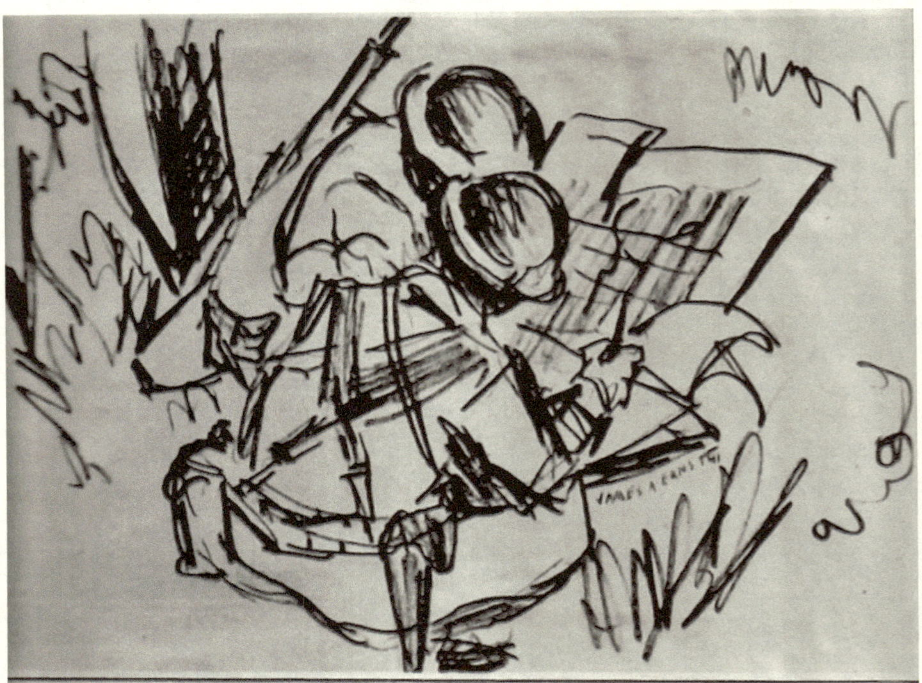

Clippings of "Soldier Art Exhibit"

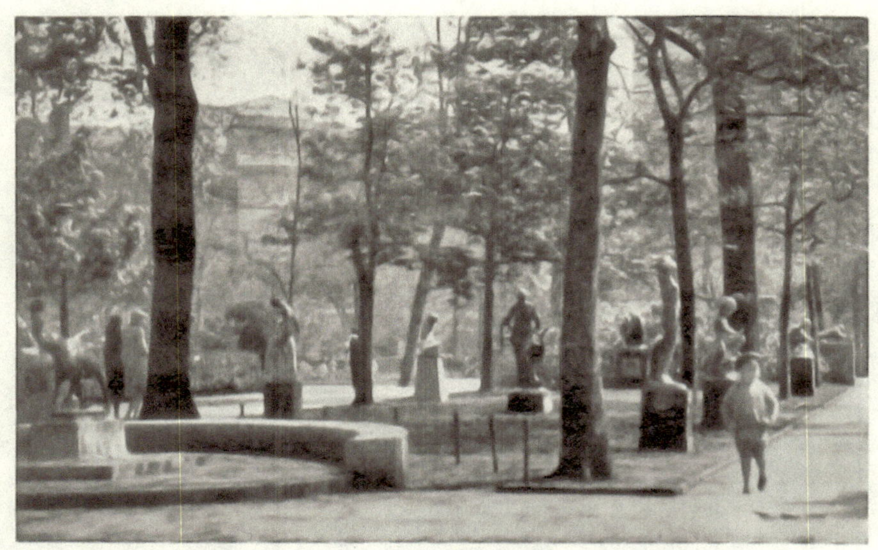

Exhibit of Sculpture-in-the-open-air, June 14-23, 1930

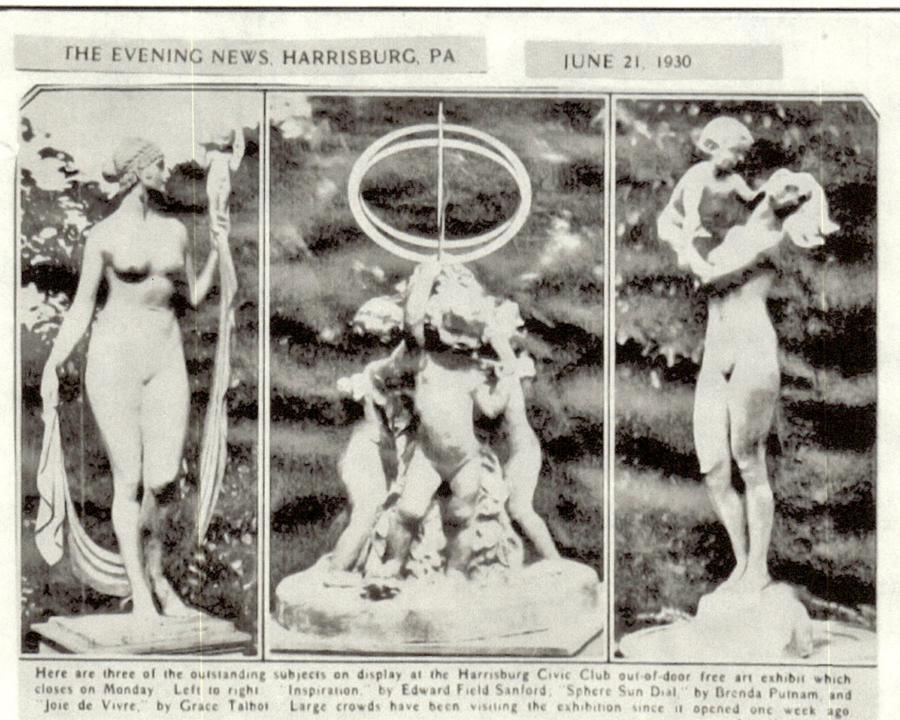

THE EVENING NEWS, HARRISBURG, PA

JUNE 21, 1930

Here are three of the outstanding subjects on display at the Harrisburg Civic Club out-of-door free art exhibit which closes on Monday. Left to right: "Inspiration," by Edward Field Sanford; "Sphere Sun Dial," by Brenda Putnam, and "Joie de Vivre," by Grace Talbot. Large crowds have been visiting the exhibition since it opened one week ago.

Clipping of Civic Club outdoor sculpture show

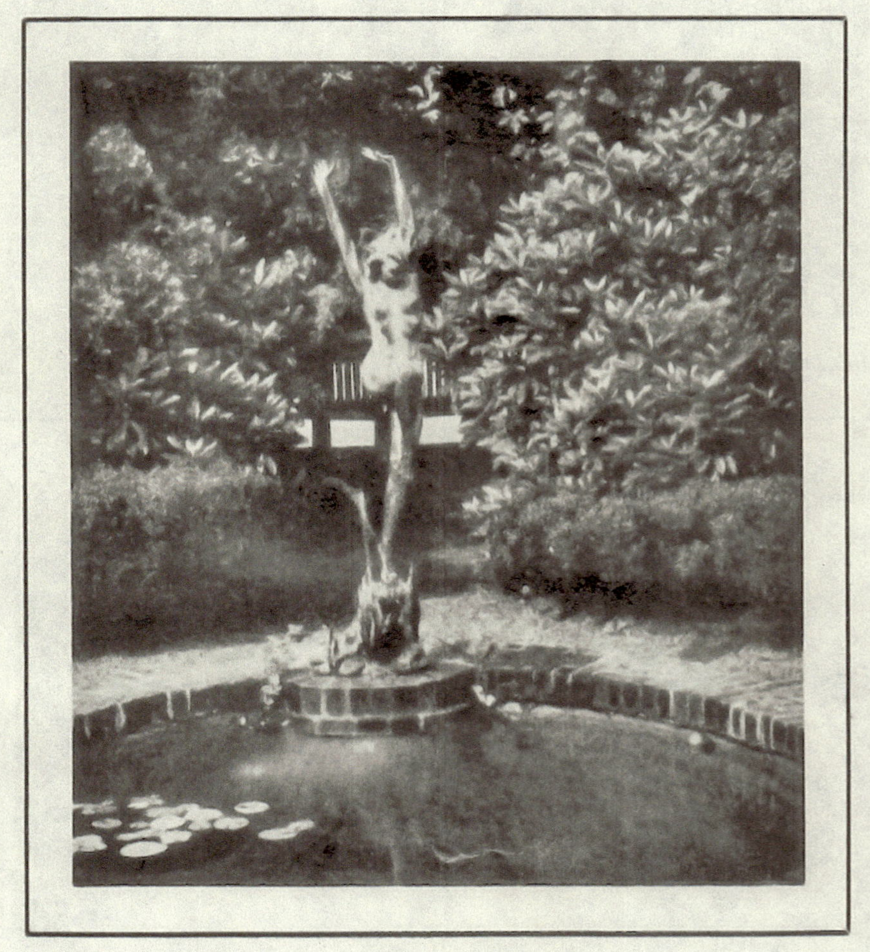

Exhibit of Sculpture-in-the-open-air

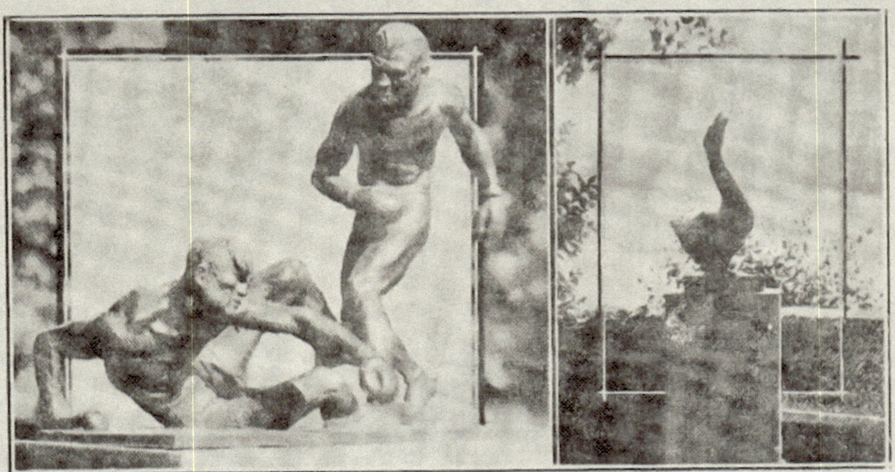

Harrisburg Morning Telegraph, Wednesday, October 4, 1933.

Statues Shown in Civic Club Gardens

The exhibition of sculpture which opened today in the gardens of the Civic Club is the first of the fall and winter events scheduled by the Harrisburg Art Association. The exhibition is open to the public and will continue till October 18.

At the left is "The Knockdown" by Mahonri Young, and at the right, we see "The Goose" by Robert Laurent, silhouetted against the Susquehanna River and the hills beyond.

Statues in Civic Cub Garden Exhibit

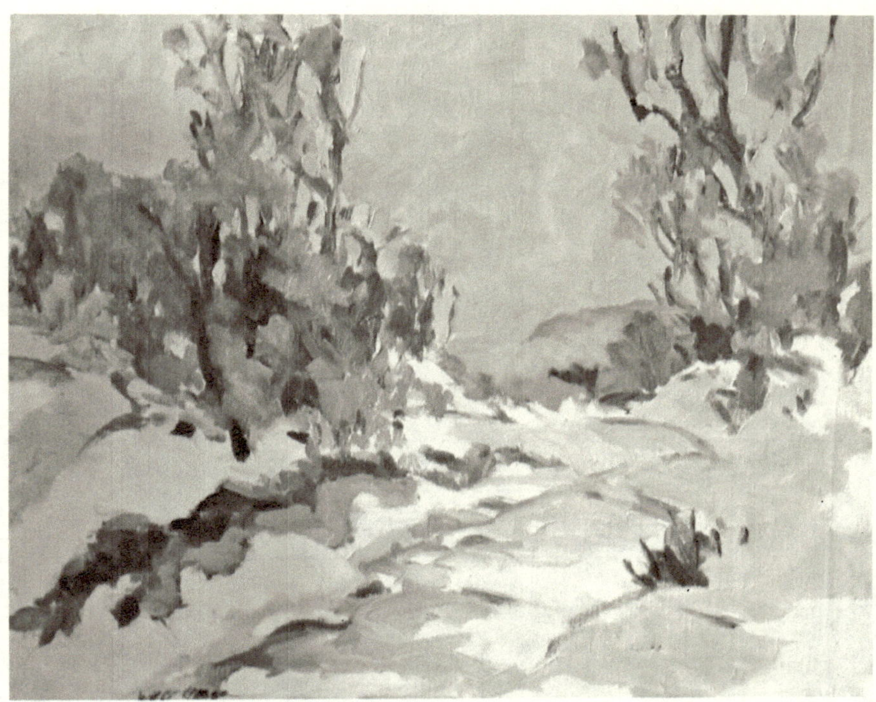

"Early Snow" painting by Walt Huber

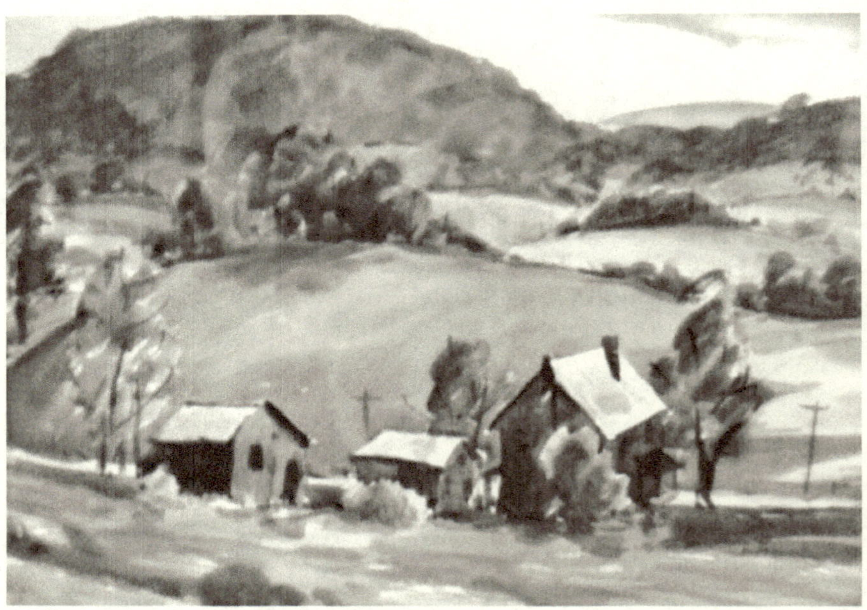

"Effie's Place" painting by Alden Turner

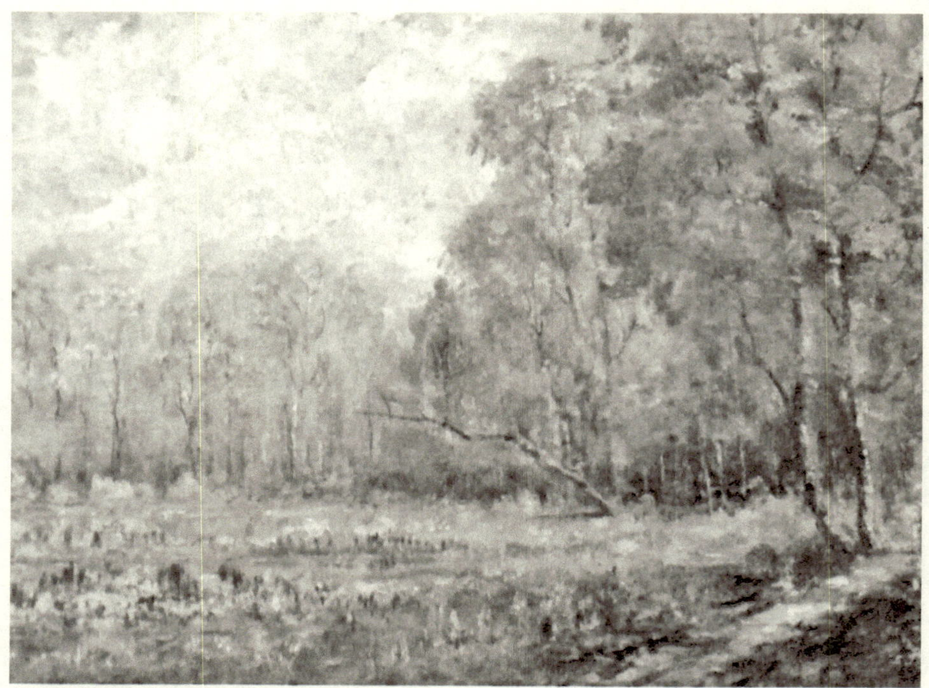

"Fall Scene" by Ira Deen

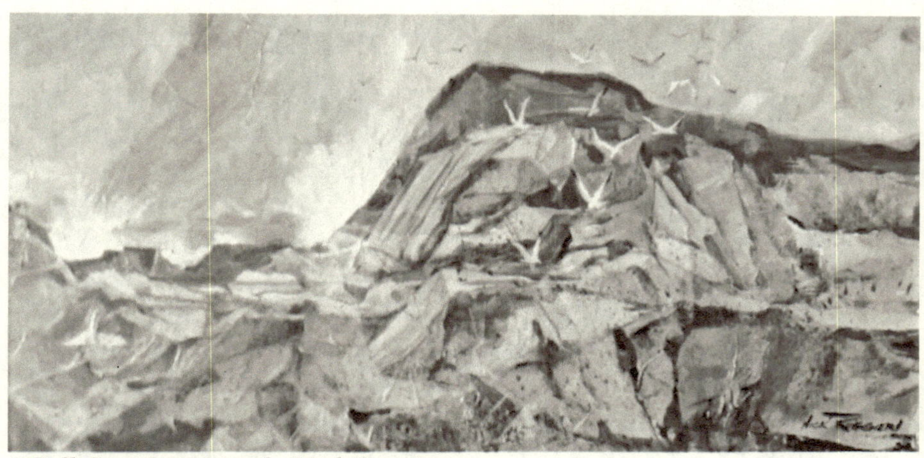

"Gull Cove" painting by Nick Ruggieri

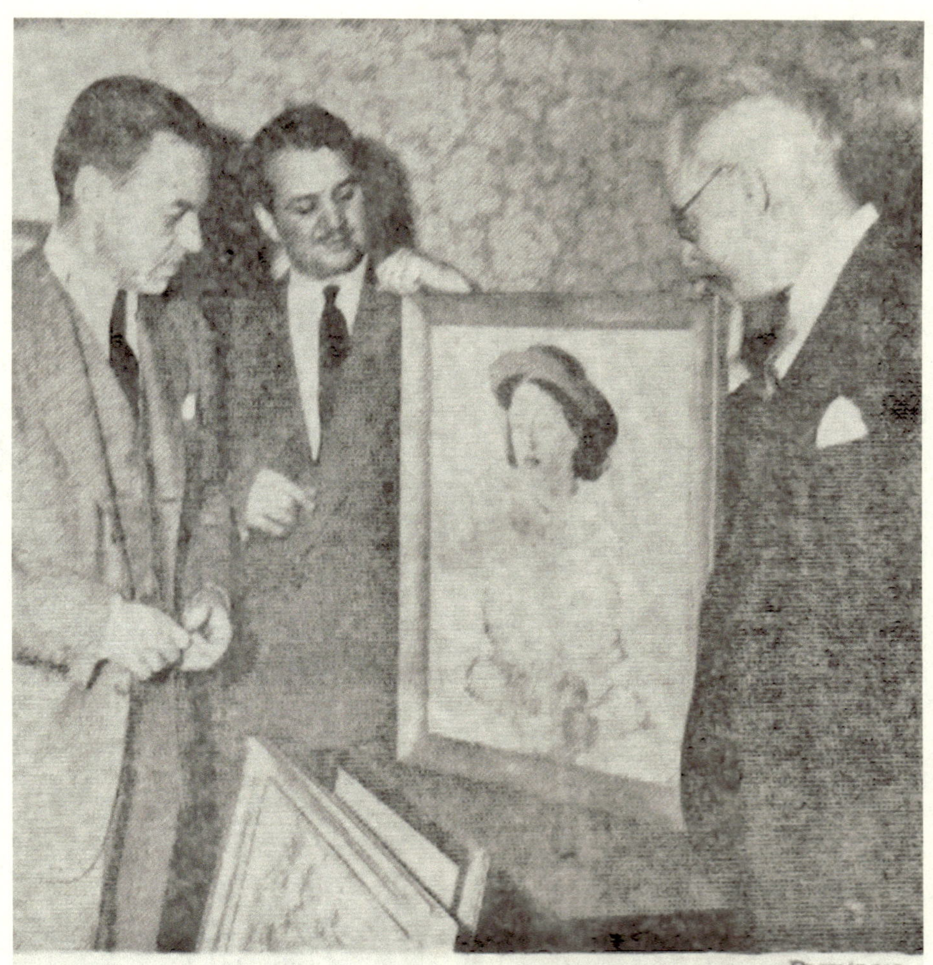

—Ensminger.

Judges are shown examining the painting which received third prize in the 20th annual local art exhibit sponsored by the Harrisburg Art Association. The show opened last night in the McCormick Annex of the Harrisburg Public Library, Front and Walnut streets. The oil is called "Margaret" and is the work of Mary Mowrey of Camp Hill. The judges, from left to right, are: Blanchard Gummo, director of the art department at Bucknell University; Dr. John Richard Craft, director of the Washington County Museum of Fine Arts, Hagerstown, Md.; and Dr. Earle L. Poole, director of the Reading Public Museum and Art Gallery.

Judges selecting painting of local artists, 1948

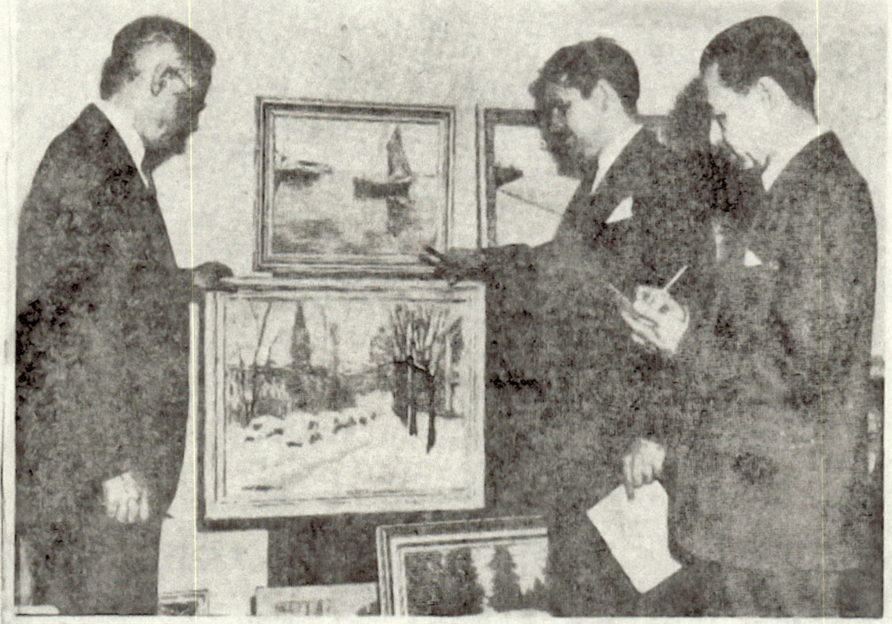

10—THE EVENING NEWS, Harrisburg, Pa., Friday, February 20, 1948

Judges Select Winners in Art Exhibit

Judges are shown while selecting winners at the 20th annual local art exhibit of the Harrisburg Art Association at the Harrisburg Public Library Annex, the McCormick home, Front and North streets. Winners will be announced at a preview of the exhibit tonight at 8 o'clock. The exhibition of more than 100 entries will be open to the public beginning tomorrow at 1 p. m. and continuing through Sunday, February 29. The judges, left to right, are: Dr. Earle L. Poole, director of the Reading Public Museum and Art Gallery; Dr. John Richard Craft, director of the Washington County Museum of Fine Arts, Hagerstown, Md., and Blanchard Gummo, director of the art department at Bucknell University.

Judges selecting the winning pic of a local artist, 1948

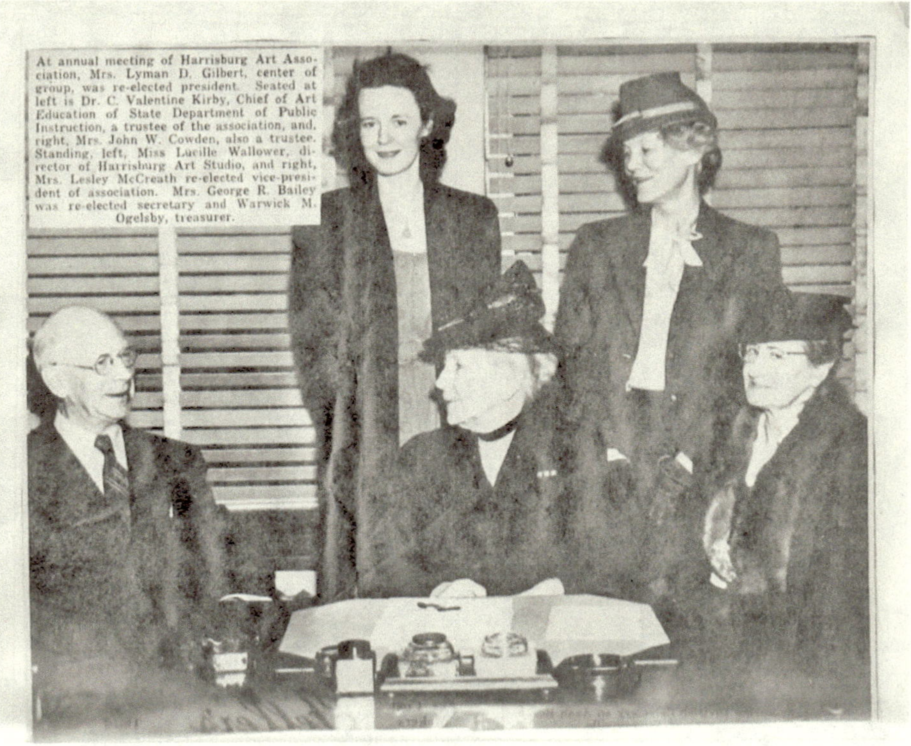

At annual meeting of Harrisburg Art Association, Mrs. Lyman D. Gilbert, center of group, was re-elected president. Seated at left is Dr. C. Valentine Kirby, Chief of Art Education of State Department of Public Instruction, a trustee of the association, and, right, Mrs. John W. Cowden, also a trustee. Standing, left, Miss Lucille Wallower, director of Harrisburg Art Studio, and right, Mrs. Lesley McCreath re-elected vice-president of association. Mrs. George R. Bailey was re-elected secretary and Warwick M. Ogelsby, treasurer.

1944 Art Association Members

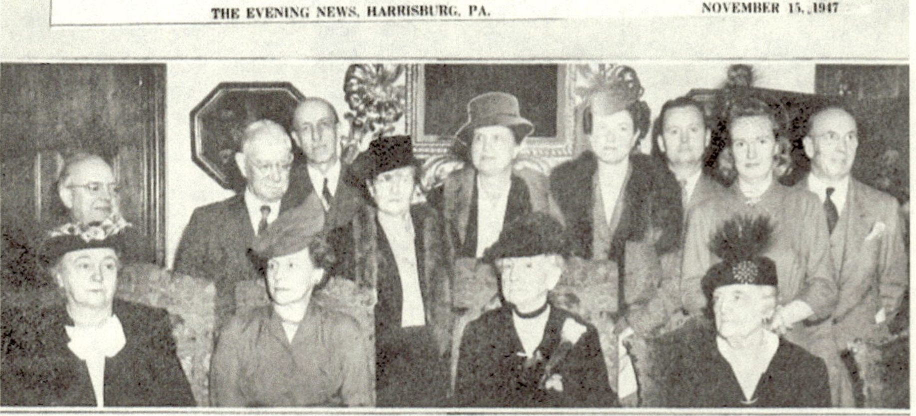
THE EVENING NEWS, HARRISBURG, PA. NOVEMBER 15, 1947

This group picture of officers and trustees was taken at the annual meeting of the Art Association of Harrisburg at which it was decided to appoint a committee in the near future to study the practicability of establishing a permanent home for the association. All those shown in the picture are members of the board of trustees. Left to right, seated are: Mrs. William H. Earnest, Mrs. Frank M. Masters, Mrs. Lyman D. Gilbert, who was re-elected president of the association, and Miss Letitia G. Brady. Standing: Walt Huber, Dr. J. Horace McFarland, David R. Shotwell, Mrs. John W. Cowden, Mrs. L. A. Burkholder, Mrs. Henry B. Gilbert, Edward C. Michener, Mrs. Daniel Hastings Hickok and Edgar Z. Wallower.

1947 elected committee members

THE EVENING NEWS, Harrisburg, Pa., Saturday, December 10, 1955—3

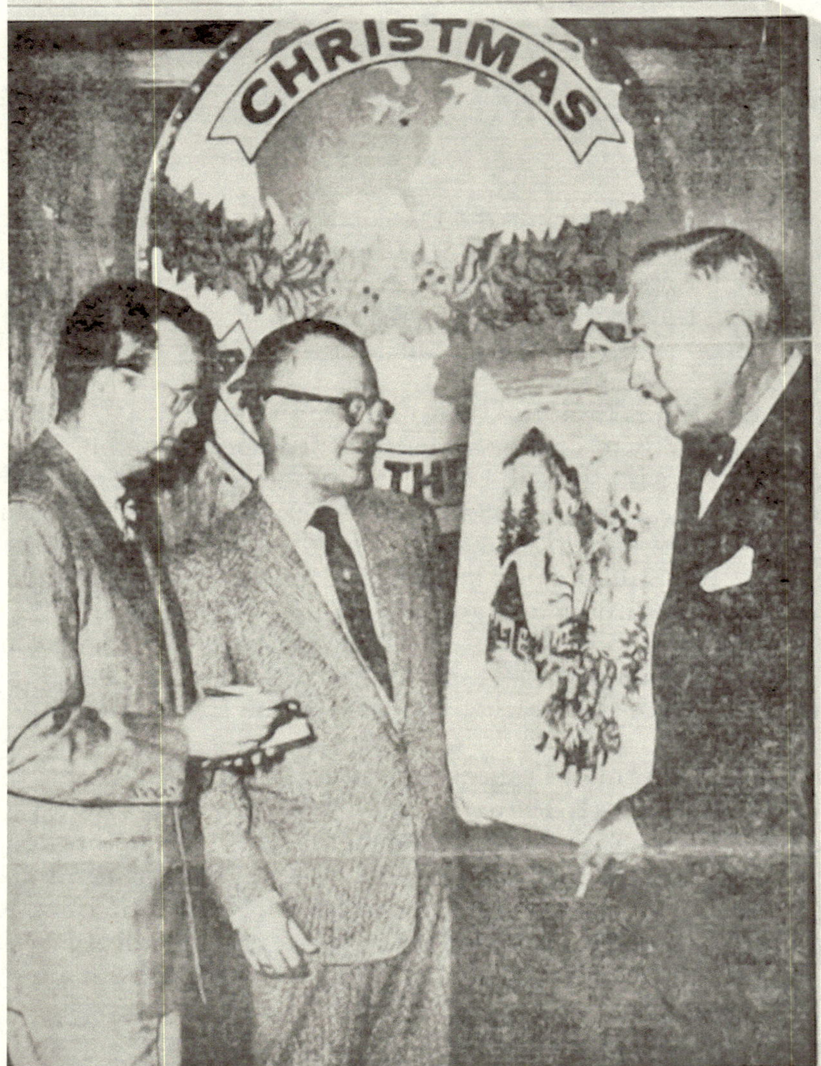

JUDGES CHOOSE WINNING PAINTING—Edward C. Michener, Russell J. Charles, and Franklin Moore make their final choice of the winning painting in the Harrisburg Art Assn's "Christmas Around the World" contest. Mrs. Virginia O'Rourke, 512 E. Keller St., Mechanicsburg, is artist of the winning painting, "Sing for Christmas," depicting Yuletide caroling in Czechoslovakia.

* * *   * * *

Mechanicsburg Artist Gets $35 First Prize in Contest

Christmas Judges choose winning painting, December 1955

AFTER THE MERGER: 1955 – 1979

Nick Ruggieri served as the President of the newly-re-organized Art Association from February 24, 1954, until November 30, 1954, when Robert Bartlett, another artist, was elected to the position. On November 15, 1955, Wilbur Nisley succeeded him. The Association was located at this time at 414 Spring Street, Harrisburg.

In the minutes from the Board meeting of April 6, 1956, it was noted that Mrs. Ivan Lenker announced the spring exhibit dates as May 21-26, with the exhibition committee consisting of Mrs. Richard Walker, Mrs. Betty Snow, and Nick Ruggieri. Vid Petrasic was in charge of hanging the show. Betty Snow was at this time Director of the Studio, and she reported that the enrollment for the semester beginning on February 1 was 115 students.

An interesting note in those minutes concerned a letter from Ed Michener, asking Mrs. Walker to "investigate where the paintings of Sir John Lavery are located in the Harrisburg Library"!

Program Chairman Frances Wrobel reported to President Nisley on November 1, 1956, that an exhibit of works by local artists had been presented in November called "Let's Paint the Town," organized by Mrs. Ivan Lenker. A series of films ran the last Friday of each month from November through April, obtained from the Philadelphia Museum of Art, University of Pennsylvania, and the Princeton Film Library. On April 13, there was an art auction, run by Betty Snow. These were all admirable efforts, although not attaining the grandeur of the exhibitions and lectures of the early years.

December 12, 1956, Dr. David Johnson was elected President. Minutes are very sketchy for 1957 and 1958, but Ed Michener was President for 1958, and then on May 28, 1959, Nick Ruggieri was again elected President. At the Sunday, October 11, 1959, Board meeting, Ruggieri discussed the proposed purchase of a house at 2949 North Front Street in Uptown Harrisburg, owned by a Mrs. Dale, for $40,000. A Mr. Richey was called upon to express his opinion of the property. He stated that "the building consists of 2500 sq. feet of space not including the garage and basement. He felt it was not large enough; however partitions could be moved to make rooms upstairs larger. Location and parking facilities excellent. Grounds expensive to maintain. Exterior hard to keep up. He felt the asking price too much for the amount of space."

After lengthy discussion, the Board agreed to appoint a committee to explore three options: the purchase of the Front Street house, the purchase of another suitable building, or buying land to erect a new building.

At the Board meeting on November 19, 1959, another option was discussed, namely, that of building an addition to the Community Theatre building on Vaughn Street. New officers were elected at the June 7, 1960, meeting, with Mrs. W.Carl Hartmann chosen as President. Exhibitions were presented at the Harrisburg Community Theatre building and were very well received.

On May 19, 1961, President Hartmann reported that the "first juried Local Artists Exhibition" was successful but "showed some errors to be corrected next year. (It must be made clear that there can be no refunds of entry fees, and that no painting may be taken down while the show hangs.)" She also mentioned that the annual art auction "was a very poor one." The Board moved that at the next year's auction, artists should be offered 50% of the sale price of their paintings.

At the May 24, 1961, Board meeting, Mrs. Hartmann read eight recommendations made for the Association by a "professional fund-raising specialist." These consisted of the following:

(1) Establish a definite goal for the Association.

(2) Move out of the alley.

(3) Have a more business-like school.

(4) Establish an Auxiliary, which can do such things as have trips and visit an interior decorating shop.

(5) Have more lectures and demonstrations.

(6) Keep a list on hand of all practicing artists.

(7) Stop having the Bal for the benefit of the Building Fund.

(8) Have a better set-up budget.

At the same meeting, Hain Wolf was elected President. Then at the October 27, 1961, meeting Earl Blust reported as Exhibition Chairman that there would be a memorial exhibition of Walt Huber's paintings from November 26 to December 2. Another member of the old guard to die. This Huber exhibition was reported to have been a success in the January 15, 1962, minutes, with $1226 in sales going to Huber's widow.

In these same minutes, it was noted that a letter from Mrs. Chester M. Sheffer had been received "criticizing the Studio as not being clean." This seems to be the first reference to Mrs. Sheffer in the records... a woman destined to become a force of nature for the Association.

An interesting bit of information was entered in the March 28, 1962, minutes, stating that "the word 'local' be stricken from the name of the Show and that it be called the 34th Annual Exhibition of the Art Association of Harrisburg, and that the radius for entries be extended to 75 miles." Progress was being made!

Progress on most fronts, but not on all, as a review by *Evening News* writer Bill Doran indicates in the summer of 1963, regarding a three-day art show by local artists sponsored by The Downtown Harrisburg Association. Doran emphasized "It's always a pleasure to walk into an art show and see something on canvas you can recognize. In fact, in these days of modern abstract painting with its paint dripping and sculptor (sic) straight from an auto junkyard it is almost a surprise to walk into an exhibition of current artists and find you can recognize the objects in nearly every painting." Doran continues his diatribe with, "Omitted from the show are the automobile parts school of sculptor (sic) and 'pop art.' Neither is missed."

Will Brown was President from 1963 through 1966, and it was during his tenure that the long awaited plans to acquire a building for the Association finally came to fruition. A letter was sent to all AAH members, dated May 20, 1964, inviting everyone to the annual meeting and banquet to be held on June 3 at the New Penn Harris Motor Inn, Camp Hill By-Pass. The letter stated, "The program has been carefully prepared to brief you fully on plans for our new building and Harrisburg's New Art Centre. Prominent State and Municipal officials have been invited. It will be a stimulating evening marking a new giant stride in the 36-year-old history of our association."

The June 4, 1964, *Patriot* ran a big article extolling the fact that "City Group Plans Art Centre." The article quoted Will Brown as stating, "We are embarked on a sound cultural investment, one that will provide Harrisburg with its first art centre."

Former Harrisburg Mayor Daniel Barry stated that the city is "proud and honoured that the association has invested in this downtown property." Nick Ruggieri outlined the group's long search for a permanent home, explaining that he and his building committee had explored "abandoned churches, unused school-houses, and private homes, but the house at 21 North Front Street was immediately the choice of the association."

The article went on to say that "plans for the financing of the new venture are being made under the leadership of Mrs. Maurice Shaffer and Edward C. Michener." Ruggieri was in charge of the building committee. On Saturday, June 20, 1964, the Downtown Harrisburg Association announced that they would make a "substantial contribution to our BUILDING FUND for participating in a clothesline exhibition along Market Street, Third Street, and in Market Square."

On November 1, 1964, a full-page article by Anthony Arms appeared in the Sunday *Patriot News*, complete with photos of the house at 21 North Front Street, an art class held in the new studios, and member artists selecting works for the premiere exhibition. The premiere exhibition to be presented in the 21 North Front Street galleries consisted of paintings by nationally-known artists Greta Kempton Walker and Wang Yinpao, shown in the Vance C. McCormick Gallery and Gallery A on the first floor, with AAH member artists' works in the other galleries and the M. Louise Aughinbaugh working studio on the second floor. Also on view was the Annie M. Rodearmel German room, so-called due to Miss Anna M. German's donation of her mother's paintings. In an article in *The Evening News* on October 13, 1964, it was noted that Mrs. German had done most of the paintings when she was about 16 years old and a pupil in a young ladies' academy known as the Harrisburg Female Seminary. Mrs. German was born in Harrisburg in 1850, and lived all her life at 25 North Fourth Street. Although the writer of the article, Edna Nash, noted that Mrs. German's paintings were almost all copies of 17th and 18th century Dutch artists' works, there was one inspired by a poem by Lord Byron.

In total, Miss German donated 27 paintings to AAH, done mostly by her mother, but several by her contemporaries. Several selected pieces of furniture and statuary were also donated for the room to be called the Annie M. Rodearmel German Room. (This room is now my President's office. The German collection was later removed and re-donated to the Historical Society of Dauphin County after a contretemps with the Board and President Mary Sheffer, but that's a later story.)

The new art centre officially opened on November 9, 1964, with Harrisburg Mayor's wife Mrs. McBride cutting the ribbon, and over 200 people in attendance. It was reported that, together with the purchase price, the Association had put more than $50,000 into the building and its improvements.

During the ensuing months and years, numerous articles and photos filled the Harrisburg newspapers, regaling readers with images of artists at work in AAH classes, exhibitions, and winning artists. The annual art auction continued to bring in funds for the Association, as well as garnering a great deal of publicity. Some of the winners listed in these articles went on to future fame, including Maya Shock, who founded the Doshi Gallery; Edith Socolow, who became an influential instructor at Harrisburg Area Community College; Earl Blust, who continued his AAH involvement until 2011; and Wanda Macomber, who became a well-known abstract precisionist painter.

All through these years, the annual Bal Masque figured highly in publicity and AAH records... the Bal Masque was first held in 1941 as a fundraising event for the Association, and after a hiatus during World War II, it was begun again in the 1950's and held annually at the old Penn Harris Hotel in downtown Harrisburg.

Presidents of the Board in those years included:

(1) Will Brown—1963-1966.
(2) Russell J. Charles—1966-1967.
(3) Mary McEnroy Sheffer—1967-1975.
(4) Shim Lehrman—1975-1976.
(5) George Logan—1976-1977.
(6) Nancy Horstik Greenawalt—1977-1978.
(7) Peggy Berliner Ottens—1978-1979.
(8) David F.Lenker—1979-1980.
(9) Carrie Wissler-Thomas—1980-84.

The minutes from the December 6, 1972, Board Meeting have an interesting comment: George Logan "questioned when the German paintings became a gift to the Art Association and was there a record of acceptance by the Board. Consensus of opinion was they were not formally presented but officially became property of AAH when Miss German took them as a tax deduction in 1971." Later in the minutes Mr. Haughwout, Chairman of the special committee appointed to investigate the grievances of Miss German relative to the agreement entered into between Miss German and AAH, read a letter from Miss German to President Sheffer, outlining her grievances as to the lighting and maintenance of the German Room. Also in the minutes, it was noted that Gallery Doshi, owned by Maya Shock, was presenting a $25 award for Best Professional and $10 for Best Amateur paintings submitted for the Ninth Annual Membership Exhibition.

These minutes of 1972 also referred to the Greater Harrisburg Arts Council, and the fact that all organizations were requested to contact the Council before scheduling major events to avoid date conflicts. (An interesting concept that continues, in 2014, to be an issue for art organizations.)

In the Board minutes of February 7, 1973, Karl Foster moved, seconded by George Logan, that the Board concur "with Miss German's request that her contract with AAH be terminated and paintings and other contents belonging to her be removed from the gallery in which they now are and also that Miss German release or discharge all claim or demand to AAH for the $3000 Patron Agreement and release all other claims, suits, or accounts, because growing out of the agreement of 1964 and the addendum dated July 7, 1966, be concurred with."

The June 6, 1973, minutes observed that Mrs. Sheffer had been re-elected yet again as Board President. Mrs. George Ebner was the School Chairman during this period, and her reports indicate the classes offered were varied and numerous, and well attended. In the minutes of the January 2, 1974, meeting, Mrs. Ebner reported that a new class in film production would be offered on Wednesday evenings with John Hudak as instructor. This innovative class was to be a "program of comprehensive understanding of motion picture medium and production techniques." Mr. Hudak was the Executive Vice President of Walter O'Connor Co. Advertising Agency in Hershey. Classes were advertised in the newspapers and via posters.

The Board at this time, 1974, consisted of President Mary Sheffer, Mr. Drum, Mrs. Ebner, Karl Foster, Nancy Greenawalt, Juanita Hostetler, Enid Keen, George Logan, Helen Messic, Peggy Ottens, Vid Petrasic, Bea Redmond, Mrs. Reisman, Nick Ruggieri, Richard Walker, Earl Blust, Mimi Conrey, Mr. Forbes, Mr. Gilbert, George Lackhove, Shim Lehrman, Mr. Johnson, Rachel Ratowsky, Mrs. Murray, Mr. Schlosser, George Tschamber, and May Voight. (I had joined AAH as an artist member in 1972, and I became familiar with many of these people.)

It was recorded in the February 6, 1974, minutes that "because of careful expenditures and good investment policies, the Association is one of the few of its kind in sound financial position." To fill a vacancy on the Board, David Lenker was nominated by Richard Walker, seconded by Karl Foster. Kathleen Ebner nominated Mrs. Eliza Curry, seconded by Peggy Ottens. Both nominees were duly elected.

In the March 6, 1974, minutes it was noted that Rachel Ratowsky thanked the Board for "voting to help defray Chamber Music Series expenses in the amount of $500. Fortunately the Series to date has been self-sustaining. Therefore, it was unnecessary for AAH to contribute. Series has 54 sponsors. Consensus of opinion that last concert (Temple Trio) one of finest ensembles ever brought to Harrisburg." The Art Association has always promoted fine music as complementary to the fine art on display, something that continues in the present era.

At this time, 1974, dues consisted of $10 for Associate, $15 for Active, and $25 for Sustaining. In the same March minutes, mention was made of a "new Art Lending Service at Kline Village Library," with all the paintings by AAH members. The program was sponsored by Friends of the Library. This comprised a predecessor of the AAH Community Exhibition program, which was instituted in the 1980's.

The minutes of the May 1, 1974, Board meeting include a description of the censorship issue that artist Gene Suchma elaborates upon in his "Art Association Memories" section of this book. In the minutes it was stated that, "Karl Foster, Exhibit Ch., announced the Annual Juried Exhibit was judged by Wm. A. Smith, AWS, replacing Henry Pitz who is ill; Mildred Kratz, AWS, Pottstown; Jeanne Dobie, AWS, Wayne. 218 entries were submitted; 80 were hung. Mr. Foster stated there being a controversy about one painting, he asked for the opinion of Board."

The Chair Mrs. Sheffer announced that following several requests, "the Professional Artists' Committee, the AAH Executive Committee, (including the AAH attorney), had been reached and consulted with the decision that the painting in question be withdrawn. Authority for withdrawal was based on AAH rules incorporated in each entry blank that 'AAH reserves the right to reject any work not in good taste.' The decision of above Committee had been disregarded and controversy had arisen. After discussion, Chair called for vote. Mr. Walker moved painting be removed and not hung in exhibit. Mrs. Redmond seconded motion. The vote was three against and 18 for removing painting. Chair pointed out that the affairs of AAH are under the jurisdiction of the Board of Directors and requested that the controversy in question not be released from the Board."

However, word did get out. The artist whose work was censored was Gene Suchma, and his painting was a nude self-portrait. He describes the incident in his essay in this book. The censorship incident, for that's what it was, pure and simple, drove a number of artists away from the Association. Maya Shock, founder of the Doshi Centre for Contemporary Art in 1972, withdrew her membership from AAH, telling the Press, "I stayed in the Harrisburg Art Association in the hope that I could change some things. So after twelve years I gave up." This was not the Art Association's finest hour, and gained the organization an unsavory reputation for censorship, from which 1980 onwards

AAH has been adamantly opposed. Since 1980, AAH has been known as an organization that stands tall against censorship in all its ugly forms. But in 1974, it was a different era.

At the June 5, 1974, Board meeting, all the officers were re-elected for another term, with Mary Sheffer again as President. Two new Board members were elected: Rhea Reese and Doris Dunlap. Mae Johnson was Studio Director at this time. At the July 3 meeting it was noted by Richard Walker that Harristown, the city's re-development authority, would not be able to carry through many of its proposed projects, so "therefore AAH will not be affected." It was also mentioned at this meeting that Mrs. Redmond "read copy of letter sent to Maya Schock accepting with regret her resignation from AAH and thanking her for past services." (This resignation came as a direct result of the censorship incident described above.)

In the March 3, 1975, minutes more discussion ensued concerning Harristown's intentions regarding AAH. Richard Walker, AAH solicitor, "advised that Harristown Redevelopment Corp. has appraised AAH property at $96,000. They do not state how much property this will include, whether this is to include all of or only part of building. We cannot accept or reject the proposed appraisal until we know definitely what they are going to do. Will await for further development." Also in this meeting it was reported that AAH now had $10,000 insurance coverage on all paintings "previously in its permanent collection."

The minutes from the July 2, 1975, meeting state that Shim Lehrman was now President... Mary Sheffer had finally stepped down after serving nearly eight years, from 1967 through 1975. In Doris Dunlap's School Report, Charles Hickok was announced as a new wood sculpture teacher for the fall semester. In the building report, David Lenker said that he thought "we should not put any more money into the building than necessary; will bring in paint chart for third floor studio (will do painting himself)." One assumes this is a result of the vaguely threatening Harristown plans?

At the October 1, 1975, meeting Mrs. Sheffer informed the Board of two break-ins at the building and the theft of the typewriter. On March 3, 1976, it "was announced that the membership drive is to be headed by Mrs. Ottens and Mrs. Welker." (Interestingly enough, I was recruited to help to prepare the membership brochures for mailing! I remember standing in the first-floor Aughinbaugh Gallery, sorting brochures to mail.)

At the June 16, 1976, meeting, George Logan was elected President, with Dave Lenker elected Vice President of Buildings and Maintenance, Martin Laibow—Vice President of Exhibitions, DorisDunlap—Vice President School, May Voight—Recording Secretary, Rachel Ratowsky—Recording Secretary, and Mae Johnson—Treasurer.

At the November 3, 1976, meeting, it was stated that Richard Walker, Shim Lehrman, Martin Laibow and Dave Lenker had met with Mr. Haas of Harristown to discuss the AAH situation. "Plans are for back section of building probably being removed but entire building will not be. If necessary, a loading dock would be built. Only original portions of buildings would be retained which includes building next door, now owned and used by Bankers' Life. If needed additional space for classrooms, etc.it might well be that part of that building would be available. A new Arts Building is projected, possibly on Second Street, with possibly a second floor walkway connecting to our building and a parking entrance added. The police station will be back of us. Mrs. Warren Heisey, newly appointed to have charge of the Arts would in all probability be very much against our moving away and would do everything possible to make it pleasant for us." This astonishing plan, fortunately, never came to fruition.

The proposed "Arts Building" finally came about when Whitaker Centre was constructed in 1999, but didn't have a visual arts component, and AAH was left intact, both organizationally and structurally.

Another item of business covered at that November 3 meeting was discussion on demolishing the former carriage house/garage at the rear of the garden, due to its poor state of repair. This discussion continued at the December 1 meeting with no firm decision being reached.

The minutes of March 2, 1977, observed that there were 274 paid-up members, and a committee was appointed to "investigate possible headquarters for Association in event it is deemed advisable to move from present location." The chairman of this committee was Martin Laibow, with members Dave Ottens, Paul Long, Dave Lenker, Mimi Conrey and Helen Messic. At the annual meeting on May 18, 1977, Dave Lenker, House Chairman, reported that various plumbing leaks had been repaired, and the garage had been finally removed, with a fence erected across the back of the property at the garage line.

At the June 1 meeting, I was "suggested by Peggy Ottens for publicity." I was listed in this first record of me in the minutes as "Caroline Thomas." At the same meeting, the Board Chair George Logan complained that the organization was not being run efficiently. It was noted that "We must have a fulltime Studio

Director who will be in charge of school, also supervise and be in attendance at exhibits. Applications accepted from anyone interested in applying for this position."

Due to the resignation of Bob Lackhove there was a vacancy on the Board. Peggy Ottens proposed me (now called "Carolyn Thomas") for consideration. The stage was being set for commencement of The Modern Era...

On August 3, 1977, President Nancy Greenawalt announced, "immediate action must be taken to engage full time Studio Director." She stated, "Earl Blust has indicated he will be advisor on this," noting that she, Peggy Ottens, and George Logan all had done "cover-up for office help" during the past year. She went on to state, "We need volunteers who will come in to do studio-type work; we must have a better school, not only a good school but the best, which means better teachers."

Nancy Greenawalt said, "I do not believe we did our best last year. I worked in the office two or three days a week doing things someone else should have been doing. This was work that cannot be done at home: new projects can be tried under a good Studio Director. The building is only used 30% of the time. The rest of the time the walls are empty. We could possibly take one room such as the Aughinbaugh Gallery, and charge a reasonable fee to anyone wishing to rent it for an exhibit. This would give us additional income. We only made $1000 last year and it took $1000 per month to open the doors. We should take money already allocated for a Studio Director and come up with a good Studio Director at an estimated $7000 per year."

Mary Sheffer apparently took a different view of the situation, requesting to be recorded in the minutes that during the considerable time she had worked with both Mrs. Johnson and Miss Domain in the office, she found both to be very efficient. "If by chance anything ever came through incorrect, it was because they had been given incorrect directions." The Chair then replied that there is a "breakdown between what they do and where the public is involved." Discussion ensued concerning where the money would come from to pay a full-time Studio Director, with Peggy Ottens emphasizing, "We do have funds. There is money available, which would be taken out of capital. We should be using it to generate more revenue."

Mrs. Sheffer retorted with, "Specific funds of the Association were set up during my Presidency with the understanding at that time that the interest could eventually help take care of various activities while the capital should be left untouched so that it could grow. We should live within our income."

President Greenawalt suggested that the several $4000 certificates of deposit could possibly be used to hire a full-time Studio Director, "as an experiment?" The upshot was that a committee was formed to set up the requirements for a Studio Director, and to examine the feasibility of doing so. Ann Fitzpatrick was appointed as chairman of this committee.

Peggy Ottens was elected President of the Board for 1978-1979. In her President's message in the July/August 1978, Newsletter she itemized several community exhibitions in which AAH artists were exhibiting, including a solo show I had at Penn State University in Middletown. The September 1978, Newsletter announced that the fall semester classes would begin with 19 scheduled classes, and two bus trips were touted... one to the East Wing of the National Gallery in Washington, DC, and one to the Museum of Art of the Carnegie Institute in Pittsburgh. The Fall Membership Show, with Kathleen Piunti as Exhibition Chairman, opened to high acclaim.

In the October Newsletter, I was mentioned as Publicity Chairman. "Christmas in the Governor Findlay Mansion" was announced for December 2 with carol singing, a doll and train display, and a 19th-century Christmas tree promised. The November Newsletter added to the description with notice that Dave Keefer would be the town crier and Bill Rohrbeck would perform the traditional "Boar's Head" carol. A chamber music trio was to perform. The chairman of this holiday extravaganza was Doris Dunlap.

The ever-popular annual art auction was promoted in the Newsletters, and the Bal Masque, with theme "Anything Goes," was heralded for February 24 at the Penn-Harris Motor Inn, Camp Hill.

I well remember attending this Bal Masque as Mary, Queen of Scots, in a costume created for me by Charles Schulz. Another thing that made this Bal memorable was the news that long-time member and supporter Louise Aughinbaugh had died. She always was present at the Bal entrance, and her absence was noticeable. Her death was noted in the April Newsletter, along with that of artist Bob Bartlett, one of the original Seven Lively Artists.

In the May, 1979, Newsletter, Peggy Ottens wrote a farewell address as outgoing President. She noted that the committee chairmen and office staff were "responsive and responsible." She said that Sibby Hill is the new co-studio director with Mae Johnson, who time-shared the workweek. Nominees were announced for the Board, to be elected at the May 23 Annual Meeting. The nominees were Bernadette Barattini, Leslie

Carricato, Marisa Charles, Mary Kay Fager, Janet Foner, Rhea Reese, Dr. Irwin Richman, Jack Slepicka, Mary Zimmerman, and me, now listed as "Carrie Thomas." At that Annual Meeting I remember Mae Johnson was nominated from the floor, and was elected instead of Dr. Richman, which was not well received by many people, especially since Mrs. Johnson resigned shortly thereafter.

The minutes of the June 6, 1979, Board meeting announced the election of new officers: David Lenker was elected President, with Dick Walker as First Vice President. It was noted that, "with the resignation of Mae Johnson, it was necessary for Margaret Hill, office secretary, to work full time." A discussion ensued concerning increasing her wages and changing her title to Studio Director.

A memorable occurrence at the July 11 meeting was my motion to accept a portrait of Mrs. Vance McCormick (AAH founder and first President) from her grandson Spencer Nauman, donated as a gift to AAH.

The October 3, 1979, minutes reflected a number of disturbing situations: Building Chairman Karl Foster was attempting to identify a reliable custodian, and a section of the garden fence had been stolen. Termites were suspected in the building, and School Chairman Janet Foner said that most of the scheduled fall classes, especially those in new suburban locations, had been cancelled. Money was also lost on the Ranulph Bye watercolour workshop. Things were not going very well. In the November 7 minutes, I made a motion that we explore the possibility of hiring a professional cleaning service.

The minutes of December 5, 1979, recorded a momentous occurrence. Margaret Hill resigned as Studio Director, and I proposed Charles Schulz as a replacement. I made the motion and Leslie Carricato seconded. The motion passed and Charles Schulz was hired. A new era was beginning.

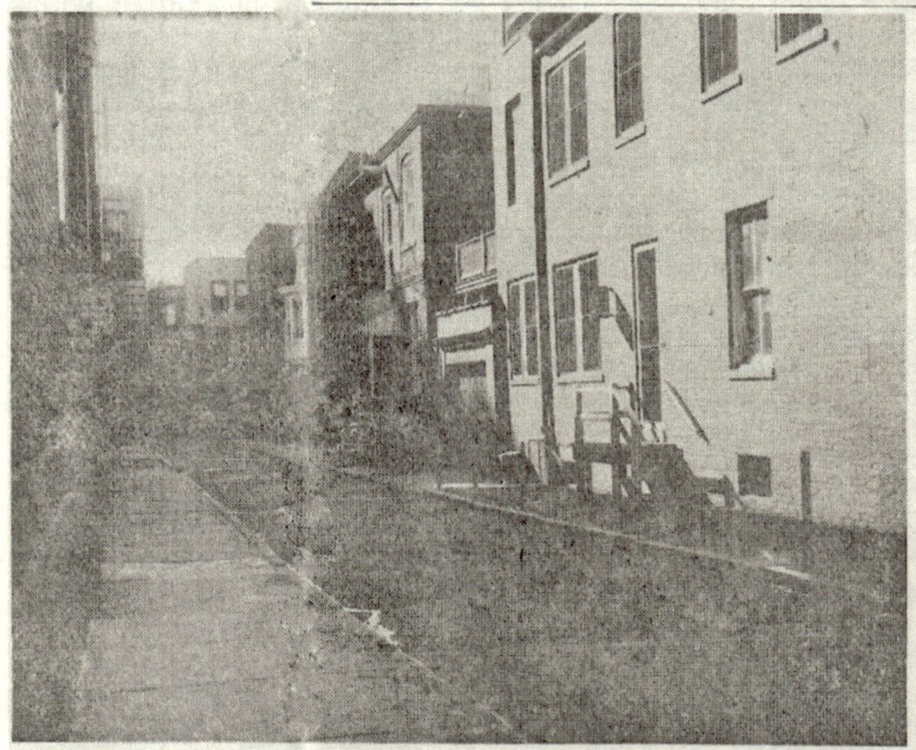
The Evening News, Harrisburg, Pa., Wednesday, Oct. 22, 1958—47

—Evening News Photo

ART CENTER—The "studio" of the Harrisburg Art Assn. on 414 Spring St. is the center building on the right with a white porch. In a thriving city of marble structures, this is the center of art. To some artists, it is the cynical incarnation of the importance of art in the life of the city.

414 Spring Street Art Association Studio

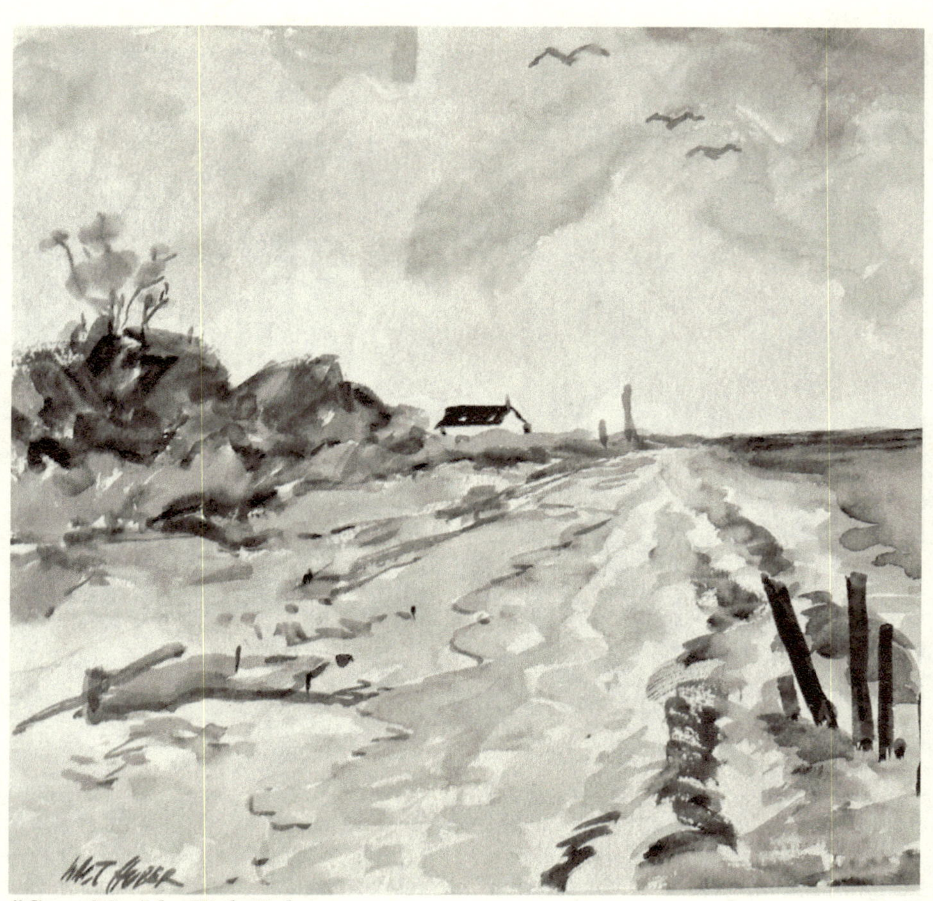

"Cape May" by Walt Huber

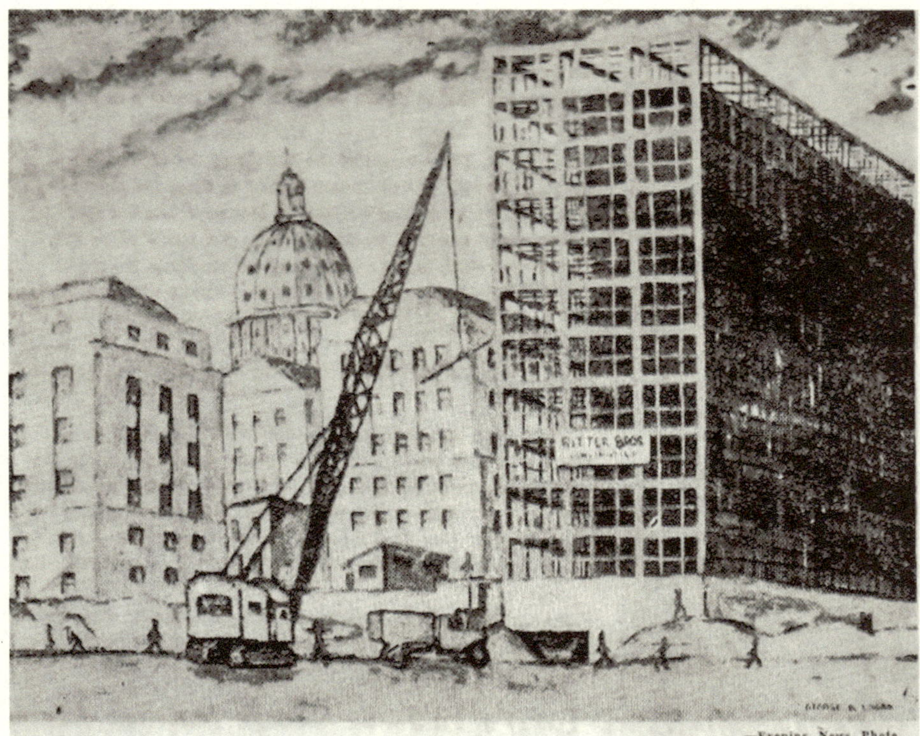

—Evening News Photo

'CAPITOL BUILDINGS UNDER CONSTRUCTION'—This oil painting entitled "Capitol Buildings Under Construction" was given first prize in the competition among members of the Harrisburg Art. Assn. It was painted by George Logan.

"Capitol Buildings under Construction" by George Logan

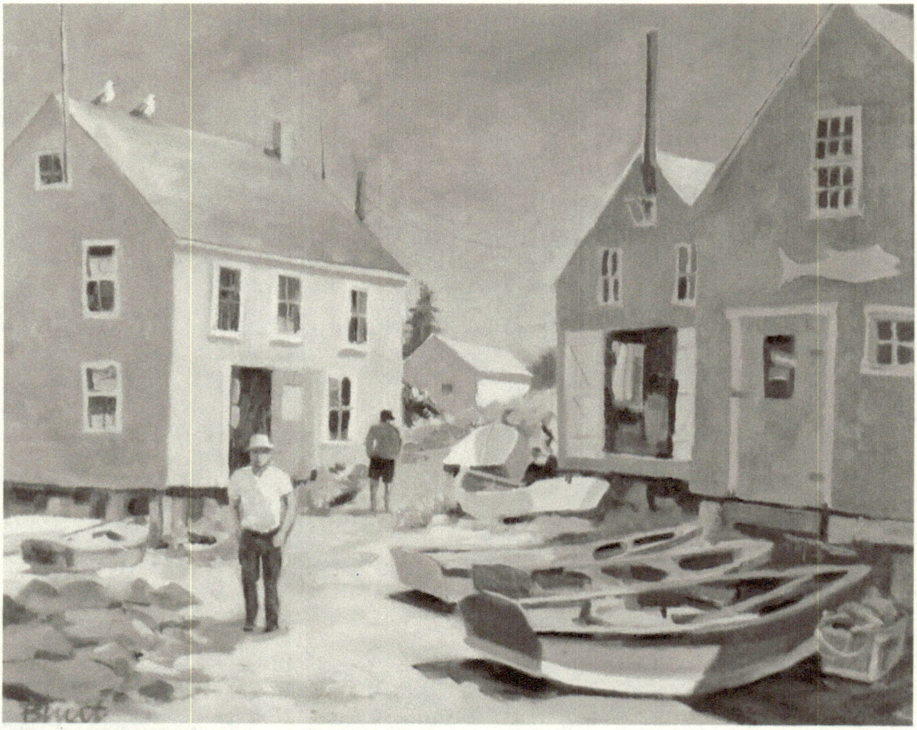

"Fish House" by Earl Blust

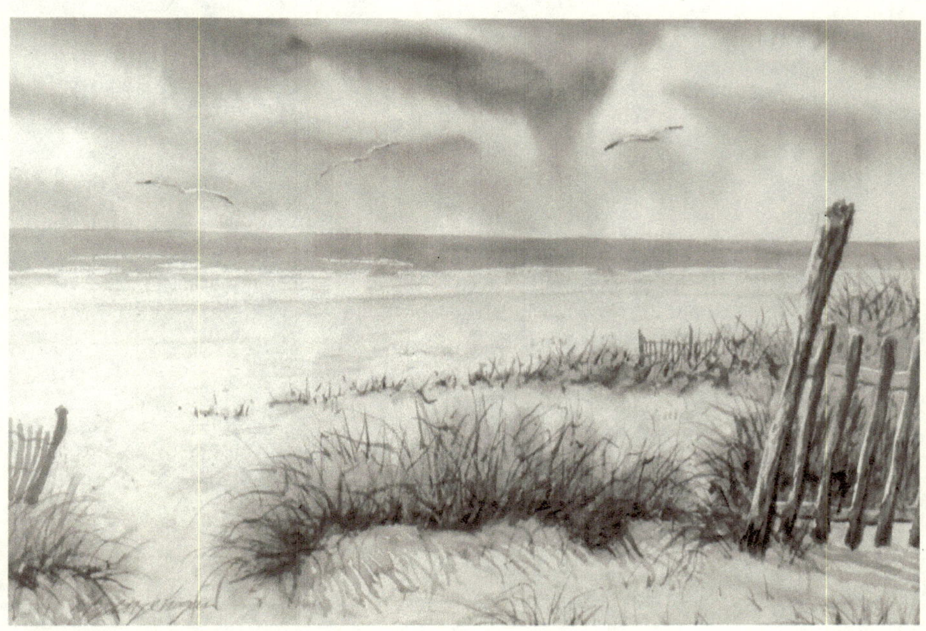

"Seascape" by George Logan

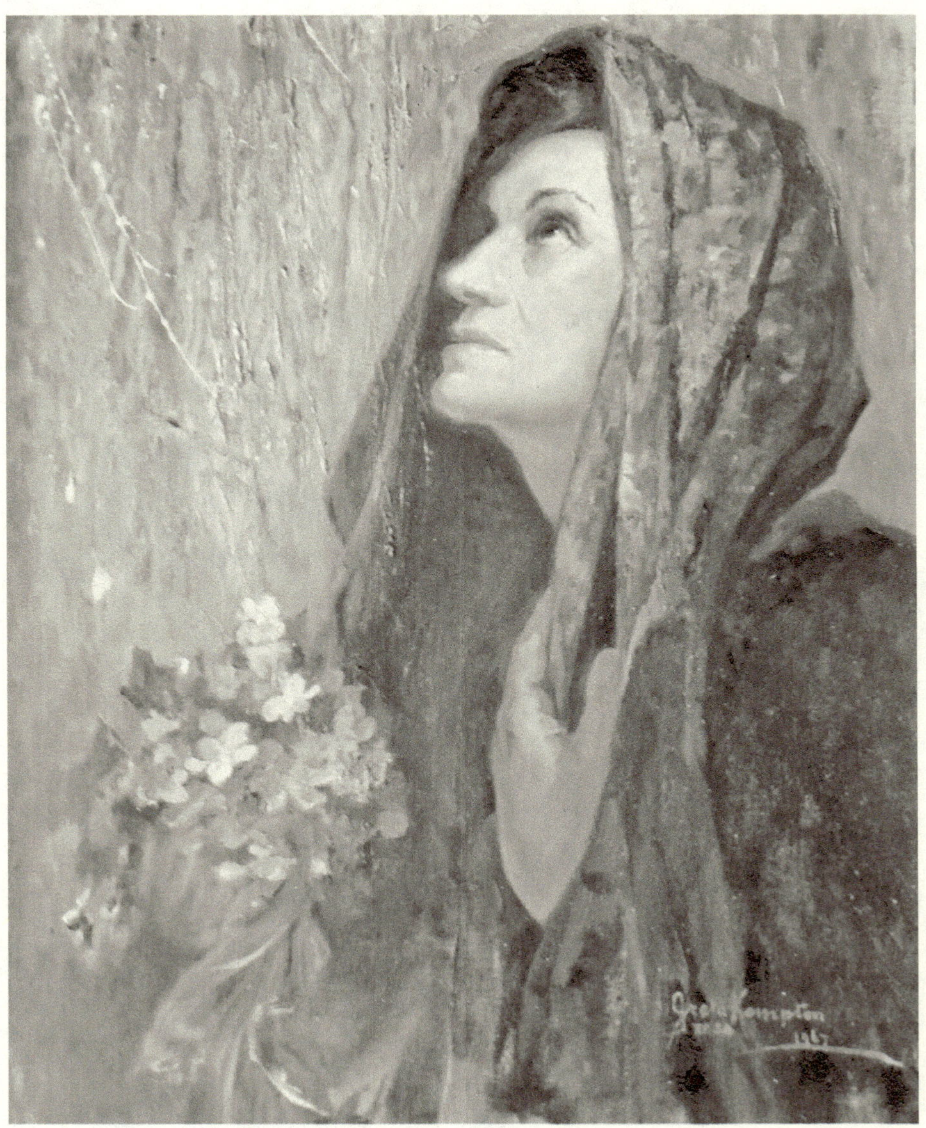

"Lady with Violets" by Greta Kempton

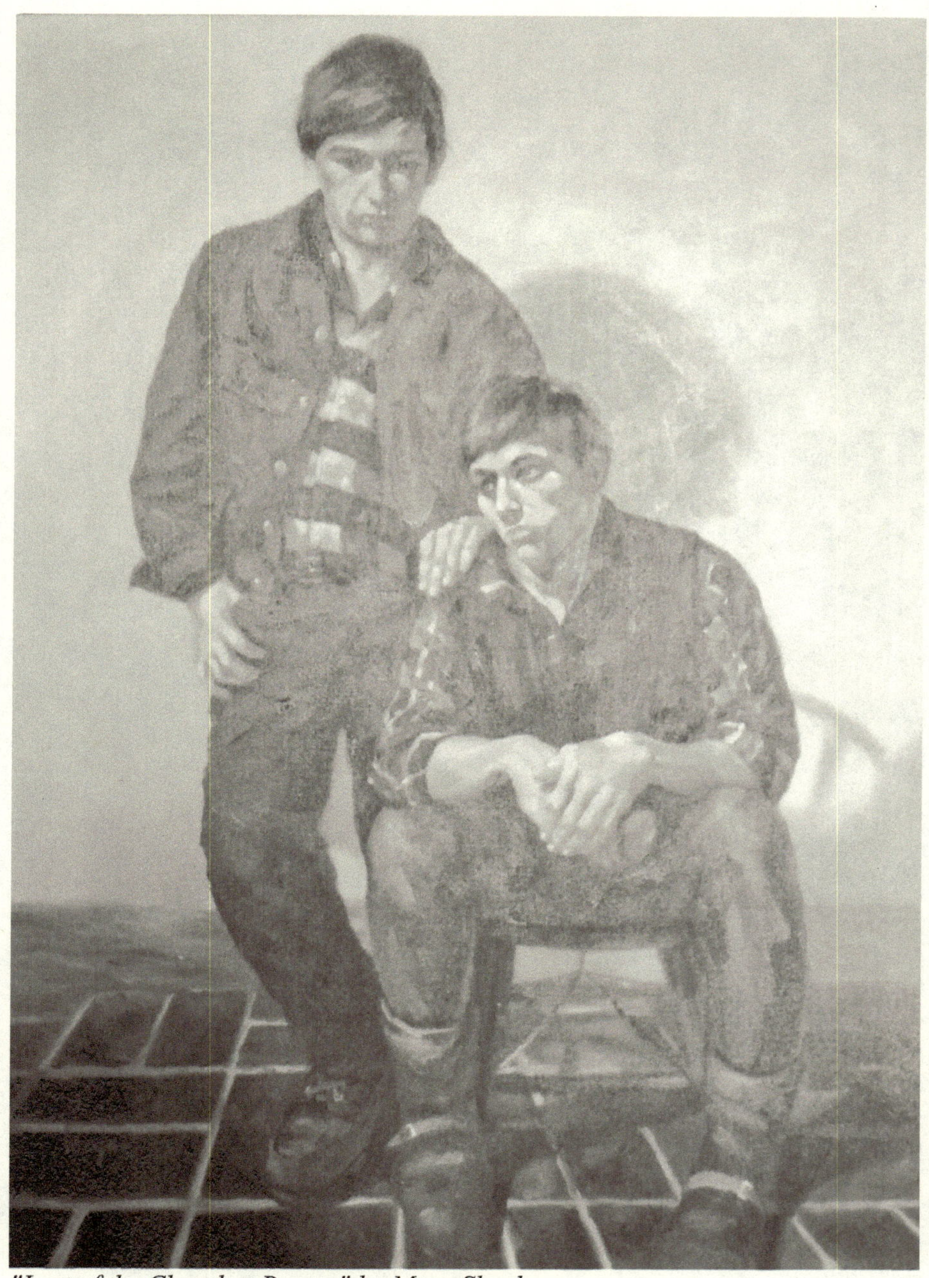

"Last of the Cherokee Braves" by Maya Shock

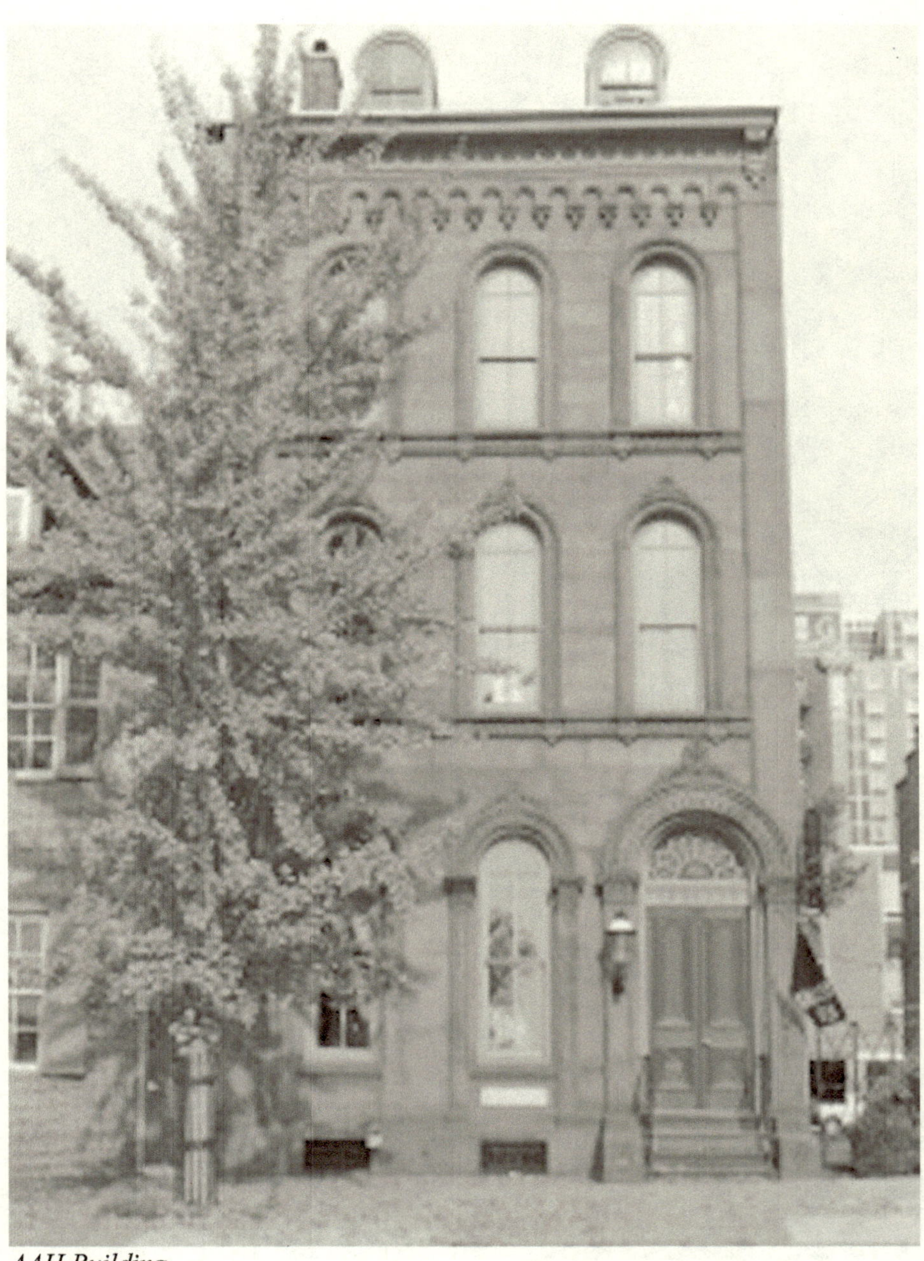

AAH Building

THE MODERN ERA COMMENCES: 1980-1984

The minutes for the January 2, 1980, Board meeting, noted that a Figuratively Speaking winter membership exhibition would be held from February 3 through 15, with entry fee of $2, limit three per member. This innovative exhibition had taken the place of the annual Flower Exhibition. Peggy Ottens nominated me to fill the vacancy of Vice President, and I was duly elected to be Dave Lenker's VP. New Executive Director Charles Schulz "said he would like to have newsletter mailed out one week after Board meetings and also ask for people to help with mailing." I was also named Chairman of a committee to revise the By-Laws.

At the March 5 Board meeting, Peggy Ottens and Rachel Ratowsky both resigned from the Board, and architect Milford Patterson was elected to fill the unexpired term of Ms. Ottens. Motions were made to have the drapes cleaned and a Coke machine installed in the basement, both of which were completed, as Schulz reported at the April 2 meeting. At the March meeting a committee was formed, including me, to have the building appraised and to check into the possible "relocation of AAH." I remember we toured the Janet Gannett house, the Spanish-style home at the corner of Division and North Second Streets, which was for sale but totally inappropriate for our needs.

However, a detailed appraisal of the building done by William Daylor was presented to the Board on April 2, giving the value at $125,000. The committee had visited Harristown to yet again try to discern what plans that entity had for the Front Street Governors' Row mansions. The committee was instructed to continue to look for a possible new location.

The money situation remained very dicey at this time. In the May 7, 1980, minutes Treasurer Peg Brown recounted that the general account had very little money, and AAH still owed the Penn Harris for the Bal Masque, and the teachers had not been paid. Juanita Hostetler moved that "we clear up all our bills by borrowing enough from the Kunkel Fund at Commonwealth National Bank." The proposal was accepted.

Then, at the June 4, 1980, Board meeting I was elected President. Karl Foster was elected Vice President; Mary Davis, Recording Secretary; Rhea Reese, Corresponding Secretary; Peg Brown, Treasurer; Gene Suchma and Jack Slepika, Professional Arts Committee. As the new President, I "stressed certain priorities such as helping to solve financial problems by applying for a grant" and identifying other fundraising activities.

The Board at this time was composed of the above-mentioned officers, and the following Members: Bernadette Barattini (Legal Counsel), Leslie Carricato, Janet Foner, Mary Kay Fager, Leo Gilroy, Ann Marie Lukesh, Dave Lenker, Joanne Miller, Milford Patterson, Linda Smith, George Tschamber, May Ireland Voight, Marybeth Walkowiak, and Nancy Greenawalt.

At the July 2, 1980, Board meeting, Treasurer Peg Brown stated that our accountant Harold Sheetz was close to finishing the audit, and a certificate of deposit, which was due to mature on July 8, was decided to be reinvested at the best rate possible. Milford Patterson, now in charge of the building's upkeep, "reported many things to be done, but first the galleries will be painted." Susquehanna Paint Company would give a discount on the paint. Also, on July 19, the locks on the doors were to be changed... no reason given.

The new Professional Arts Committee announced plans to "standardize judging procedures" ...an excellent intention. In the interest of bringing in badly needed funds, the Ways and Means Chairmen announced plans for a Monte Carlo Night for November 15, with the Lions Club setting up the games at $150. A proposal was also made to sell tote bags with the AAH building on the front. Joanne Miller was authorized to order the bags. Leslie Carricato announced that the Bal Masque would be held in Strawberry Square with the theme: "300th Birthday Party in Penn's Woods." Governor Thornburgh and his wife were to be asked to serve as honorary chairmen of the Bal. In another fundraising attempt, a flea market was planned for July 4 and 5.

However, at the August 6 meeting the Monte Carlo Night concept was scratched because "the work involved outweighed the profit expected." A Kipona Café and Sidewalk Artists event was planned for Labour Day weekend, with Charles Schulz's mother Pat Treon handling food sales, and Leo Gilroy and Robin Forbes doing portraits. Also notable at that meeting were the announcements of the donation of a splendid carved chair to AAH by Dr. George Martz's widow, and the County Commissioners' permission for AAH students and visitors to use their parking lot on weekends. (The chair now sits prominently in my President's office.)

A sign of the times was recorded in the September 3 minutes, when I "mentioned that there should be no smoking in the building, particularly in studios because of fire hazard"! I also reported that an application had been filed with the Office of Historic Preservation for a grant to help with termite control, repointing of the brownstone, sealing windows and building bins for the permanent collection. We also applied for a grant to the Pennsylvania Council on the Arts to pay our Executive Director's salary. (This was not approved, however.)

The AAH building was to be on the Historic Harrrisburg Candlelight Tour on December 14, the October 1 minutes reflected. The Board also decided at that meeting to only send out a newsletter every other month, rather than monthly. The Membership Committee began to make a concerted effort to recruit new members, as noted in the November 5 minutes. The Bal Masque theme had been altered to "Party in Penn's Woods," but at this point there was no emcee nor a business patron chairman in place. The Bal that year was definitely a struggle. Jack Slepicka and Marisa Charles both resigned from the Board.

At the December 5, 1980, meeting Bob Bissett, a photographer, and Sue Hoenshield were elected to the Board. The Professional Arts Committee determined to have one "big-name" judge rather than three for the Juried Exhibition, and contact had been made with the Philadelphia Museum of Art. The Herm Miller Orchestra was identified to provide the music for the Bal, with media personality Jim Sinkovitz to be emcee. Charles Schulz reported the plans for the Candlelight Tour on December 14, including an antique doll and silver collection as attractions, which required the hiring of a policeman guard at $7 per hour.

By the January 7, 1981, meeting, some positive developments were reported, including a $4600 grant from the Kunkel Foundation for building repairs, and one of $100 from the McCormick Trust.

As Chair, I pointed out at that meeting that 1981 would be the 55th anniversary of the Art Association's incorporation, and "something ought to be done to celebrate it." Anne Percy, Director of Drawings for the Philadelphia Museum of Art, was announced as the Juried Exhibition judge. Although not noted in the minutes, I well remember Charles Schulz's letter to Ms. Percy, because I helped him in the office with correspondence and typing. He inquired in his letter to her whether she would be "travelling via automobile or by locomotive"! (I clearly recall the amusing image of our juror arriving at the station in Harrisburg, clinging to the engine's cattlecatcher!)

At the February 4, 1981, meeting *Patriot News* columnist Paul Beers was announced as the Honorary Chairman of the Bal Masque. Board member John Cherundolo reported on a series of planned AAH bus trips to art museums, and the Ways and Means Committee said that the upcoming art auction would have a professional auctioneer at the fee of $100.

At the March 4, 1981, meeting, Leslie Carricato moved that the Bal Masque be scratched from the calendar for 1982. The Bal in February at Strawberry Square had lost money. It would not be revived for ten years. At this meeting the issue of parking was once again raised, with Nancy Greenawalt moving that we look into the "possibility of increasing the parking space even if it means getting rid of the garden." By this time, fortunately, Harristown seems to have lost interest in threatening to make us move to tear down the building.

On April 1, I announced that at the suggestion of Lauren Welker, former Board Member and former Studio Director, AAH would present a "Miniature Show" as a moneymaking project on September 20. Participants would be charged $20 for booth space, with an admission charged for attendees. A total of $3398 was raised from the art auction, with artists receiving $1364 of that. At the May 6 meeting, I reported that the AAH 55th Anniversary would be celebrated at the Annual Meeting, with Louise Walker as the speaker. *The Evening News* was doing a full-page article on the anniversary. Nancy Greenawalt was working on the creation of a plaque of AAH Presidents, which was to be presented at the anniversary dinner. The plaque was to be donated at the expense of the Board. (That plaque continues to hang in the AAH front hall, duly updated as new Board Chairs are elected.)

At the June 3, 1981, Board meeting, the following officers and committee chairmen were elected:

President—Carrie Thomas
Vice-President—Leo Gilroy
Recording Secretary—Louise Linden
Corresponding Secretary—Mary Beth Walkowiak
Treasurer—Rhea Reese
Exhibition Co-Chairmen—Bob Bissett and Erna Tunno
Membership Chairman—Valerie Ciana
Buildings—Milford Patterson
School—Janet Foner
Finance—John Cherundolo, with committee members Leslie Carricato,

Joan and Dennis Miller, and my husband Scott Thomas
Publicty—Carrie Thomas and Charles Schulz
Social—Pat Treon
Historian—May Voight
Legal—Bernadette Barattini
Auction—Frank Hebert and Nancy Greenawalt

It was at this meeting that the Board decided exhibition reception costs would be borne totally by the artists involved, with coordination of logistics with Social Chairman Pat Treon. The checking account balance was recorded as $762.57. We were living on the edge! The Board was composed of dedicated individuals, many of whom were artists, but none of whom were especially adept at raising funds.

At the July 1 meeting, Membership Chairman Valerie Ciana was pleased to announce that 23 new members had joined since June 1. Because of the diligent efforts of Charles Schulz and Dave Lenker, the Harrisburg Jaycees were noted as donating $1000 to AAH and would become a Business Patron. Staffing the building was a difficulty in those days, as reflected in the comments in the August 5 minutes in which Erna Tunno was thanked for securing volunteers for Saturdays to open the AAH galleries, and Charles Schulz reported on the "volunteer persons that are supposed to serve as receptionists but did not."

At the September 2 meeting, Gene Suchma's resignation from the Board was accepted and Julie Goodrich Benbow was elected to fill the position. She was a photographer and an art history instructor at Harrisburg Area Community College. Valerie Ciana reported the total membership was now 236, with 78 new members! Building Chairman Milford Patterson and his volunteers were thanked for their painting of the galleries, and the termite problem in the entranceway was discussed.

AAH artists participated in a special celebration of the State Capitol's 75th anniversary, and Pennsylvania's 300th anniversary on October 19, with Charles Schulz and his mother creating the gigantic cake depicting a map of PA with all the counties for the event. Lengthy discussion ensued at the October 7 Board meeting on the state of AAH finances, with Chairman Cherundolo describing the importance of wise investments of our limited funds. Releasing the various AAH "restricted funds" for use in meeting expenses was a hot topic, with Legal Counsel Bernadette Barattini agreeing to look into the issue.

At the November 4, 1981, meeting, it was mentioned that slides and resumes were being sought from artists desirous of applying for Invitational Exhibitions… this was a far cry from the previous relative free-for-all in selection of artists to exhibit. Discussion again ensued concerning the need to preserve our historic building, and the lack of funding available. Membership Chairman Valerie Ciana announced we now had 262 members, and that Steve Morgan and his fiancé were to be married in the AAH galleries on November 27, and would become Patron Members. This was to be the first of numerous weddings to be held here in future years.

Mayor Steve Reed was elected and a congratulatory letter was sent to him, stating that AAH looked forward to working "with the Reed Team in the promotion of art in the city, etc." And work with Mayor Reed we did, as the years went on!

On December 2 further advances were announced in the enhancement of the prize-jurying process for exhibitions, with Valerie Ciana moving that Board Member artists be permitted to enter all shows and receive awards for their work, as long as "these artists would not be permitted to be present at any time during judging proceedings." This was accepted, along with Nancy Greenawalt's motion that there should be a "monitor in all galleries and that no outsiders be permitted in these areas during any phase of official judging."

At the January 6, 1982, Board meeting, I made one of my on-going pleas for Board Members to each submit names of business-people who could become Patron members. It was noted in the minutes that Charles Schulz and I had attended Mayor Reed's inauguration and had "re-confirmed the Association's desire to work with his staff to continue the promotion of Arts in the community."

In the February 3 minutes it was announced that Mrs. Ginny Thornburgh, the Governor's wife, had accepted our invitation to present the judge's awards at the Juried Show reception. I remember how excited we all were at this honour. Another sign that AAH was moving into the future was the mention that "slides were still being accepted for the Juried Show." Prior to Charles' tenure as Executive Director, artists hand-delivered their entries for the Juried Show, and the range of eligibility was within driving distance of Harrisburg. It was he who instituted the procedure of accepting slide entries for the show, making it an international exhibition.

At the March 3, 1982, meeting, a number of motions were made by John Cherundolo of the Finance Committee to consolidate several of the small memorial funds in existence, to help with the ongoing problems with solvency. At the April 7 meeting I thanked the Exhibition Committee for their fine efforts in "making the Juried Exhibit such a memorable event." I also again requested that Board Members give me names of businesspeople to contact about becoming Members.

On May 5, I thanked the Art Auction Chairman Frank Hebert for the great job he'd done with the event held at the Hotel Hershey. Besides the monies generated by the Auction, I announced a grant of $1000 from Kline Foundation to be utilized on building maintenance. Building Chairman Milford Patterson reported that the silicone treatment on the front of the building had been successfully completed, and the procedure to eliminate termite damage had been finished with less structural damage found than expected. All were urged to attend the Annual Meeting at the West Shore Country Club on May 26.

On June 2, 1982, new Board Members Larry Hartman of Dauphin Deposit Bank and artist Charles "Li" Hidley were introduced. The third new Board Member, Dr. David Bronstein, was unable to attend. I was re-elected Board President, with Leo Gilroy (portrait instructor) as Vice President, Rhea Reese as Treasurer, and Louise Linden as Recording Secretary. The Board decided to eliminate the position of Corresponding Secretary as no longer necessary.

The committee chairs named at that meeting were Valerie Ciana—Membership; Milford Patterson—Building; Erna Tunno and Li Hidley—Exhibitions; Charles Schulz and Carrie Thomas—Publicity; Dave Lenker—By-Law Review; Julie Goodrich-Benbow—Professional Arts; Leo Gilroy—School; John Cherundolo—Finance; and Bernadette Barattini as Legal Counsel.

The Art Association has been soliciting friends in the corporate community for years to contribute the prizes for the membership, juried, and school exhibitions. This practice began in the summer of 1982, as in the August 4 President's report I said that I'd contacted businesses for prizes for the Fall Membership Show, but had been told by most businesses that it was too short notice. However, Nationwide Insurance did promise $275 in prizes, and would provide a representative to attend the awards ceremony. Bob Fuller was recorded as providing a $50 watercolour prize... the first of his decades-long tradition of sponsoring prizes for the Fall Show.

Dr. Bronstein suggested asking businesses for prizes a year in advance, which was an excellent proposal. He and Li Hidley voiced their opposition to yet another proposal that the garden be torn out to create additional parking. The subject of lack of parking continued to be a sore one.

Electing Dr. Bronstein to the Board had been a very wise decision, because he brought a fresh perspective and a window into the business community the artists on the Board had lacked. At the September 1 Board meeting, Dr. Bronstein suggested that the image of the Art Association be "upgraded so that more members would be interested in joining." Also at that meeting the Board discussed the desirability of concentrating efforts on a larger, more profitable fundraiser than our meagre efforts of selling food and flea-market items during City festivals.

Changes were being made in the building in that the Executive Director's office was moved upstairs to the former Anna German Gallery, and a grant from the Ann McCormick Trust enabled us to purchase a kiln for the basement in order to start a pottery program. I'd applied for a grant from the Whitaker Foundation for cabinets for the classrooms as well, and was seeking grants to pay for a copier and an alarm system for the building.

Much discussion occurred during the Board meetings in the early 1980's concerning the need for volunteers to keep the building open weekends and to work at receptions. At this point, Charles Schulz was the only employee of AAH. Funding continued to be a tremendous challenge, with the Treasurer's reports listing monthly bank balances as low as $200 at times. A "major" fundraiser was identified as a benefit performance on January 19, 1983, of "Romantic Comedy" at Harrisburg Community Theatre, with Board members requested to sell tickets. The total profit from this event was listed as $726 in the February 11, 1983, minutes.

At the March 18 meeting it was announced that the Annual Art Auction would not be held. A new dues schedule was a subject of discussion, and Valerie Ciana, Membership Chairman, announced that our total membership was now 435... quite an accomplishment since the number had been barely 200 in 1980. John Cherundolo, who had performed so ably and with such dedication as Finance Chairman, tendered his resignation from the Board due to career demands. It was also announced at that meeting that the contract for constructing the new cabinets for the classrooms had been awarded to Woodlore.

An amusing anecdote about an incident during this time involved a bogus classified ad someone placed in *The Patriot News*: "MODELS WANTED TO POSE NUDE for evening drawing class. $9 an hour, 9 a.m. to 5 p.m. 6 days a week. Apply in person, Hbg. Art Exchange, 21 N. Front St., Mon. thru Fri. 9 a.m. to 5 p.m., see B.Foster." This ad, replete with misinformation, generated a plethora of phone calls and visits from would-be models, with Charles fending off importune individuals intent on earning that $9 per hour, many of whom may have been "strippers"! I finally called local radio stations and announced to the public that the ad was a hoax. The ad did attract a LOT of publicity, albeit the wrong kind!

By this time, AAH was presenting community exhibitions at First Federal, Four Seasons Townhomes, and the VIP in Strawberry Square, and Li Hidley was reporting good attendance at the in-house exhibitions. There was definitely a feeling that progress was being made. Complaints were regularly made at meetings, though, about mailings going out late, such as the class brochures. Charles Schulz always countered with saying that there was a need for competent clerical help, either volunteers or from Temporary Help. Mary Beth Walkowiak made a motion at the April 8 meeting that AAH should hire someone to come in on at least a weekly basis. Dr. Bronstein seconded the motion. Charles said he would do his utmost to find someone. He was utilizing the services of Senior Employment people as receptionists and custodians, but none of them had clerical skills.

The new dues schedule was agreed upon as follows: Artists and Supportors at $20; Patrons at $100; Sponsors at $500; and Friends at $1000. Interestingly enough, the two latter categories remained at the same level in 2014.

The June 15, 1983, Board meeting was held at the Maverick Restaurant, and new Board Members were welcomed who had been elected at the Annual Meeting in May. Businessmen Charles Stoup, Morris Schwab and Brian Sann were appointed to the Finance Committee, and would lend their expertise to finally bringing AAH into solvency. I was re-elected President, with Dr. Bronstein as First Vice President. Hidley was elected Second Vice President of Exhibitions, with Leo Gilroy Third VP of School. Leslie Carricato was elected Fourth Vice President, a position now combined with that of Treasurer. Sally Adelman was elected to the Board as Secretary. Also elected to the Board were Frieda Gover and Rona Javitch.

Interestingly, at this meeting Dr. Bronstein commented that AAH artwork should be on the Maverick's walls, and then Charles Stoup inquired, "Where do companies get their paintings?" Bernadette Barattini suggested that "maybe we could contact local directors." The seeds were planted that night for the AAH Sales Gallery...

At the July 8 meeting mention was made of a slide file for artists' works, with Dr. Bronstein asking why we couldn't have the actual artwork instead of slides. No storage space was Hidley's reply. Then at the August 12 meeting, Dr. Bronstein reported that the Building Committee had invited Robert Keys and Mary Knackstedt to be on the committee, with the latter as Chairman, in the hopes that it will "be possible to extend the facilities of AAH."

Charles Schulz reported at the August meeting that Milford Patterson was terminally ill, and I asked that the Board do something to show our appreciation for his long and dedicated service to AAH. I asked that someone make a motion to name one of the galleries in Milford's honour, and Brian Sann moved that the front upstairs gallery, formerly the Ruggieri Gallery, be re-named The Milford Patterson Gallery. Morris Schwab seconded the motion, which was carried. Neither of the proposers knew Milford personally, but were convinced of his service to AAH. Charles and I subsequently visited Milford to tell him of the gallery being named for him, and he was very touched.

Mary Knackstedt, interior designer, was invited to attend the September 16, 1983, Board meeting and pronounced that she'd done a thorough walk-through of the building, and found that it definitely needed to be "jazzed up." She said that storage space for the permanent collection was needed, the outside lamp needs to be fixed, and there were many areas where the building could "be developed." She basically outlined the description of a Sales Gallery, in which people could "come in off the street to purchase artwork," and each artist could supply at least ten paintings. Mary K. explained that the art need not be framed, and that the AAH commission should be between 25 and 33.3%. The Sales Gallery should be on the first floor, have regular hours, and perhaps could be run by volunteer Junior League people.

Again a complaint was made about the class schedule arriving right before classes started, and again Charles said this is "because there are not enough people to do the work." Charles then reported that he was trying to get someone from the Federally-funded Senior Employment program that could type, hopefully four hours a day. He then requested that since he'd worked for four and one-half years with no vacation, he wanted to work half days for the month of October. His request was approved.

At the October 14 meeting I reported that Milford Patterson had died, and that all memorials had been requested to be made to AAH. Frieda Gover reported on a proposed membership drive, which was going to include phone calls to prospective members as well as a brochure that Charles was designing. More discussion ensued concerning the "Gallery Shop," with the position of Shop Director to be filled with Valerie Fleschhaker, who had been interviewed by Morrie Schwab, Dr. Bronstein and Charlie Stoup. It was decided that artists would receive 2/3 of the sales and AAH 1/3, with the Director receiving 1/3 of "what is left." Dr. Bronstein moved that the Sales Gallery be approved, and work be started to develop inventory.

At the November 11 meeting it was decided to open an account for the Sales Gallery at Dauphin Deposit Bank. Bernadette Barattini promised to have a contract ready for Board approval for the Sales Gallery Director, Mrs. Fleishhaker, and Charlie Stoup recommended that all shelving needed to begin the project should be charged against the AMP Fund. A tea was being planned for November 17 for "prospective Sales people," organized by Peg Brown, Betty Bronstein and Rhea Reese. A plaque committee was formed to explore having a commemorative plaque made for the front hall.

At the December 9 meeting Charlie Stoup reported that the person selected as Sales Gallery Director had moved to Washington, DC, and a second person approached had not taken the job. The search was continuing.

I requested at that December 9 meeting that everyone should coordinate with Charles Schulz when "something is happening at AAH so he will know what is going on." It was a time of flux, with many strong and determined personalities working on a number of initiatives simultaneously.

It was noted on January 13, 1984, that poetry readings would commence at AAH on January 15 and continue on future Sundays. The Building report outlined areas in need of paint, and a motion that Deitzel Brothers be contracted to replace the roof was made and accepted.

At the February 10 meeting Dr. Bronstein's Building Report outlined six to seven pages of projects, including the new roof, lighting, painting, air conditioners, fourth-floor storage, etc. Charlie Stoup even suggested that the galleries' hardwood floors be carpeted... Looking back, it was fortunate that no funds were then available to accomplish the latter!

A Sales Gallery Manager had still not been identified, but someone of interest was being interviewed. At the March 9 meeting, the Manager was introduced as Shari Brandt, a graduate of the Art Institute of Pittsburgh. More discussion ensued concerning the parking dilemma, with Hidley asking for suggestions on "how to get the public into the building." A banner or sign on the front of the building was debated. Discussion also concerned re-instating the annual art auction as a fundraiser, with Hidley denigrating the concept by saying art auctions are not profitable..." There are too many auctions now, people with cheap art." The Sales Gallery was reported to be open on May 12, 1984.

At the April 13, 1984, Board meeting Sally Adelman's resignation from the Board was accepted, and Legal Counsel Bernadette Barattini was appointed acting secretary until the June re-organizational meeting. Discussion ensued concerning a "social committee" to help with receptions, and it was suggested that the next President appoint two persons to act as co-chairmen of such a committee. My term of office as Board President was drawing to a close after four years. The membership drive was reported to be doing well, as had the Juried Exhibition, bringing in over $1000.

Charlie Stoup was now Building Chairman and discussed a Capital Campaign to bring in the funds necessary to restore the building. The Sales Gallery's opening was announced for May 12, to coincide with the opening of the exhibition of Barry Cohen's and my paintings.

However, at the May 11 Board meeting in my President's Report I expressed my great disappointment that the Sales Gallery would NOT be opening on May 12 as announced. I told the Board that I had done a great deal of publicity for the opening, contacting the newspaper's art writer Sharon Johnson, as well as local radio stations. I stated, "Then, meetings were held to which I was not invited by the Gallery Committee, and the date of opening was changed." I concluded my report by stating that I no longer would make any effort to publicize the Committee's venture." This was an unsettling time in many respects. At this same May meeting, Valerie Ciana-Hand resigned from the Board due to her marriage and pregnancy.

At the June 8, 1984, meeting I reported that AMP was constructing a large plaque for the AAH front hall, which would honour those who have served the organization through the years. I suggested that it be dedicated at the September Membership Exhibition, which was to be the 20th anniversary of AAH acquiring the building.

The Sales Gallery Committee announced that the Gallery was finally to open on July 11, with inventory to be displayed throughout the entire building.

The following new officers were then duly elected:

Charles Stoup—President
Dr. David Bronstein—First Vice-President
Charles "Li" Hidley—Second Vice-President
Leo Gilroy—Third Vice-President
Brian Sann—Fourth Vice-President

Bernadette Barattini—Secretary

So my four-year term as Board President had come to an end. Little did I know that I would return in another two years.

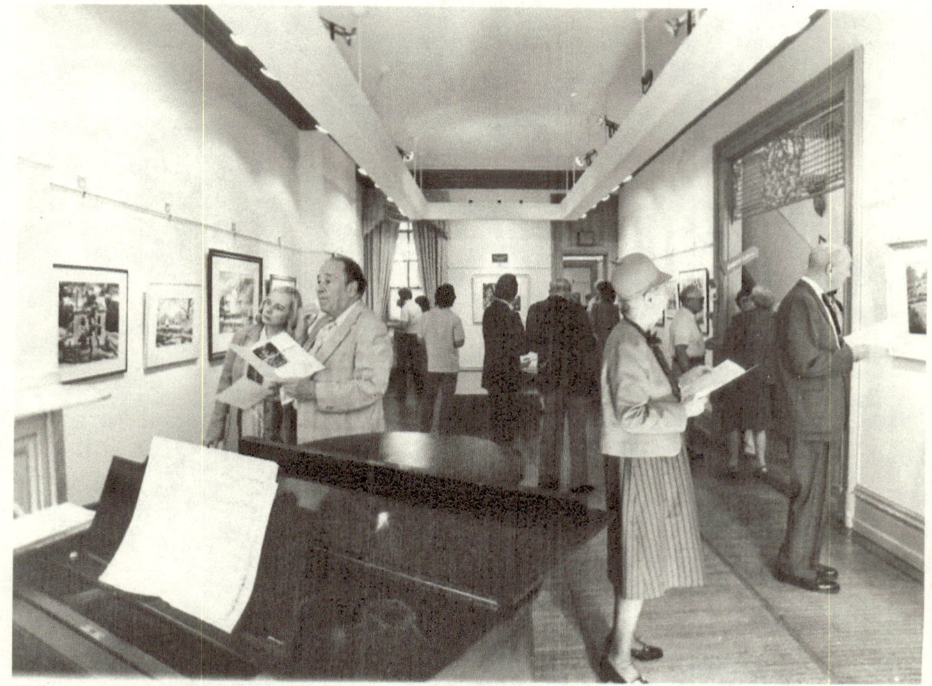

Edward C. Michener Exhibition in the 1960s

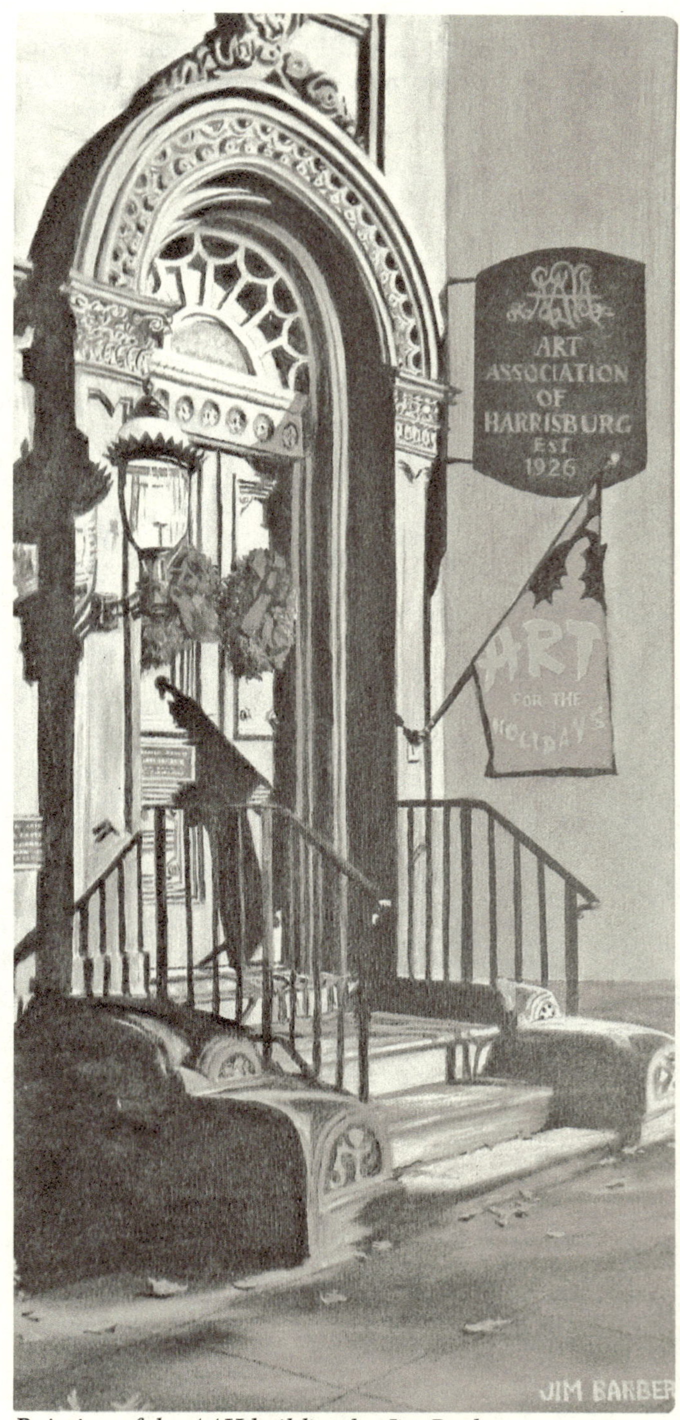

Painting of the AAH building by Jim Barber

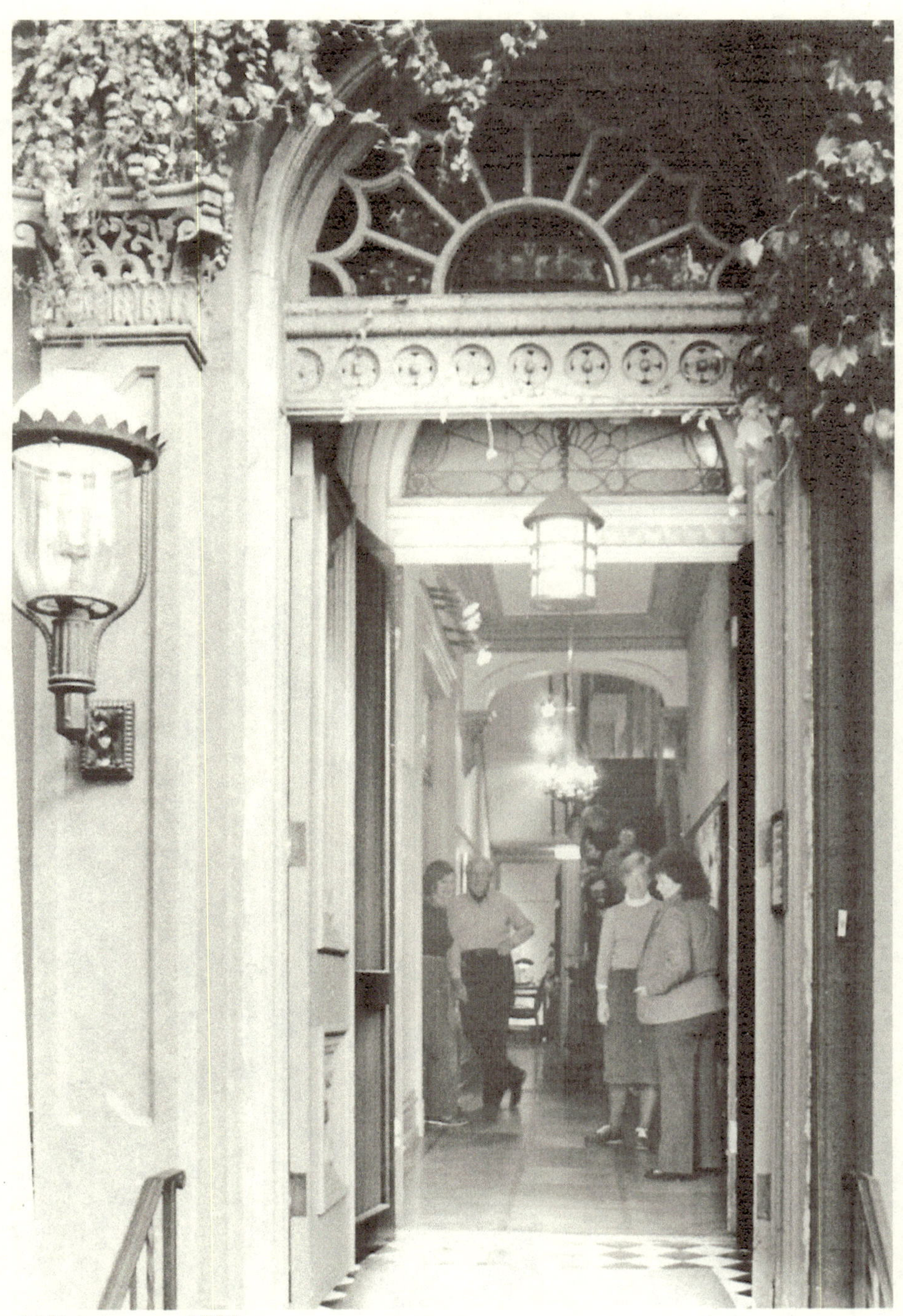

AAH entryway, 1980s

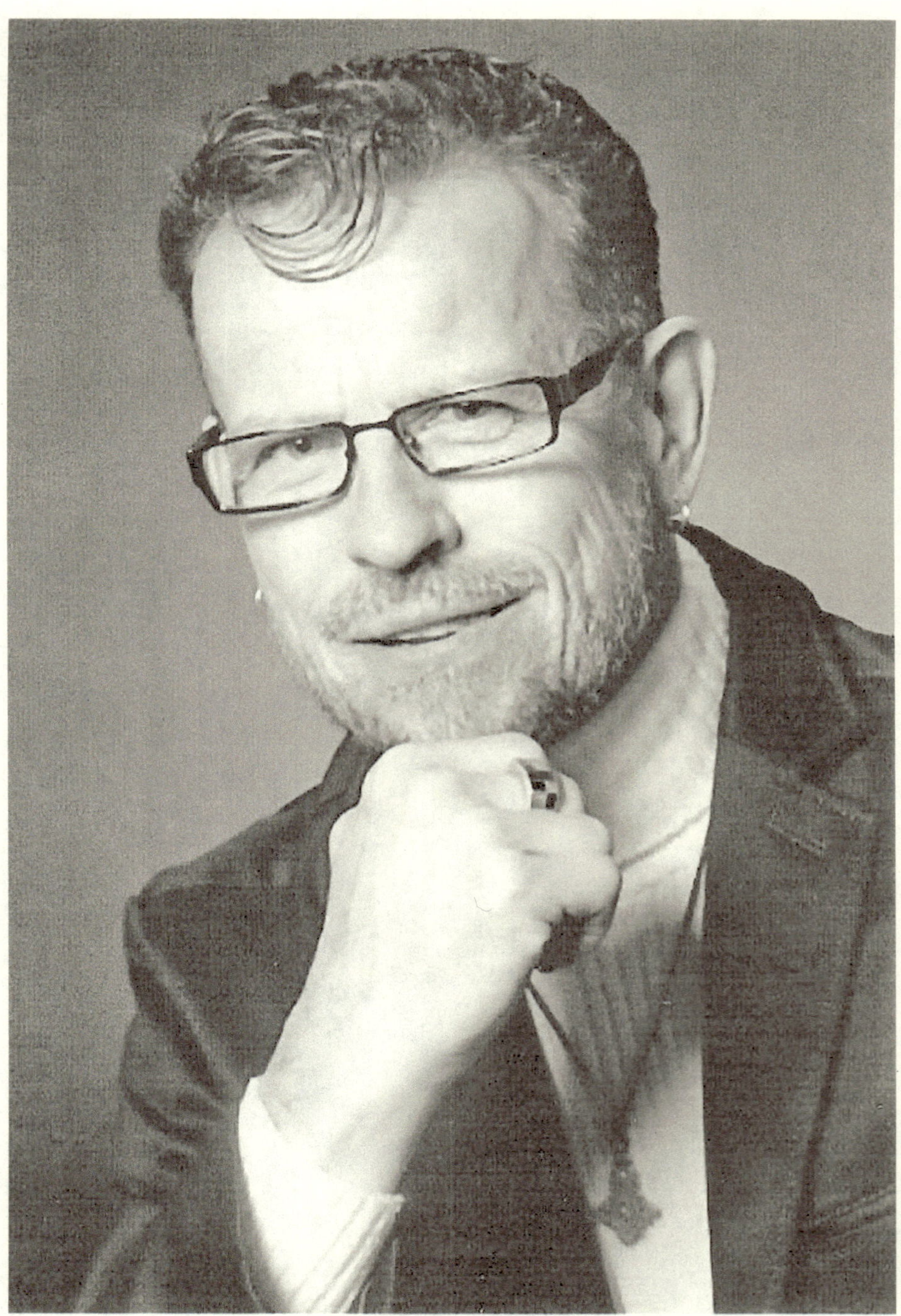

Charles Schulz, Executive Director, 1979-1985

THE INTER-REGNUM: 1984-1986

Charlie Stoup was elected President of the AAH Board in June, 1984, but I still served on the Board. The Board had been meeting at Goldsmith-Flanigan's furniture store on Market Square for several years, and continued to do so under Charlie's leadership for the first several meetings. After a few months, Board meetings were held customarily at the AAH building itself. The Sales Gallery continued to be a major topic of discussion during Board meetings, with new Board member Elsie Swenson being named Chairman of that committee.

Elsie Swenson was the wife of former Harrisburg Mayor Harold Swenson, and an excellent choice to head the committee. At the August 1984, Board meeting she was absent, but her report was distributed and announced that the July 11 premiere of the Sales Gallery had been highly successful. The Sales Gallery Manager's contract had been changed, with now 7-1/2% of the first $100,000 in sales being paid to Manager Shari Brandt, instead of 10%. Five percent of any income over $100,000 was to be given, taken from the 1/3 share of sales retained by AAH and not paid to the artists.

Erna Tunno continued as Exhibitions Co-Chairman, and reported community exhibitions at the VIP Club, Four Seasons Townhomes, First Federal Savings & Loan in Colonia Park, and Sheraton Inn East.

Her Co-Chairman Li Hidley reported that attendance had been low at the in-house exhibitions and invited suggestions on rectifying this situation. Leo Gilroy remained School Chair, and reported about 120 students were expected to enroll in the fall semester.

President Stoup announced that the Capital Campaign, which had been discussed during my Presidency, would officially commence in mid-September. He said that not only the Board and general membership would be solicited, but also foundations and businesses, with a total projected of $69,000.

To save money on printing in the future, Board Member Bart Milano, President of Central Penn Business School, offered to have printing jobs done by his students. This offer was met with enthusiasm by the entire Board. He also very graciously offered to assist in the purchase of more modern office equipment.

Under new business in the minutes, President Stoup said that he had attended a fundraiser group meeting at the West Shore Country Club and had learned of potential funding sources, including the possibility of Harrisburg's creating a "united way for the arts," as Hartford had done very successfully. He went on to predict that "this is a very promising idea for AAH." (This was the first mention of the concept, which eventually developed into Allied Arts, which now has morphed into The Cultural Enrichment Fund.)

At this same meeting, Charlie Stoup recommended that Charles Schulz's salary be adjusted from $9000 to $10,000 annually, and that the "budgeted supplemental secretarial help be changed from $4000 to $3000. He also suggested that a bonus be added to his salary of 2-1/2% of the Sales Gallery proceeds on a quarterly basis. This recommendation was accepted following a motion by Leslie Carricato, and seconded by Frieda Gover.

The Board at this point in 1984 consisted of Charlie Stoup, Bernadette Barattini, Leo Gilroy, Brian Sann, Frieda Gover, Charlie Hickok, Bart Milano, Elsie Swenson, Charles Li Hidley, Rona Javitch, Dr. David Bronstein, Erna Tunno, Bruce Slaff, Rhea Reese, Alyce Spector, Morris Schwab, Leslie Carricato, and me. Staff consisted of Charles Schulz, Executive Director, and Shari Brandt, Sales Gallery Manager.

I was no longer Publicity Chairman... Charlie had asked me to continue, but I was attempting at this time to strike out as a freelance arts writer and didn't want to do it as a volunteer Board Member anymore.

At the September 14, 1984, Board meeting Elsie Swenson and Shari Brandt reported that the Sales Gallery was meeting with success, in that fifteen pieces of art were sold in the last one-and-a-half months, and individuals were beginning to visit regularly. A meet-the-artist series was announced by Elsie as well. President Stoup suggested the coordination of all sales activities for AAH, and appointed a committee for this purpose, consisting of Li Hidley, Elsie Swenson, Erna Tunno, and Charles Schulz as ex-officio member. Dr. Bronstein expressed the need for larger pieces in the Sales Gallery, but I countered with the fact that artists are concerned "with safe storage of larger pieces." For October and November, the AAH galleries would be turned over to the Sales Gallery for exhibiting inventory.

Charles Schulz reported that Bart Milano and Elsie Swenson were assisting in an AAH application to PHEAA for students to assist with general office work and with the Sales Gallery.

At the October 12 meeting, more Sales Gallery successes were noted by Elsie Swenson. Total sales of $4325 had been made since the inception of the Sales Gallery, representing the sale of 37 pieces by 21 artists. The parking spectre was once again raised, with presiding First Vice President Dr. Bronstein instructing Charles to contact the Chairman of the Harrisburg Parking Authority to inquire about subsidized parking for AAH visitors and students. The Capital Campaign was well underway, with letters having been sent to all AAH members as well as area foundations.

By the November 9 Board meeting, AAH had received pledges in the amount of approximately 1/3 of the projected Capital Campaign goal. Changes were reported for the School, namely tuition increases and daytime parking for students at a fee of $10 at the Walnut Street Garage. The AAH roof was finally scheduled for replacement, thanks to the influx of funds for the Capital Campaign. Charlie Stoup did a terrific job in raising the funds for the building repairs... As a retired AMP executive, he knew absolutely everyone, and played golf with a great many movers and shakers.

My contribution at that particular meeting was to suggest that we contact the Paxtang-Lenker-Manor Women's Club as a source to decorate the building for the holidays. Leslie Carricato offered to decorate the front door, and I vividly recall the lavish "della Robbia" arrangement with real fruits she created above the door. At this meeting, Elsie Swenson recommended assigning Board members to host each exhibition... Elsie was ahead of her time, because this fine concept was finally implemented in 2009!

At the December 12, 1984, Board meeting Elsie reported that the Allied Arts Fund, which had been a mere "twinkle in Charlie Stoup's eye" earlier in the year, was about to be incorporated, with an office to be located at 27 North Front Street. The Capital Campaign continued to be successful, as did the Sales Gallery. Charles Schulz announced that the Basic Oil Painting class would be held at the University Centre, which was the class I taught... I remember it well. Leslie Carricato's resignation from the Board was accepted with reluctance at this meeting.

It was discussed that 1985 would be a "Founder Year Celebration," since AAH's charter had been granted 60 years ago in 1926. How the time had flown! Margaret Anderson Brown said that AMP had designed a large plaque for the front hall, listing the original incorporators and others at the first organizational meeting, as well as others who contributed much to the Association. The plaque would be installed in May, with June being named Founders' Month. Peg Brown went on to say that there would be an exhibition of artwork by retired artists in conjunction with the celebration. Elsie Swenson, ever logical, suggested that the Civic Club be contacted for additional information on AAH founders—which indeed I did for this book!

At the January 11, 1985, meeting the Treasurer's Report generated more than the usual commentary. Several of the admonitions resulting from the discussion including requesting Schulz to try to reduce the monthly mailings to members, and for Hidley to study the cost of receptions, entry fees, and commissions on art sales. Shari Brandt was told to talk to JC Penney's about their contributing the best-of-show award for the juried Show, and Morris Schwab agreed to contact various businesses for show prizes. Elsie Swenson was requested "to study how to increase the volume of sales in the Gallery." Artists' membership fees were raised from $20 to $25.

Membership Chairman Frieda Gover reported that we now had 365 Artist members, 136 Supporters, 34 Patrons, 9 Sponsors, 2 Friends, and 2 Honorary Life Members. Charlie Stoup said that $27,600 had been pledged to date for the Capital Campaign.

Ellen Hughes was nominated at the February 8, 1985 Board meeting to fill the unexpired term of Leslie Carricato, and Tom Rouen was nominated to fill that of Alyce Spector, who also had resigned. At this same meeting, Charlie announced that we had received $5000 from the Kunkel Foundation for the Campaign, $250 from Herco, and would receive $1000 from AMP... all good friends in the business community. He reported that Elsie Swenson had been named Chairman of the Allocations Committee for the new Allied Arts Fund, although funds from the group would not be distributed until 1986-87.

At the March 8 meeting, Charles noted that our membership now stood at 738, which was outstanding. The General Fund at that point was $2625, with the School Fund containing $5647. Although those figures were a far cry from those during my early Presidency, the downside was that he also reported we owed $8817 in bills from the General Fund, and $1939 from the School. Hidley noted that 99 pieces had been accepted into the Juried Exhibition, but lamented the fact that we'd had an "abysmal showing" at the March 2 reception. It was speculated that perhaps we should only present membership exhibitions, dropping the invitationals, due to the poor attendance at the latter.

The concept of soliciting businesses to contribute prizes for the membership and juried shows was bearing great fruit, with Charlie Stoup reporting six entities had committed to providing the Juried Show prizes: CCNB, Commonwealth Bank, *The Patriot News*, D&H Distributing, Pomeroy's, and Sutliff Chevrolet. He also was in touch with Rite Aid for the Best-of-Show Award.

Charlie Hickok explained that it was be highly unlikely that we could hold a Juried Exhibition at the State Museum, due to the Museum's policy of exhibiting only historic objects. Hidley suggested that we contribute something to the Museum's permanent collection to be included in that exhibition. On a good note, Charles Schulz reported that we'd made $3000 profit from the school for the winter term!

It was at this March meeting that the resignation of Shari Brandt as Sales Gallery Manager was announced, along with the hiring of Linda Horowitz. She would meet with Schulz and attend the next Board meeting. Charles said that Ellen Arnold, Executive Director of the new Allied Arts Fund, had visited him and left information about the organization, which he distributed to the Board.

As a segue to that, Charlie Stoup, Dr. Bronstein and Brian Sann said that they had met with Allied Arts on March 1 to present our budget, as well as proposed budgets for 1986/87. He pointed out that by joining Allied Arts, AAH could potentially lose from $2000 to $5000 in contributions we currently receive, but we could "gain a large amount of money in return, to enable us to increase our budget considerably." Erna Tunno then moved that AAH apply to membership in the Allied Arts Fund, with Charlie Hickok seconding. The motion was carried in spite of Hidley's questioning the advisability of joining "an organization without reading all the information on it carefully."

It was also at this landmark meeting that Charlie reported that AAH could join the Greater Harrisburg Foundation for $300, which would then become the nucleus of a trust fund for AAH. The GHF would retain .6 of 1% annually to maintain the AAH Fund, with interest being paid to us annually. Ellen Hughes moved that AAH join the GHF, with Rona Javitch seconding. This motion was also carried. Both of these Board decisions would have far-reaching financial benefits to The Art Association.

Then at the June 14, 1985, Board meeting Charlie Stoup was re-elected President, David Bronstein lst Vice President, me Second Vice President of Exhibitions, Bruce Slaff as Treasurer, Bernadette Barattini as Secretary, and Tom Rouen as 3rd VP of the School. Outgoing officers Leo Gilroy, Brian Sann and Li Hidley were thanked for their service. New Board members John Guarnera and Mary Wesoloski were introduced and welcomed.

The Board as of June 14, 1985, was composed of Charles Stoup, Bernadette Barattini, Bruce Slaff, Frieda Gover, Brian Sann, Dr. Bronstein, John Guarnera, Charlie Hickok, Mary Wesoloski, Kathleen Ebner, Leo Gilroy, Li Hidley, Ellen Hughes, Rona Javitch, Frank Masters, Bart Milano, Tom Rouen, Morris Schwab, Elsie Swenson, Erna Tunno, and me.

Regarding the Sales Gallery, it was stated that new Manager Linda Horowitz would be away for the summer, so Keith Schaffer was scheduled to manage the Gallery during her absence. It was also noted that the Jewish Home and Susquehanna Centre had both agreed to pay the Association $100 and $75 per month, respectively for the use of artwork exhibited from the Sales Gallery. Linda Horowitz said that she would like to set a policy to increase this financial support to AAH through community exhibition fees… the beginning of the policy still in place today.

At this meeting it was also proposed by Tom Rouen that a mural be painted on the south wall of the AAH building, and Charles was instructed to get an estimate for the removal of the ivy there. Charlie Stoup reported that pledges and cash received to date amounted to $39,000 of the $69,000 Capital Campaign goal. He suggested that we extend the campaign from three to four years, and his motion was carried. A new roof was now in place, and new office equipment had been purchased. Charlie said that he'd received an estimate on painting the building's exterior for $2500, with the Building Committee having to select the colours for the trim and doors. (It was Charlie Stoup himself who finally removed the ivy from the south wall. He appeared at AAH one hot summer day and amazed Charles and me by cutting and pulling all the ivy down, all single-handedly!)

Although Charles Schulz's contributions to this Board meeting do not indicate that he was leaving as Executive Director, by this time the wheels were in motion. Dr. Bronstein announced that over 30 applicants had responded to an ad for a new Executive Director, and that three applicants would be interviewed. Regarding this situation, a special Board meeting was held on July 12. Present were Bernadette Barattini, Charlie Stoup, Frank Masters, Kathleen Ebner, Elsie Swenson, John Guarnera, Erna Tunno, Ellen Hughes, Mary Wesoloski, and Dr. Bronstein. I did not choose to attend.

Dr. Bronstein, Chair of the Search Committee, reported that his Committee had advertised for the position of executive director and had received 33 applications. These had been screened down to 10 applicants, and finally, only two remained under consideration: Linda Horowitz, AAH Sales Gallery Manager, and Ernest Morrison. Dr. Bronstein said that the ultimate choice was Ms. Horowitz, who would be employed as AAH Executive Director and Sales Gallery Manager combined, effective September 1. The Committee recommended that the new Executive Director be paid $10,000 per year, plus a 10% commission on sales, plus basic health benefits.

Because copies of Charles Schulz's letter of April 12 were not available to answer questions raised by some of the new Board Members concerning the "circumstances surrounding Mr. Schulz's continued employment," it was decided to continue the meeting on July 30. A letter that I had written about the situation was read at the meeting and attached to the minutes.

In my letter, I wrote that I deeply regretted that a Search Committee had been formed to find a new Executive Director, when we already had one with six years' experience and an excellent rapport with both the membership and the community. I lamented the fact that Charles Schulz's employment was being terminated, after his six years of loyal service to AAH, but my words fell on deaf ears, and Linda Horowitz was officially hired to replace him.

At the July 30 meeting, President Stoup explained that he had attempted to acquire health benefits for Charles Schulz, and was trying to find funding to increase his salary, but at the April 12 meeting Charles had presented a letter to the Board requesting either to double his current salary plus health care, or to reduce his hours to two and one half days per week and overtime pay. The Board refused either option, and considered Charles' letter to be one of resignation. Ergo, the Search Committee had been formed. It had been decided that Charles would work three days per week at his current salary until a new Executive Director was identified. Therefore, he continued to work through the summer, until September 1. It was a very uncomfortable situation for everyone.

At the September 13, 1985, Board meeting Linda Horowitz was in attendance as the new Executive Director. Charlie Stoup announced that he had met with Sid Reese from the Dauphin County Commissioners concerning AAH using the parking lot next to our building for evenings and weekends... This adjacent lot has proved a godsend to AAH in the subsequent years for our classes and events.

In my report as Exhibitions Chairman, I gave a detailed schedule of exhibitions selected for the year, and said that our

Committee had decided to charge artists a fee of $15 when they applied for the invitational shows with their slides. For the April 5-May 10, 1986, Juried Exhibition I said that Tom Rouen had been helping to create and print the prospectus, which would be mailed before Thanksgiving. This would encourage more entries. And for the jurors, I had approached US Air to donate free plane tickets, and had arranged with the Host Hotel to provide free rooms. President Charlie Stoup and the Board expressed their satisfaction with all the work of the Exhibition Committee, and the help provided by Tom Rouen with the printing jobs.

Membership Chairman Frieda Gover reiterated my oft-repeated refrain that "if each board member got 3 new members, we could raise $1000 to offset the projected budget deficit"! It was agreed by all that the membership list system should be streamlined, and Morris Schwab said he would provide some help. Charlie Stoup reported that we had $45,000 in cash or pledges for the Capital Campaign.

New Executive Director Horowitz asked the Board for help in staffing the Sales Gallery with volunteers, and requested guidance as to "priorities" in her position. The answer was fundraising and membership.

It was also at this September 13 meeting that a motion was approved to give a plaque and an Honorary Life Membership to Charles Schulz, commemorating his six years of "dedicated service to AAH."

At the October 9, 1985, meeting, held at the Riverfront Inn on South Front Street, Treasurer Bruce Slaff informed the Board that an application had been submitted to the Allied Arts Fund requesting $30,000, which would cover the Executive Director's salary and that of a secretary/book-keeper. He said that he, Ms. Horowitz and Charlie Stoup were meeting with the Allied Arts Fund to make the official pitch for the contribution on November 5.

In my Exhibitions report, I thanked all the Board members who had procured prize monies for the Fall Membership Show, which had attracted 135 entries and had generated $1035 in revenue. I said that our charging a fee of $15 for artists applying for invitational shows had not discouraged entries, and 16 artists had been chosen for the next year's shows.

Charles Hickok itemized a number of crucial improvements needed for the building's interior to professionally display artwork, including new track lighting, painting, etc. Charlie Stoup suggested that the Exhibition Committee study this.

At the November 13 Board meeting, Treasurer Bruce Slaff said that the meeting with Allied Arts had gone well, but "the prognosis is vague" as to whether or not our request would be honoured for the $30,000.

Charlie Stoup reported the unfortunate news that Charles Schulz had applied for Unemployment Compensation, and it was discovered that AAH had been noncompliant for years, never having paid "into the system." Under the advice of counsel, AAH paid $1650 for 1985 and the four previous years, "to insure that we would not have to pay claims now or in the future." He cautioned that "we may be called into a hearing if Schulz's claim goes forward."

A job description for the Executive Director had been created and presented by John Guarnera. Kathleen Ebner stated "that the Board needs to know their responsibilities in giving directives to the Executive Director, so as not to overburden her." The Board approved the new job description, the first "definition of the position." The job description is essentially still valid today, stating that the Executive Director, under the supervision of the Board President, is responsible for the "day to day operations, administration and the community's awareness of the Association." The Director was also announced to be responsible for the operation and management of the Sales Gallery, and to be in charge of the scheduling and supervision of all personnel, both paid and volunteer, the coordination and oversight of the use of the facilities, and the coordination of the general maintenance of the grounds and building.

Furthermore, the Executive Director was instructed to be in charge of all public relations for the Association, both with the community and the media. All these responsibilities so outlined are still a true reflection of my Presidency today, in 2014.

Another matter brought up at this meeting concerned the Capital Campaign, and the fact that Ramsey Davenport was finishing up his work on repairing the foyer. An appeal had been made to the "Historical Society" to replace the front windows with "aluminum thermopane" ones, but fortunately this concept was rejected. The windows would have to be replaced with historically accurate wooden ones, mirroring the originals. The Capital Fund had expended $30,000 thus far.

Dr. Bronstein nominated Jane First to the Board, and she was approved. Linda Horowitz described the plaque to honour the late Mary Sachs, whose sister Hannah Cantor donated $500 annually to AAH for scholarships. Recipient organizations of the Mary Sachs Foundation were all required to purchase and install such a plaque. Ms. Horowitz went on to report that a mentally challenged young man who had been doing the cleaning in the building had been let go due to his inability to do the job. Andy Cater, one of our Senior Employment receptionists, was willing to do the work for $4 per hour.

Morrie Schwab said that Don Jenkins, a computer system consultant, would volunteer to help to evaluate the need for a computer, and the feasibility of using equipment lent by D&H. Linda Horowitz said that Tom Rouen was designing a sign for the front of the building, and brought up the suggestion, made apparently in the spring, that the AAH name be changed to “another name which might generate more interest.” Fortunately, several Board members “expressed preference to generate interest in other ways.”

At the January 14, 1986, Board meeting, several staff problems were discussed, namely that we no longer had a night watchman, due to injury, nor a maintenance person, both provided by the Federally-funded Senior Employment program. Director Linda Horowitz reported that she would like the gallery to be open Sundays, but no volunteers were available. She also said that students from Central Penn Business School were helping with some office work. (Although no mention was made at this point in the minutes, Terrie Hosey, now AAH Curator, must have been working at AAH during this period as temporary office help as well.)

Another item of interest mentioned at this meeting was the description of the new sign for the front of the building: a 3x5’ maroon wooden sign with gold lettering and the AAH logo. It was noted that a building permit would have to be acquired for the installation of the sign, as well as the approval of The Architectural Review Board, since the building is in the National Historic District of Governors’ Row. More comments were made about the unexpected expenses entailed by the unemployment compensation situation, and about the continued success of the Capital Fund Drive.

In my Exhibitions report, I noted that *The Patriot News* was doing an article about the Figuratively Speaking Exhibition, and that entries were coming in steadily for the Juried Exhibition, including inquiries from artists in India, Poland and Saudi Arabia. The two jurors were flying in on US Air, and would stay at the Holiday Inn, “with those businesses covering the costs.”

John Guarnera made an “Exhibitions Extraordinaire” report concerning a potential lecture series by nationally acclaimed artists, such as Louise Nevelson, Phillip Pearlstein and Helen Frankenthaler. (This did not materialize, unfortunately.)

At the February 14, 1986, meeting Charlie Stoup made the exciting announcement that the Allied Arts Fund had agreed to contribute $15,000 to AAH in quarterly payments. He said that the first $7000 would cover the deficit, with the remaining $8000 being utilized for a part-time secretary and an increase for the Executive Director's salary. When Charlie expressed concern that the AAH memberships from corporations may be eroded as a result of the AAF campaign, Elsie Swenson suggested that if this happened, we should document the loss of donations and submit this to AAF so that they could re-evaluate the needs of AAH.

In Linda Horowitz's report, she stated that Middletown Lumber had constructed new sculpture bases for us, and thanked Morris Schwab for the computer terminal and modem in our office. She also said that the Mary Sachs plaque was finished and ready to install in our front hall.

Then, Linda submitted her letter of resignation as Executive Director, due to her poor health. Everyone expressed their sadness at this announcement. (Linda, although appearing very fit and an avid runner, had debilitating allergies, which were exacerbated by traffic fumes in the city.) Dr. Bronstein was again appointed head of a search committee. Linda had told me privately that she was resigning, and advised me to apply for the job, because she said, "You are doing most of the work here anyway." I was there pretty much full-time during her tenure, as running the exhibitions was a very time-consuming job.

In my Exhibitions report, I commented that the 58th Annual Juried show had generated $6000 income from entry fees, with 500 entries having been received from 40 states, 5 provinces of Canada, Poland, Sweden and West Germany! The champagne reception, scheduled for April 5, was to be a posh affair, with Bob Bissett engaged to photograph the proceedings, and Tony Perry of *The Patriot News* promising to do an article.

On March 13, Jane First suggested that the Art Association should consider presenting a "Treasures of Harrisburg" exhibition for the next year, but it was pointed out that since we had no security system in place, this would not be feasible. (The concept came up again a year or so later...) Concerning staffing, Linda Horowitz announced that AAH would be open on Saturdays going forward, from 9 AM to 3 PM, and from 6:30 to 10 PM the evenings when classes were in session. The building was to be watched over by a "night janitor" during those hours.

Charlie Stoup reported that approximately 48 inquiries had been received concerning the Executive Director position, and the committee had reduced that number to 15. After a job description and salary level letter had been sent out to those individuals, 7 responded who wanted to be considered. I was among that seven.

At the April 10 meeting, Dr. Bronstein announced that four candidates had been interviewed by the Search Committee: Linda LeFever, Susan Lott, Delores Kiely, and me. He said, “Thomas was unanimously selected by the committee.” The Board then moved that I be hired at $14,400 per year and would start working on April 15, with Linda Horowitz working with me for two weeks. After the Board officially approved my employment as Executive Director, I submitted my letter of resignation from the Board, and asked for suggestions for a replacement instructor for my Basic Oil Painting class. The terms of my employment forbade my teaching a class for AAH... and I would find very quickly that my new position would consume almost my every waking hour.

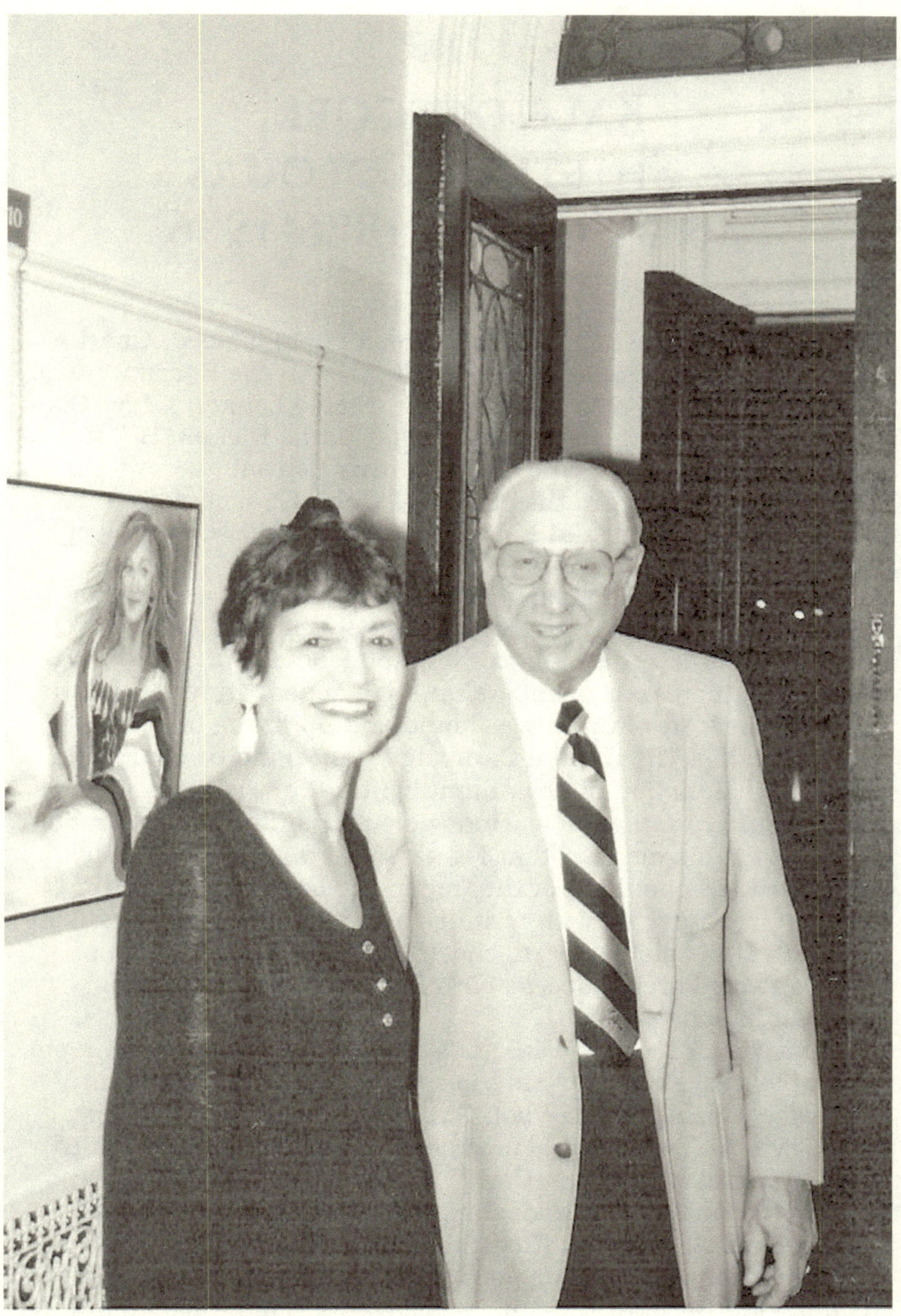

Helen Middleton and Charles Stoup

KALEIDOSCOPE – SHIFTING COLOURS AND SHAPES: 1986-1996

When my tenure as Executive Director commenced, Charlie Stoup was still President of the Board. Also on the Board were Dr. Bronstein, Suzie Merrill, Frieda Gover, Nancy Lenker, Bruce Slaff (Treasurer), Frank Masters, Max Mills, Charlie Hickok, Brian Sann, Elsie Swenson, Erna Tunno, Morris Schwab, Leroy Robinson, Jane First, Kathleen Ebner, John Guarnera, Tom Rouen, Ellen Hughes, and Bernadette Barattini (Secretary/Legal Counsel).

At my first Board meeting as Executive Director in June of 1986, the Treasurer's report was extremely encouraging, with Bruce Slaff stating that due to show sponsors for prize exhibitions, increased membership, high school attendance, and the new Allied Arts Fund, "we should end up in the black next year"! Amazing! The Capital Campaign projects to be completed included: installation of new "night lighting" by Dauphin Electric; a new security system; new windows, and painting inside and out.

It was at this meeting that Frank Masters, Building Chair, questioned the condition of the tree in the front of the building, fearing it was infested with termites and might fall down, causing a lawsuit. I was instructed to check into this. My Exhibitions report reflected great success both financially and regarding jurors and sponsors.

In my first Executive Director's report, I listed the following as our employees: Receptionists Viola Clark (Senior Employment) and Joyce Haufnagle (Tri-Vac); Custodian—Chung Ee ($32 per week); Typist—Twila Perry (once per week—a former student of mine); General Volunteer—Carole Lewis; Sales Gallery (Sat. and Sun. afternoons)—Deb Goldschmidt (Central Penn student); Typist—Marikaye Snyder (Central Penn student—Mondays).

Community shows were going well at this time, and I said that I'd contacted Barbara Berk at Pennsylvania Blue Shield about mounting two-month-long shows there. The shows at Highmark Blue Shield continue to be our most popular with our artists today. I announced that I'd joined the PA Society of Association Executives, and the minutes reported, "Thomas says she loves her work." I said that I had to take a week's vacation from July 28 through August 1 in order to finish my Master's Degree work, and Viola was working full-time during my absence.

Another highlight of June 1986 meeting was my comment that PHICO representatives had visited the gallery and were considering the purchase of several paintings and pieces of sculpture from the current exhibition... This was to be my first big sale of my career managing the Sales Gallery.

At the September 19, 1986, meeting I happily announced that PHICO had purchased four sculptures for over $11,000 and needed additional artwork for their new facility, with me as their consultant. This major sale was to be promoted in the PHICO report. I was invited to speak at The College Club, West Shore Rotary, and The Civic Club about AAH, a subject on which I've continued to wax eloquent for over 28 years.

Charlie Stoup congratulated me on my "fine job as Executive Director, on behalf of the Board."

The Capital Campaign progressed well, and on November 14, Charlie Stoup explained that $72,500 had been raised. He said that the building would be closed for two weeks in February for painting of the first floor, but would not affect the classes. The indoor shutters would be completely refurbished, and the drapes would be removed. The intent was to make the galleries brighter and more open, the better to display the artwork.

Frieda Gover, Bruce Slaff and I had made the presentation to the Allied Arts Fund on November 13, and we had requested an annual allocation of $25,000, a big increase over the $15,000 received the previous year.

It was noted that the Special Events Committee was planning a "Harrisburg Collectors' Show" for September 1988, chaired by Jane First. Questions were raised concerning security for such a show, the willingness of collectors to lend their treasures, guards, school sessions, etc. More would be discussed on this topic in the months to come.

To celebrate the newly painted galleries, a play about Mary Cassatt was to be presented on Sunday, March 8, with actors Mr. and Mrs. William Sommerfield of Philadelphia.

In my report, I noted that since April 15, when I began my job, the commission on art sales to AAH was $6738. Morris Schwab and "all the others complimented Thomas on the great job she is doing." It was hard work, but so exciting, with all the Capital Campaign projects, the art sales, the successful classes, and all the work with the artists. The Board was hardworking and we made a great team.

Other good news at this meeting included the new (historically correct) front windows were finally being installed by Ramsay Davenport, and new security system was in place. Besides two Central Penn interns helping at the office, it was noted that "Terrie Tedeschi is now a part-time secretary." At last Terrie appeared in the minutes, even though she had been doing temp work for Charles Schulz earlier.

This meeting was a real roller-coaster... Charlie Stoup asked everyone to consider changing the name for the Art Association to the "McCormick Art Centre, " and then Frank Masters brought up the subject of the public sculpture across the street from AAH —"Egyptian Gate." He felt that AAH should take a position on the subject of whether it should be moved. This was extremely perplexing to me, as I had chaired the committee that had selected the sculptor and the design, prior to my being hired as Executive Director. I was very proud of the sculptor Ike Hay and his stunning creation, and in fact I had written a letter to the editor of *The Patriot News* in the sculpture's defense after a writer had grumped that "Gate" resembled a "cross between MacDonald's Golden Arches and Benihana of Tokyo"!

I was requested not to send my letter to the editor, despite artist Board Members Charlie Hickok and John Guarnera speaking up in defense of the sculptor. In fact, Charlie Stoup was asked by the Board to write a letter to the "appropriate parties indicating that the board recommends serious consideration be made in finding another location for the Egyptian Gate sculpture." I was not pleased, but my hands were tied. Fortunately, the sculpture was NOT moved, and continues to stand as a landmark across the street from AAH today, albeit in dire need of a new coat of paint.

That summer of 1986 another unfortunate incident occurred, concerning an exhibition of Philadelphia artist Larry Stearns' works. Stearns painted large canvases with semi-clothed male figures posed in the foreground, with sections of famous paintings in the background. His paintings had been shown at the State Museum of Pennsylvania in The Art of the State, and he was a highly respected artist. However, one of the Board members saw the show in our gallery the Saturday morning before the opening reception, and he called me at home, aghast. He shouted angrily that he would "never take his wife and daughters to view an exhibit like that!" He apparently was disturbed by what he perceived as a homoerotic feel in the artwork, and he demanded that I take the entire exhibition down and replace it with works from the Sales Gallery. I refused, and called Exhibition Chairman John Guarnera, who also refused. Finally, our President Charlie Stoup asked me to move one small painting of a man in a bathtub from the main gallery to the second floor middle gallery, which he said would enable him to mollify the complainers. I moved the painting, which I did not regard as censorship, but mere re-arranging. Since the people who were upset never visited the gallery, but just expressed their disapproval because of what they heard, this smoothed over the situation. Crisis averted.

In the subsequent months, substantial progress was made on the Capital Campaign projects. Discussion continued to crop up from time to time about taking garden space to increase the parking lot, but luckily this was dropped. As of January 1987, Charlie Stoup announced that $74,000 of the $84,000 Campaign goal had been raised, and that the floors would be refinished in June and new stair carpets installed. He said that the galleries would be painted in February. He commented that interior designer Mary Knackstedt, who had assisted in the formation of the Sales Gallery, was helping with suggestions as to paint colours, etc. (This caused a major run-in between Charlie and me, when I declined to accept Mary K's advice that all the galleries be painted deep red. Mary K ceased her advice, and Charlie stormily told me, "You've lost us a powerful friend.")

We got a computer of our own that January, a Tandy, for $1399... Don Jenkins and my husband Scott Thomas worked on getting it operational, with Frank Masters' friend Wilbur Lawrence having downloaded all our membership information onto a disc for the new computer. Terrie Tedeschi-Hosey was noted as the person who would do the data entry. Progress was being made on all fronts.

The Allied Arts Fund was extremely helpful in putting AAH on a firm financial footing, along with the efforts of the business people on the Board.

It was at the March 27, 1987, Board meeting that Jane First again brought up the subject of the "Treasures of Harrisburg" exhibition for September of 1988. Elsie Swenson and Susie Merrill were named as co-chairmen, and Mrs. Merrill went on to say that a gala benefit would be held in conjunction with the exhibition.

We had officially hired Viola Clark by this point as a part-time receptionist. She had worked for us for 5 years as part of the Federal Senior Employment program, but at last we put her on the payroll. In March I told the Board that our second receptionist, from Senior Employment, was Carolyn Jones. Viola was a character, gruff-voiced and opinionated. People who phoned often said to me, “That man who answered the phone told me...” And I would reply, “That was no man; that was Viola!” Carolyn Jones was the opposite, very “genteel” and soft-spoken in her phone manner. They did not get along. Viola handled our bulk mailings in those days, and ruled her volunteers with an iron fist. An original, was Viola, but very loyal to the Association.

The annual meeting in 1987 was held at the Sheraton East, with President Charlie Stoup asserting that the past year had been good, with AAH ending the fiscal year in the black. The program that year consisted of a play by Paper Sword President Gene Hosey entitled, “Just One of the Boys,” as well as a slide show by Bob Bissett called “That Was the Year That Was: Art Association 1986/87.” (The Paper Sword was the poetry group, founded by Gene Hosey and Tom Giannelli, which met on Sundays in the AAH main gallery.)

At the June 26, 1987, Board meeting the officers elected were Charlie Stoup, President; Bruce Slaff, Treasurer; Dr. Bronstein, First Vice President; John Guarnera, Second Vice President, Exhibitions; Tom Rouen, Third Vice President, School. Bernadette Barattini was again the LegalCounsel/Secretary. Charlie Stoup noted that the Capital Campaign fundraising was officially over, thanks to a $5000 pledge from Dauphin Deposit Bank & Trust Co., bringing the total pledges to our goal of $84,000. However, plans were afoot to re-do the garden, naming it The McCormick Garden in honour of our founders Mr. and Mrs. Vance McCormick, and the generousity of the McCormick Foundation throughout the years.

Discussion continued about the “Treasures of Harrisburg” exhibition project, with a tent in the parking lot next door being proposed for the night of the gala, Saturday, September 25, 1988. Admission to the exhibition was planned to be $5 for the public, $3 for AAH members. The funds to be raised were to go towards restoring the permanent collection and for scholarships.

We were holding a great many special receptions for other groups in the galleries in those days, including events for PA Blue Shield, Pre-Trial Services, Rotary Clubs, etc. We used Central Penn Business School interns as our evening receptionists, and had volunteers in the Sales Gallery on Saturdays. Our evening “security guard” for many years was Johnnie Johnson from Senior Employment. Senior Employment people were supposed to be in “training” to eventually take real jobs on payroll, as Viola Clark had done. Mr. Johnson was theoretically “in training” for about 15 years. He wore a uniform of sorts he’d acquired somewhere, and sat out on the front steps on a chair, eating his nightly ice cream, and watching for students arriving so that he could open the parking lot gate. Unfortunately, Mr. Johnson habitually kept a flask in his battered valise, and all too often our interns would call me at home saying he was incoherent. So, I would have to come in and confront him, and send him home. Sometimes his daughter would come for him; sometimes he staggered off on his own. Once, he'd left in a very bad condition in a snowstorm, and when he didn't show up for several weeks, we assumed the poor chap had succumbed. One of our artists painted a portrait of him as a memorial and I ran an article about his death in the newsletter. Then he re-appeared, and I had to do another article on his miraculous return. Johnnie Johnson was an institution here for many years.

On Senior Employment payday, Mr. Johnson's buddies would show up, looking for "Pops" to borrow money. I'd send them away, and once a very inebriated guy yelled at me, 'I'm going to report you to the Big Boss!' I replied very coolly and firmly, "I AM the Big Boss. Get out of here!" And off he went. It helped that I was usually taller than these cronies of Johnnie's.

Once, however, Carolyn Jones was at the receptionist's desk and called me to come downstairs. There sat a very odd-looking chap in long flowing white robes and gold chains, scribbling incoherently on a paper. His eyes were glazed and his speech slurred. I told him that we were closing and that he would have to leave. He stood up... and he towered over me! I must admit that I was scared for once. Not only was this man high on something, but he was taller than me... not what I was used to. Nonetheless, I repeated that we were closing and he had to leave. He finally wove his way out the front door, and Carolyn Jones and I locked up and I called the police. I believe he was picked up. That was the only time, I believe, that I was really worried about a situation.

I had my first college intern in 1988—Heather Davis, of Hollins College. She was with us for an entire month and wrote a brief history of the Association as her research project. We were getting excellent press in these years, thanks to *The Patriot News* arts reporter Sandy Cullen. AAH exhibitions were generating a great deal of interest, as was recorded in the January 15, 1988, minutes. Exhibitions Chairman John Guarnera expressed his concern regarding the quality of the show invitations, so it was decided to look at upgrading them. The invitations were being printed in-kind at that point by Rite Aid, thanks to Board Member Tom Rouen.

In March 1988, Robert Allen, the Board member now in charge of the Building Committee, announced that H. Edward Black Associates were designing the new garden as an in-kind service, which was lovely. More funds were being sought to complete the new McCormick Garden, which was to include paved areas and shrubbery beds, making it an appropriate space for outdoor receptions and art classes. New air conditioning units were purchased from D&H Distributing Company and installed.

Board member Charles Andrews, owner of The Garden Gallery in Carlisle, proposed raising the artist membership fee to $30, to offset the increase in printing fees after Tom Rouen of Rite Aid left the Board, as well as higher postage rates. He explained that "The Art Association is unique... there is nothing like it between here and Washington, D.C." With the services rendered to artists by AAH, the raise in membership fee seemed more than justified by all concerned.

Gene Hosey gave a report at the March 25, 1988, Board meeting concerning the Paper Sword, explaining that the poetry group was attracting writers from far and wide to read at the group's twice-monthly meetings at AAH. The Paper Sword attracted not only writers, but also avid listeners, and the group presented musical programs as well. The poets, all AAH members, were applying to the PA Council on the Arts for a grant to support paying readers, and Gene said that the PCA was "very impressed with the Art Association as the only real Art Centre in all of Central PA!"

At the June 24, 1988, Board meeting a new slate of officers was elected, with Dr. Bronstein becoming Board President, Brian Sann First Vice President, John Guarnera Exhibitions Vice President, Gene VanDyke School Vice President, Bruce Slaff Finance Vice President/Treasurer, and Steve Feinour as Secretary/Legal Counsel. Steve Feinour had been elected to the Board after his wife Bernadette Barattini had left after serving three full terms.

The School was thriving, with many new students registering for summer classes, and it was noted that the "new flyer is quite attractive, of good quality paper stock, and well laid out." Improving our printed materials was very much on everyone's mind at this time. The newsletter, unfortunately, was still being Xeroxed by generous business partners, and did not present a very professional look.

The garden project was moving on steadily, with Ed Black's firm having created a lovely design. Bob Allen presented the plan on June 24, explaining that, if fully implemented, the project would cost $21,000. However, it was hoped that many contractors would donate in-kind services. The garden was to be officially named "The McCormick Garden" in memory of The Association's founders and benefactors over the years. After the plan was accepted, Ed Black promised to make up specs to go out to various landscape firms for bids. He was extremely helpful in overseeing the entire project, which was very kind.

Supplementing a $3500 pledge from the Anne McCormick Trust Fund were $500 pledges from Board Members Bronstein, Brian Sann, Charlie Stoup, Ellen Hughes, Jane First, Morris Schwab, and Robert Allen. The plan was accepted by the Board, with the hope that the contractors would be able to clear the garden area in the fall, lay the lighting conduits and brickwork, and then do the fence and plantings in the spring.

President Bronstein praised Charlie Stoup for his excellent job as President during the past four years, and said that thankfully, he would stay active on the Building Committee and "as our star fundraiser"! I learned a great deal from Charlie, observing him calling his buddies on the phone, joking about their golf scores, and then asking them for money for capital projects.

As new Vice President for the School, Dr. Van Dyke reported that his committee was planning to offer a pilot scholarship class at a city school, funded by the $500 granted annually by the Mary Sachs Foundation. The concept was that a minority art teacher would be approached to teach the class, which would be attended by those youth who had been identified by the committee with the help of their public school teachers, as being both disadvantaged and artistically talented. Van Dyke said that if the pilot program succeeded, other entities could be approached to fund an ongoing program.

Regarding the Sales Gallery, Elsie Swenson applauded the volume of sales generated since I'd been hired. Board Members were requested to pass along contact information on potential business art clients, and then I pointed out the "advisability of remaining low-key in advertising for the Sales Gallery due to the Association's nonprofit status." I reminded everyone that we may only handle our own artist members' works on consignment, and cannot legally buy nor sell work in a retail manner. Every so often Board Members would ask why we couldn't sell commercial notecards and art supplies, and I had to remind them that we could only sell members' works as part of our mission to support artists.

It was at the September 30, 1988, Board meeting that resurrecting the Bal Masque was listed among the President's goals. Dr. Bronstein also said that he hoped to hold a show of art owned by corporations in the area, to improve AAH graphics, to involve older members who no longer attend functions, and to develop a strategic plan for the organization. These were all fine goals, and fortunately, both the strategic plan and the Bal actually came about.

One may ask why the minutes from the September 30, 1988, Board meeting didn't mention anything about the proposed "Treasures of Harrisburg" exhibition, planned so long ago for this very month? What happened was that the committee requested that the entire building, studios and galleries all be taken over for an entire month, with all classes cancelled, and with my moving out of my office for the duration. This I adamantly declined to do. I explained that cancelling classes and not permitting any visitors to the building for a month without paying a fee would radically decrease the excellent rapport AAH had built up with students and the public. I stated unequivocally that I could not run the Association's business from my home in Susquehanna Township. I stated that it would be impossible to turn the entire building over to a "Treasures" show for a month. The committee was disappointed, but withdrew their plan and turned to explore other concepts.

In the long term, their plans for the lavish gala in conjunction with the treasures show morphed into an extravagant catered, sit-down dinner for the garden's dedication, which worked fine.

At this time, the Board consisted of Vangie Gekas (wife of Representative George Gekas), Jane First, Dr. Ruth Leventhal, Brian Sann, Charley Ann Rhoads, Charles Stoup, Dr. Bronstein, Erna Tunno, Frieda Gover, Suzanne Merrill, Morris Schwab, Jody Grass, Bruce Slaff, Norma Gotwalt, Gene VanDyke, Robert Allen, Elsie Swenson, Kathleen Ebner, Charles Andrews, Steve Feinour, John Guarnera, Charles Hickok, and Ellen Hughes. However, Elsie Swenson tendered her resignation from the Board due to her being elected as new president of the Allied Arts Fund. Dr. Leventhal moved that the minutes reflect the Board's appreciation for all the fine service that she had given AAH during the years of her tenure. She was a terrific Board member!

I noted that I would spend the three days of Thanksgiving Weekend at the Farm Show Building for a large Christmas gift sale, manning an AAH booth with artwork and literature. (I can clearly remember that long, unproductive weekend... no sales, and lots of lugging of artwork in and out.)

At the January 27, 1989, Board meeting, our guest of honour was Holly Leggett, the Executive Director of the Allied Arts Fund, who praised our presentation to their allocations panel highly. She announced that AAH would be receiving an allocation of $21,000 from the Allied Arts Fund in 1989, which everyone greatly appreciated. Two other guests were my current interns Kathy Carl of Oberlin College, Ohio, and Michael Poss of Dickinson College. Kathy had been assisting our Curator Charles "Li" Hidley in cataloguing the Permanent Collection, while Michael was learning gallery management from me. Treasurer Bruce Slaff extolled that "all bank balances are good."

The Special Events Committee was by now fully engaged in planning the gala for the dedication of the McCormick Garden on May 6, with an elegant sit-down catered dinner and cocktails in the new garden. The cost per person was to be $50. I was instructed to invite the County Commissioners, Mayor Stephen Reed, the Governor, and other dignitaries.

Dr. Bronstein's dream of resurrecting the Bal Masque for 1990 was moving on apace, with his mentioning that he was contemplating inviting "old-timers" such as Tony Arms, Pete Wambach, Sr., and Nick Ruggieri to assist in the planning. Continuing with his President's report on March 31, 1989, Dr. Bronstein said that the "most rewarding thing the Art Association has done" was the ceremony celebrating the Scholarship Class we'd sponsored at Shimmel School for 15 disadvantaged city children. He thanked the School committee, Norma Gotwalt in particular, for a job well done.

Three scholarship classes were planned for 1989, thanks to grants of $500 each from Hannah Sachs Cantor, the Kiwanis Club, and the Mary Sachs Foundation.

I reported that Nick Ruggieri had informed us that a show of his work would open in Strawberry Square on May 6, the same evening as our Garden dinner. Very graciously, Nick said that he was listing AAH as an honorary "co-sponsor" of his show, and that he would give AAH $300 from his sales towards our scholarship classes. Interestingly enough, apropos of an exhibit of corporate art, Jody Grass and Vangie Gekas said that their investigation revealed very little if any national or international art in the area's businesses. However, they discovered that many businesses had purchased art from the AAH Sales Gallery and would be happy to lend some pieces back for an exhibition. I was requested to coordinate something with the exhibition committee.

The plaque for the McCormick Garden had been ordered, to include all the names of the donors who'd contributed $500 and up for the project. Couples were to be listed as "Mr. and Mrs., rather than using the women's first names, in the interest of formality and consistency." It was announced that Walter, Nisley and Walter were the low bidders on the planting, and would be doing the landscape work in early April.

The Garden Gala dinner did take place on May 6, but it rained heavily that evening and the bar outside under the canopy was very soggy. The tables with the floor-length cloths throughout the galleries looked very elegant, and the meal, catered by Wickey's of York, was delicious. An old chap spilled his coffee all over me, I recall. (Initially, the Board had requested that I pay to attend the event, but I persuaded them that I had to work while in attendance, so they relented.)

In fact, at the Annual Meeting held May 23 in the West Shore Country Club, I showed a slide program depicting the evolution of the garden from overgrown wilderness to the new brick courtyard with lovely plants and fence. Dr. Bronstein summarized the many accomplishments of AAH during the past year: the Scholarship Class program, the Juried Exhibition, the Garden project, and the work of AAH volunteers and Board. He announced that the Bal Masque would be held at the new Harrisburg Hilton on February 9, 1991.

There was a Bal Masque steering committee meeting on September 6, which consisted of Pete Wambach, Tony Arms, Fern Hetrick, Nick Ruggieri, Jean Skinner, Paul Beers, Hain Wolf, Jane First, Elsie Swenson, Dr. Ruth Leventhal, Alyce Spector, Helen Heisey and Mike Greenwald. Themes for the Bal were tossed about, including "Ellis Island," "Pictures on an Exhibition," "Night at the Opera," "Haunted Bookstore," "Night of Mythology," "Night Over a Rainbow," "Night of Comic Strips," and "Hollywood's Golden Age." Since the Bal had not been held for almost a decade, imaginations were running rampant. Board Member Jody Grass was named Bal Chair.

Another momentous decision was to hold a strategic planning session in late January, to be conducted by Dr. Leventhal. President Bronstein elaborated to those who doubted the need for the session that it "need not necessarily change direction for an organization, but would clarify the direction in which it was going, and set guidelines for future growth."

It was at the Board meeting on September 22 that the First Harrisburg Gallery Walk was announced. I explained that this self-guided tour of 15 city galleries would take place on Sunday, September 24, and that Mayor Reed had proclaimed the day "Harrisburg Gallery Walk Day." Various Board Members had agreed to serve as volunteer greeters at the door, and Chris Hurwitz was providing the refreshments for the day. Capital Area

Transit had agreed to provide the two new trolley/buses to transport visitors from gallery to gallery, and MetroArts had assisted as acting as a funding conduit for the event. I'd arranged for each gallery to have a special green flag with a gold "G" for the day, and a flyer had been designed and printed with a map.

Gallery Walk had been created as a result of a meeting I'd had with some of our Community Exhibition sites, such as Penn State Downtown Centre, Temple University, and the PA Blood Bank on Walnut Street. The people there had asked me why we couldn't hold a joint reception at some point with an exhibition opening in our main gallery, and I'd suggested that we invite other galleries as well to participate. I remember vividly how happy I was on September 24 when I'd dashed out to see how the other galleries were doing, and I'd seen dozens of people on the streets, walking purposefully from gallery to gallery, perusing their Gallery Walk flyers. What a treat to see our brainstorm actually come to fruition!

A special reception was hosted at AAH in November 1989, for an intimate exhibition of paintings by the late Anson Campbell, hosted by his partner Walter Geisey. Governor Casey and former Governor Leader were both in attendance, and Mr. Geisey donated a painting to the Permanent Collection.

John Guarnera was a highly effective Exhibition Chairman in those days. At the November 17 meeting he explained at some length how his committee had met twice to review works by 86 artists who had applied for invitational exhibitions. He said that 20 artists had been selected to exhibit in 1990/91, selected from a wide geographic area and who worked in a wide variety of styles and media. He went on to stress that the shows were "balanced between the traditional and contemporary styles," and that was no set policy to select one particular style over another. He concluded his report by saying that the proposed exhibition lent from area corporations had been dropped due to the committee's lack of enthusiasm with their findings.

It was at the January 26, 1990, meeting that I told the Board that the soon-to-be-built Hilton Harrisburg had placed an order with AAH for 189 prints for the guestrooms, and that I was in touch with the decorator concerning art for the public areas. Dauphin Deposit Bank was considering a commission for two major sculptures by our Janet Veiner, and the PA Medical Society was contemplating commissioning paintings by one of our artists. At this time, there was a Sales Gallery committee in place, and I was constantly concerned by their insistence that we "enlarge the Sales Gallery" and literally make it more commercial. I kept explaining that AAH is non-profit and we absolutely could NOT increase the size of the Sales Gallery and change its character to that of a commercial "shop."

This issue came to a head at the end of the strategic planning session on February 3. I was requested in the adopted plan to generate substantial additional art sales, and I told President Bronstein that I could meet that goal, but did not need a committee to do so. He agreed to my request and disbanded the committee. Shortly thereafter, I secured the huge commission with the new Hilton, which generated about $60,000 in art sales. I was vindicated in my wish to run the Sales Gallery solo.

Jane First's Special Events Committee had organized an elaborate show they called originally "Art for Fun," but then changed the title to "A Look at Artistic Creations," in order to add more aesthetic credence to the collection of works by non-artists. The show was to open with a private reception for artists, Board Members and guests on May 19, with Harry's Tavern supplying the liquor at cost, Wickey's donating some hors d'ouevres, and Board Members being asked to supply additional refreshments. When the show opened it was quite charming, with fabric works, a delightful doll house, and other creative objects.

There was quite an interest in "private" and preview receptions in those days, with a separate reception for patrons being held the Wednesday prior to the public Juried Show reception on Saturdays. This concept was finally dropped as far too expensive, and as detrimental to the attendance numbers for the Saturday reception.

In June we made an arrangement with the Dauphin County Commissioners to utilize the basement of their next door building, at 17 North Front Street, as additional classroom space. The rental fee was only $50 per month! The successful scholarship classes for disadvantaged city youths continued, funded by the Mary Sachs Trust, The Greater Harrisburg Foundation, and several service clubs. Robert Allen was a terrific Building Chairman, and the new garden was thriving.

The new Hilton was announced as the site for the Annual meeting on May 9, 1991.

It was in 1990 that I met with Mayor Reed concerning potential studio classrooms in the soon-to-be-refurbished Reservoir Park. I had read an article in *The Patriot News* about the Mayor's intent to have "artist studios" constructed in the Park, and made an appointment to see if it was possible for these to be enlarged for AAH to rent for classrooms. Doubling the size of the AAH School was one of my assigned goals in the new Strategic

Plan, and these new studios would enable that to be accomplished. The Mayor very graciously agreed to the proposal, and had me meet with the talented architect from Crabtree-Rohrbaugh—Rick LeBlanc. He re-designed the four small studios into classrooms: one for painting, one for pottery, one for sculpture, and one as a multi-purpose studio. I was able to procure grants to acquire all the furnishings and equipment. Additionally, we arranged with the City to be the providers of art exhibitions in the newly restored Caretaker's Mansion on the hill in the Park.

Dr. Gene Van Dyke was School Chairman in 1990, and did a fine job. The fall semester that year had 190 students, with 23 courses offered plus two scholarship classes. It was noted that minority participation was increasing in all AAH programs. Dr. Van Dyke announced at the September 28 meeting that a Summer Program for Youth in the Arts was to be offered in the new studios being created in Reservoir Park.

Plans for the Bal Masque were moving along beautifully, and the committee promised the February 9, 1991, event at the new Hilton would be "lavish and first-class." The second-annual Gallery Walk in September had attracted over 800 visitors to the AAH gallery, with $1375 in art sold. Charlie Stoup admonished the Board at the September meeting that the Hilton art sale had provided a significant windfall for AAH, which we should not anticipate for future budgets.

He pointed out, under "New Business," that the trend for area nonprofits was to alter the title of Executive Director to "President," and he suggested that AAH do the same. The By-Laws were undergoing revisions, and it was decided that this was the time to change the title, as well as changing the Board President's title to Board "Chair." Morris Schwab elaborated on the benefits of this change, saying that the Executive Director is "the real person who represents AAH all the time... the change in title is a matter of enhancement of image in the public eye."

The years 1990 and 1991 were very good years for the Art Association. The Bal Masque had been resurrected with great success, thanks to Jody Grass and her capable committee; Gallery Walk was flourishing; studios were being erected in Reservoir Park to enlarge the AAH School; and we'd sold a banner amount of artwork to the new Hilton. The AAH School classes were filled well each semester. The Board was thoroughly committed and they and staff worked together smoothly to fulfill the mission of the organization. We were all gratified when at the February 22, 19911, Board meeting Dr. Bronstein reported that I had been nominated as the recipient of the third-annual Distinguished Service to the Arts Award, presented by Theatre Harrisburg.

At the March 22, 1991, meeting much discussion ensued concerning holding the Bal Masque every other year rather than annually. Some Board Members expressed concern about the amount of work entailed in making the Bal an annual event, whereas others pointed out that before the hiatus in the 1980's, it had been held annually for 41 years. The decision was that a new chairperson would be sought.

The Reservoir Park studios were moving along, with our occupancy anticipated for August. A formal agreement was being created with the City outlining the terms of our lease, with the rent being minimal although AAH would be responsible for utilities. Frieda Gover all this time had been working hard as Membership Chair, and reported that March that AAH had 656 members.

The Annual Dinner was held on May 9 that year, with Mayor Reed as the featured speaker about downtown Harrisburg and the Reservoir Park project. Dr. Bronstein reported that making "selections for the Board is becoming more difficult because so many qualified people are interested." What a great problem to have! The Board at this point consisted of Dr. Bronstein, Charles Andrews, Kathleen Ebner, Frieda Gover, Alan Hayakawa, Charles Hickok, Brian Sann, Charles Stoup, Mary Jane Forbes, Norma Gotwalt, Jody Grass, John Guarnera, Alan Hostetler, Chris Hurwitz, Ruth Leventhal, Morris Schwab, Bruce Slaff, and Gene Van Dyke. With my new title of President, I, too, became an official Board member.

At the Annual Dinner Meeting on May 9 at the new Hilton, outgoing Board Chair Dr. Bronstein was honoured for his loyal and inspired service. I presented him with a portrait of him with his "tableau" from the last Bal Masque, in which he appeared as the head of John the Baptist, wheeled around the ballroom on a table by his entourage. The Mayor presented him with a proclamation designating Thursday, May 9, 1991, as "Dr. David Bronstein Day." In turn, Dr. Bronstein presented the Mayor with a framed print of the new Pride of the Susquehanna Riverboat by artist Kathleen Kirkpatrick. AAH had a great deal to be proud of at that Annual Meeting.

Dr. Bronstein enumerated the following accomplishments:

(1) Average enrollment of 250 students in 26 different classes per semester.

(2) Total budget of $240,000.

(3) 700 members.

(4) More classroom space than ever before, thanks to Reservoir Park's studios.

(5) Sales Gallery budget of $82,000.

(6) 10 exhibitions annually.

(7) A highly successful Bal Masque.

It was a deservedly proud and enthusiastic audience at that Annual Meeting.

At the June 21, 1991, meeting Dr. Bronstein thanked the Board for their enthusiasm and efforts during his administration. Norma Gotwalt was duly nominated as the new Chair of the Board, and elected, along with Brian Sann as Vice Chair, Bruce Slaff as Treasurer, and Christina Hurwitz as Secretary. I announced at that meeting that Charles "Li" Hidley had been added to the payroll as Curator/receptionist four days per week. Terrie Hosey's title at that time was Administrative Assistant.

New Board Chair Norma Gotwalt announced as her goal a focus on the School, just as Charlie Stoup's had been the Capital Campaign, and Dr. Bronstein's had been the Bal Masque. Norma was at this time the Director of Early Childhood Education for the Harrisburg School District, and education was always paramount in her interests. She promised that she would try to bring the school instructors and Board members together to get to know each other.

Discussion ensued concerning moving all AAH classes to the new studios in Reservoir Park and transforming the studios in our building into galleries. The consensus was, however, to wait to see how well the Park studios would be accepted before making so drastic a move. It was decided to change the second-floor studio, however, into a carpeted gallery, with an office constructed at the rear of the room for the Administrative Assistant. A conference table would be added, as well as a pull-down screen for the viewing of slides for exhibition selection. Edward C. Michener and his family were approached to fund the creation of the new gallery, and they graciously agreed to do so. Ed, who had been so important in the earlier years of AAH, was still loyal to the organization and dedicated to its success.

By the November 22, 1991, Board meeting Gene Van Dyke reported that a grant of $3500 had been received in support of a summer Art in the Park program for middle-school-age youth, to be held in our four new studios in Reservoir Park.

Exhibitions Chair John Guarnera discussed the concept of a retrospective show of the late Maya Schock's paintings. She was the founder of the Doshi Centre for Contemporary Art. John proposed that AAH borrow the artwork from Maya's widower Floyd Schock, and he said he was looking into the printing of a colour catalogue for the show. By January, George Ebner had agreed to work on the exhibition catalogue, and John Guarnera suggested an income-generating special reception/cocktail party for the premiere of the Schock exhibition. Much discussion revolved around the entire project at the January 24, 1992, Board meeting, with the Treasurer Bruce Slaff expressing concern about the expenses connected with the show.

Since all the paintings would be borrowed from collectors, there would be no selling opportunities, and all the expenses would have to be covered by donations. Guarnera assured the Board that he would submit a budget for their approval, but that he was certain he could raise the $2000 necessary to print the colour catalogue, and the $500 necessary to hire the trolley buses that were needed to transport reception guests between the main building and the Reservoir Park Caretaker's Mansion, the site of a sister exhibit of works by Maya Schock's colleagues. The Board eventually acquiesced to the plan, with Charles Andrews emphasizing that the show would be "an historic event and a tremendous opportunity and should be treated accordingly." It was decided that the reception would be held the weekend prior to the show's public opening.

At the March 27 meeting, the concept of a "Blue Ribbon Committee" to oversee renovations and other building needs was discussed, first suggested by Allied Arts Fund. Ralph Klinepeter, Ed Black and Bill Brightbill were all invited to serve on this committee, with other names suggested by the group. At this meeting the new Art in the Park program was further outlined, with Michael Starner designated to teach pottery and Kim Bowie, painting. Pat Xenos, another potter, was to work on recruiting 20 students for the program.

At the June 26, 1992, meeting, members of the Board included Patti Brinjac, Kathleen Ebner, Mary Jane Forbes, Norma Gotwalt, Charlie Hickok, Chris Hurwitz, Larrie McLamb, Colleen Prensky, Bruce Slaff, Gene Van Dyke, Gary Yenkowski, Charles Andrews. Barbara Arnold, Steve Feinour, John Guarnera, Alan Hayakawa, Alan Hostetler, Tom Lennox, Dr. Ruth Leventhal, Donald Zolan, and me.

Norma Gotwalt was re-elected Chair of the Board.

The date of the special preview reception for the Maya Schock show was announced as July 18, with the public reception set for July 26. Unfortunately, John Guarnera and George Ebner had been unable to secure funding for the printing and trolley costs, so I had gotten on the phone and was able to identify some sponsors myself. However, AAH lost money on the catalogue due to the lack of patrons. The small catalogue was very handsome, with text written by George Ebner and photographs by John Rudy of Maya's paintings. Despite the fact we made no money on the exhibition, it was highly received by the public.

In those days, AAH had a Chairman of Volunteers in the person of Chris Hurwitz. She did a great job in recruiting volunteers for receptions, Gallery Walk, and other special events. In the September 11, 1992, minutes, it was also mentioned that Carol Morris was seeking more volunteers to serve on an "Ambassadors Committee" for AAH, explaining that the group would be raise money through memberships and would not compete with the Allied Arts Fund.

In 1992, AAH was making great strides in reaching out to the wider community and to diverse ethnic groups. Gene Van Dyke's school committee was exploring ways to reach out to the Spanish-speaking and Ethiopian communities. Kinnith Washington of the Urban League was elected to the Board to replace Charles Andrews, who resigned due to his heavy involvement with the fledgling Carlisle Arts Learning Centre.

In addition to Gallery Walk, we initiated the concept of "First Thursdays," in which galleries would partner with downtown restaurants to attract more visitors to the city during the week. On the surface, the concept seemed very doable, with participating galleries stamping a flyer for visitors, who then could present it to a restaurant for a half-price entrée. However, in practice, the project didn't work because very few visitors came downtown on first Thursdays, and many of the smaller galleries closed early. We eventually dropped the whole thing. Gallery Walk, on the other hand, continued to thrive, held annually on the Sunday after Labour Day.

An interesting development occurred in January of 1993, when Pennsylvania National Bank offered AAH their unoccupied building at 1230 North Third Street. The Board considered accepting the building for various uses, including an extension of the Sales Gallery, a shared space with other arts groups, etc. After due consideration, cooler heads prevailed and we suggested that the Historic Harrisburg Association be approached to accept the building, as they were seeking a headquarters at the time. Had AAH accepted the building, it would have been an albatross on our heads, due to all the extensive and expensive repairs and restoration needed, not to mention the overhead with utilities and staffing. Also, there was no parking. So HHA took the building, and began the restoration work, and now years later, they assiduously continue to work on its restoration.

AAH did rent space in the HHA building after some renovations had been accomplished, for the nominal sum of $100 per month. We moved Hidley's expressionist painting class there from the University Centre, and called the studio "Hidley Hall." Since students had a difficult time finding parking, the space was eventually given up.

In September of 1993, we hired a School Coordinator in the person of Kim Bowie, a former art instructor at the Harrisburg Academy. She had taught for AAH in our Reservoir Park "Art in the Park" program, and it was hoped that she would visit area schools to recruit students.

In November, 1993, the Board consisted of Norma Gotwalt (Chair), Barbara Arnold, Jot Bennett, Nancy Cramer, Steve Feinour (Legal Counsel), Tom Lennox, Carol Morris, Colleen Prensky, Tina Reiley, Mary Fager, Patti Brinjac, Kathleen Ebner, John Guarnera, Chris Hurwitz, Geoff McDowell, Larrie McLamb, Kinneth Washington, Elaine Wilson, Gary Yenkowski and me.

There was no Bal in 1993, but Bal Chair Colleen Prensky and her committee were hard at work on the 1994 Bal, which subsequently proved very successful. New treasurer Mary Fager pointed out after the Bal that on the off-Bal years, our budget would be in the hole $30,000... a daunting prospect.

The Board in early 1994 was in the process of trying to establish an Endowment Fund at the Greater Harrisburg Foundation, with the goal being $300,000 to $500,000. Unfortunately, no major "lead" gifts were obtained, and the Endowment drive was put on hold. The endowment stood, in 2013, at $17,000.

Norma Gotwalt ended her term as Board Chair in July 1994, and Tom Lennox was nominated as the next Chair, to be elected at the next Board meeting. However, Tom declined the nomination in August due to changes of responsibilities at his job at Pennsylvania National Bank. Instead, Treasurer Mary Fager was elected as the new Board Chair on August 4. Geoff McDowell was elected Vice Chair, Tina Reiley Secretary, and Karen Lynn as Treasurer.

The end of an era occurred on November 22, 1994, when Viola Clark died after a very brief illness. Curmudgeon that she was, she was unwaveringly loyal to AAH, and it seemed strange without her at the receptionist's desk three days a week. School Coordinator Kim Bowie's hours were extended after Viola died to 28 hours a week, with Li Hidley serving as receptionist Thursdays and Fridays. The same weekend that Viola died there was a major water catastrophe at the building. When I arrived that Friday morning, Hidley pointed towards the main gallery intoning grimly, "Water disaster... there!" Water was cascading through the ceiling, onto the gallery floor and down into the basement.

The problem had been caused by the Life Class up on the third floor. On Thursday evening they had made coffee, which I had forbidden them to do. To add insult to injury, they had accidentally emptied coffee grounds into the sink in the bathroom by the studio, and turned on the spigot to flush the grounds away. Not only did that not work, but they forgot to turn off the water when they left after class, and water continued to flow into the clogged sink all night. The result was a flood of Biblical proportions. I charged the Life Class monitor the $500 deductible for the insurance, and his class complained bitterly at my hard-heartedness. But none of them offered to help to pay the bill.

It was at the November 23 Board meeting also that the concept of a murder mystery, written and produced by Charles Schulz, was discussed. The production was to be presented in the AAH galleries, with volunteer actors and a full dinner. In January 1995, another innovative fund-raising idea was presented, namely meet-the-artist dinners, with hosts providing the meals at their expense, and featuring different artists at each. Thus was the nucleus of the popular "Summer Soirees" introduced.

At the March 29, 1995, meeting it was announced that the three nights of the Murder Mystery Dinners were sold out, and it was expected that AAH would net $3500 with the events. Board member Keith Yancey portrayed an Irish cop in the productions, and I portrayed a Gypsy fortuneteller. My husband portrayed a nefarious doctor, and Charles Schulz himself played the hero detective "Justin Time." The murder mysteries were hugely labour-extensive to produce, but were a lot of fun.

An interesting incident was mentioned at the May 24 Board meeting. I reported that the gingko tree in front of our building (the replacement for the tree removed at Frank Master's behest in 1986) had been knocked over by a Phillips delivery truck. I had subsequently negotiated with Phillips to pay AAH $800 to remove the stump and replace the tree, as well as to install a wrought-iron tree guard to protect the new tree. Greg Black of Black Landscaping did the work. (Greg was the son of Edward Black, who had so graciously designed the new AAH garden in 1989).

I was announced as the host of the first meet-the-artist dinner with "Hidley on the Half-Shell" at my house. I had envisioned these dinners to be just that: dinner parties with featured artists, enabling paying guests to chat with the artist during the meal, and to view their artwork displayed in the host's home. However, the events quickly evolved into much larger events, true "soirees" featuring a great deal of art and hors d'ouevres in place of formal dinners. Rick and Jan LeBlanc hosted a major Soiree at their stunning contemporary house on Bali Hai Road in Mechanicsburg, showcasing Wanda Macomber's large architectural abstract paintings throughout the home. Mary Fager co-hosted one at her friend Bernie Pupo's beauty salon downtown, showing Sam Sneeder's paintings. The Soirees have been going strong ever since.

At the November 29, 1995, meeting it was mentioned that the staff has occasionally been hearing a "soft occasional knocking," which started around the time of the first anniversary of Viola's death!

By this time, the Board consisted of Mary Fager (Chair), Jot Bennett, Paul Caulfield, Sylvia Coslow, Nancy Cramer, Ben Dunlap, Rick LeBlanc, Geoff McDowell, Carol Morris, Colleen Prensky, Tina Reiley, Ted Webber, Keith Yancey, Robin Balaban, Earl Blust, Patti Brinjac, Steve Feinour, Claire Flemming, Bill Flynn, Norma Gotwalt, Alma Kretzing, Linda Luke Pincock, Kevin Shook and Bob Troxell.

One thing of great interest in 1996 was the fact that The Art Association was turning 70, and to commemorate that milestone, Ed Michener composed a history and Ted Webber created a slide show, which he and I presented at the Annual Meeting on May 23. At the May 22 Board meeting, it was announced that a new fundraiser would be held called "The Art of Food," to take place in January, 1997, in conjunction with the Winter Membership show.

At the June 26, 1996, Board meeting Mary Fager was re-elected as Board Chair, with Geoffrey McDowell as Vice Chair, Kevin Shook as Treasurer, and Tina Reiley as Secretary. The other Board members at that time were Nancy Cramer, Diane McArdle, Earl Blust, Bill Flynn, Robin Balaban, Jeffrey Roof, Kendall Marcocci, Rick LeBlanc, Sylvia Coslow, Ted Webber, Steve Feinour, Ben Dunlap, Linda Luke Pincock, Keith Yancey, Paul Caulfield, Jot Bennett, Norma Gotwalt, Claire Flemming and me.

That year Paul Caulfield was Chair of a Marketing Committee, and put together a backdrop for us to use at business fairs and trade shows. Terrie Hosey and I took turns staffing the AAH booth at the Chamber of Commerce Business Fair at the Farm Show Building that fall, and several years afterwards, but with limited success. We found to our dismay that many attendees were only on the hunt for "goodie bags" with candy, pens and other souvenirs, and few wanted information on the art AAH was offering to sell to businesses.

Kendall Marcocci, whose husband was a chef, worked hard on the "Art of Food," and prospectuses were sent to area restaurants to recruit participants in November. A French knife was acquired from United Restaurant Supply to award as second prize, with a plaque created by Levin's as first. The concept of The Art of Food was to honour chefs as artists rather than "cooks." Their entries in the competition were created as works of art made of food, and were not to be tasted. Their entry fee was hors d'ouevres to serve 50 people. The artistic food creations were displayed on our six-foot tables throughout the galleries, with the edible hors d'ouevres presented on smaller tables. The Art of Food continued annually for ten years, but entrants dwindled the last few years with the advent of Restaurant Row in downtown Harrisburg. Fewer and fewer chefs had time off on Saturday evenings to participate in our event, and when they did, they usually dropped off their entries and left, and their contributions of hors d'ouevres became less and less impressive, consisting largely of bruschetta!

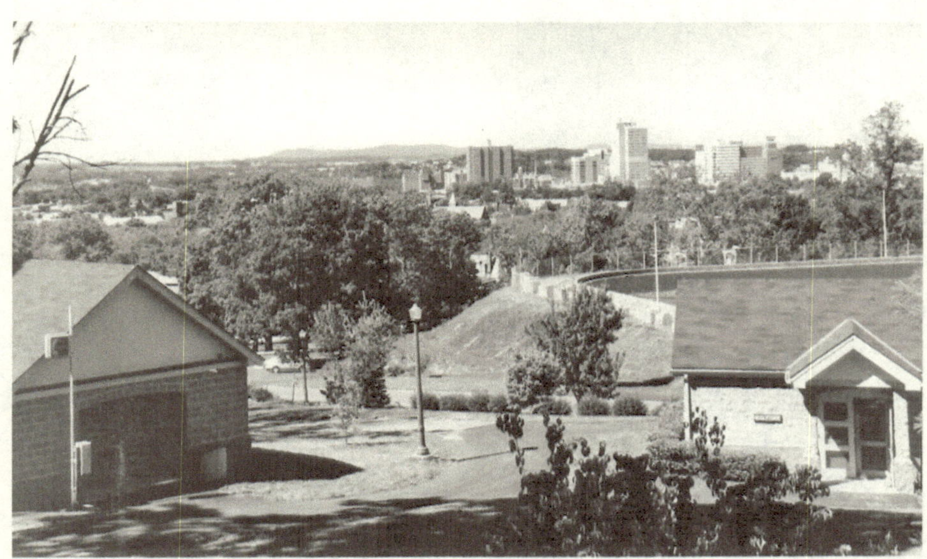

Reservoir Park Art Studios

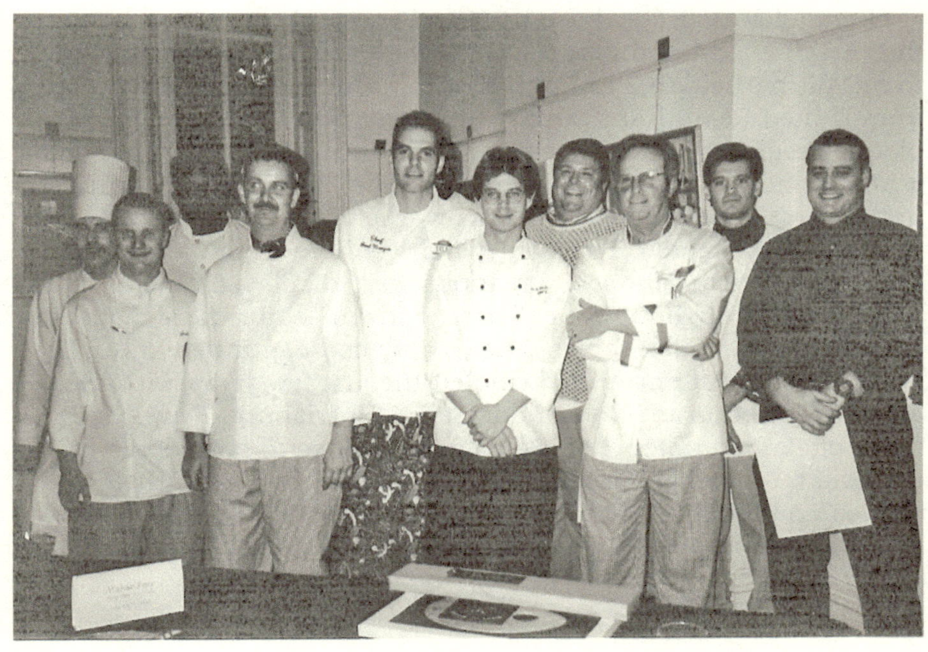

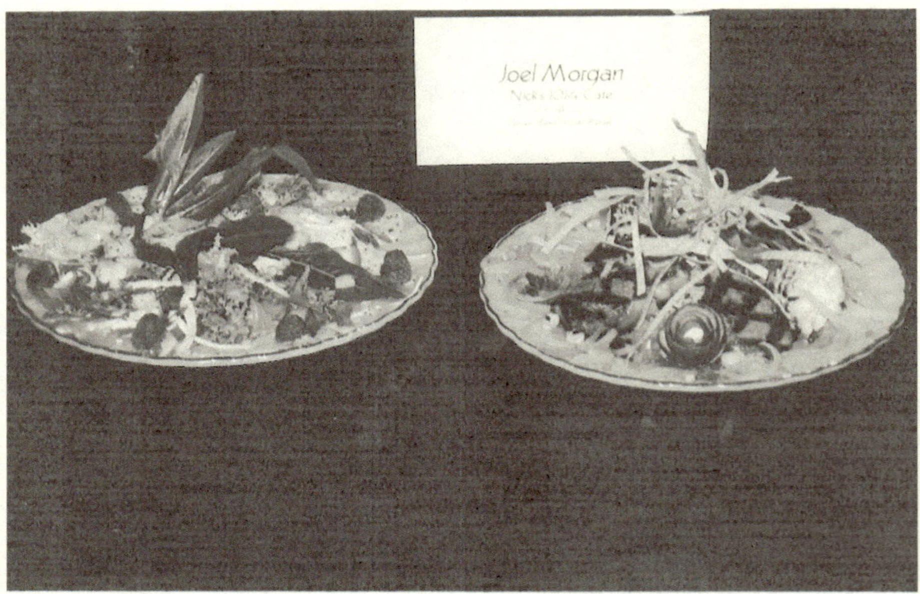

The Art of Food event

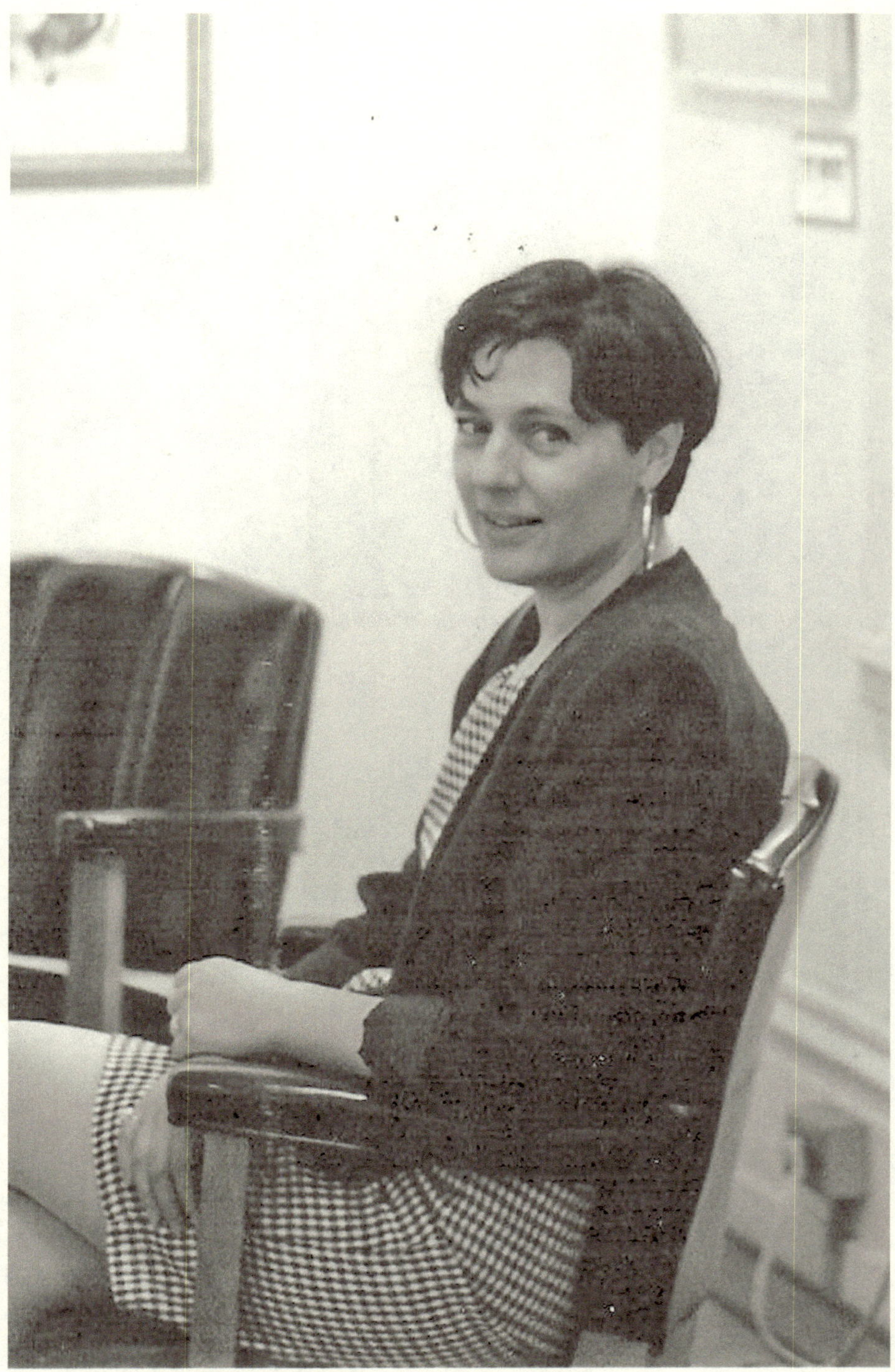

Terrie Hosey, AAH Curator, in the 1990s

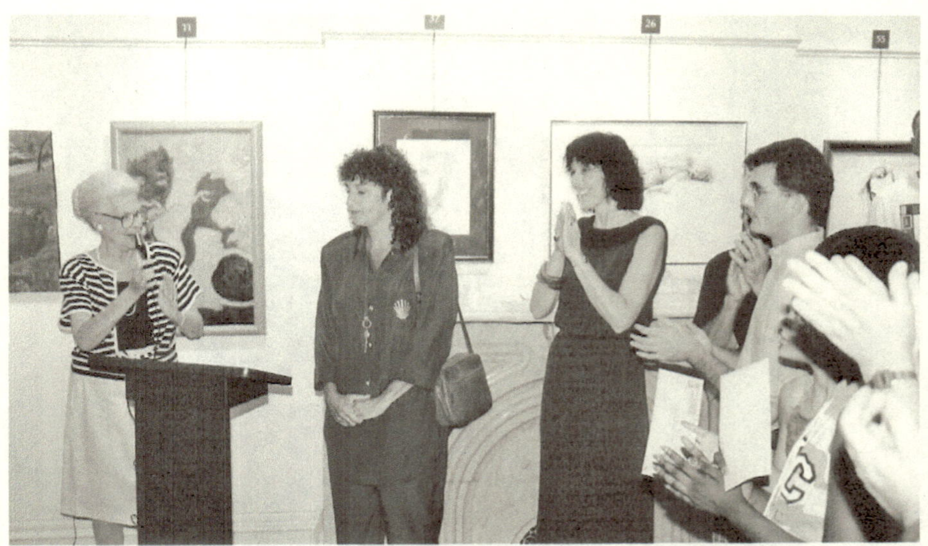

Norma Gotwalt and Carrie Wissler-Thomas conduct awards ceremony

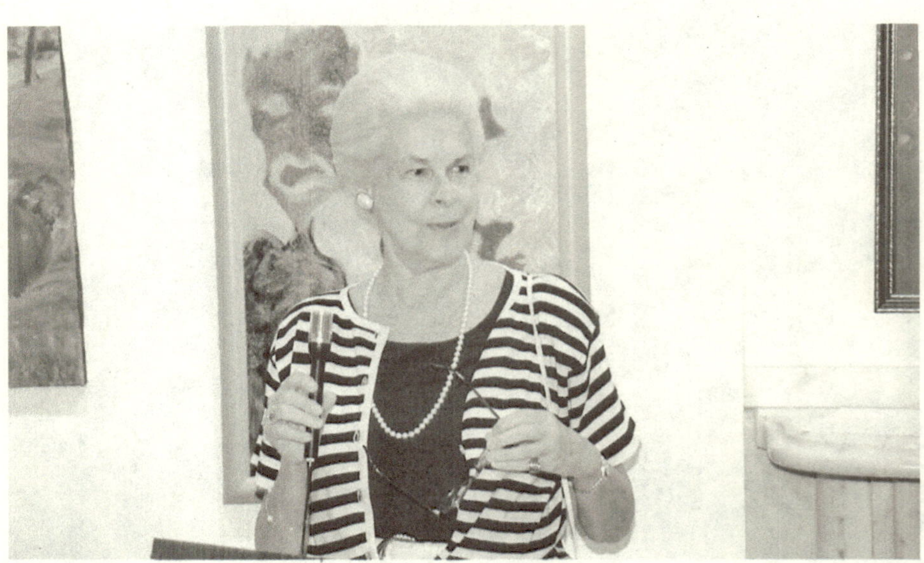

Norma Gotwalt, Board Chair, 1991

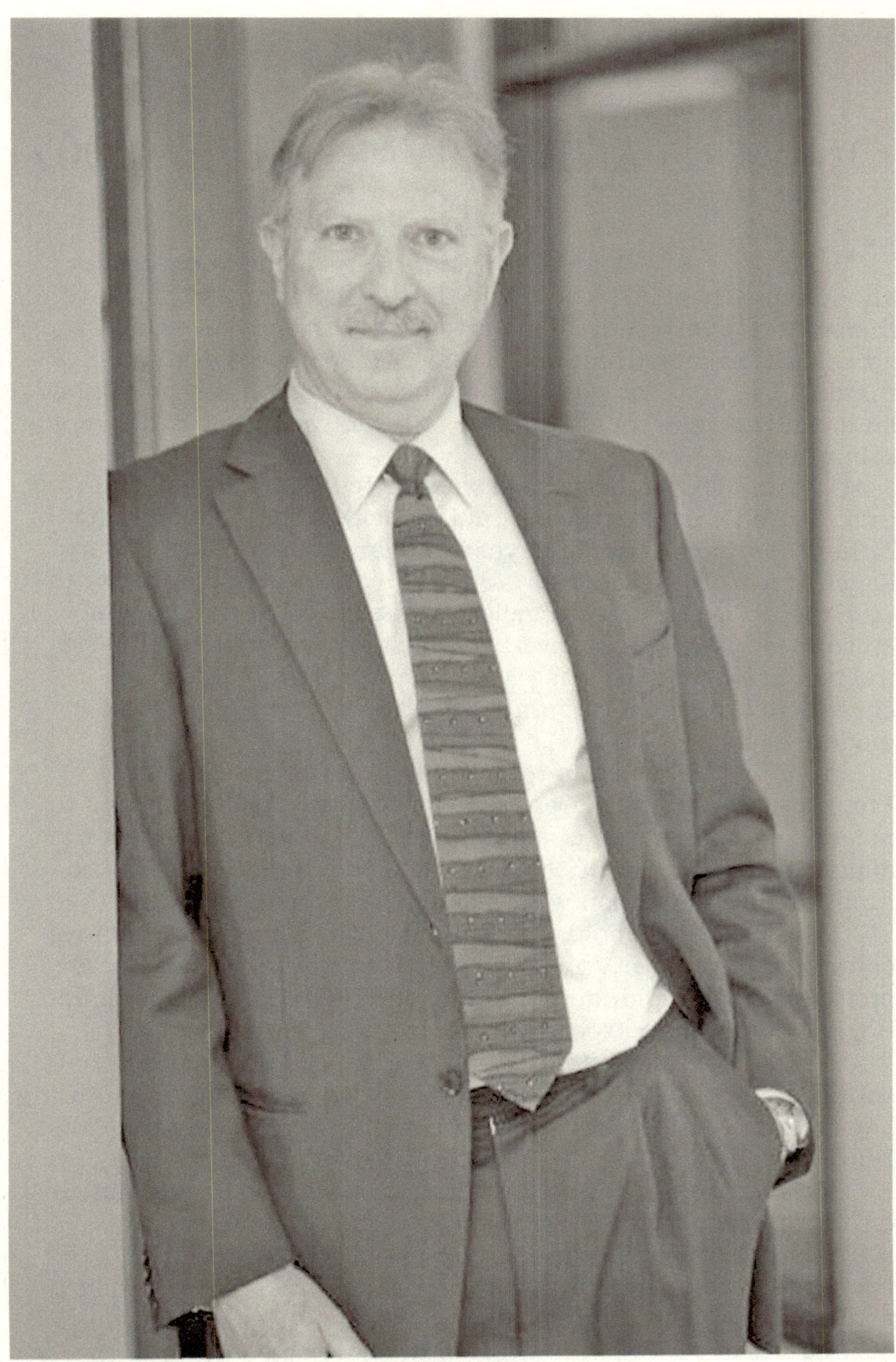

Rick LeBlanc, AAH Board Chair, 2009-2014

ONWARD AND UPWARD: 1997–2007

In May of 1997, Board Chair Mary Fager ended her term by announcing that AAH would end the fiscal year in the black, thanks to the record-breaking art sales, with the Sales Gallery grossing even more than in the year of the Hilton sales. She thanked everyone for working with her during her stint as Chair, and said that she would continue to be active on the Bal Masque committee.

On June 26, Paul Caulfield was elected Board Chair, and said that future Board meetings would be held at the AAH building rather than in the Coopers Lybrand boardroom as during Mary Fager's term. That would give Board members an opportunity to view the art on view in the galleries. He predicted that the Bal Masque for 1998 would "overtake most other activities." Indeed, the theme for that Bal was "Blast from the Past," which engendered the most elaborate decorations ever known for the modern Bals!

In 1997 AAH hoped to receive $48,000 from the Allied Arts Fund, but Paul Caulfield explained that since the Fund failed to meet its campaign goal of a million dollars, it was likely that our allocation would be reduced. (This was as a direct result of the fundraising competition with the new Whitaker Centre and the YWCA's project to renovate Sylvan Heights.) Nonetheless, things continued to prosper, thanks to the strenuous efforts of Board members soliciting underwriters for the Bal. Geoff McDowell and Roger Ceritelli were especially successful in this effort.

Besides the Bal Masque, the Board determined in 1998 to continue to hold "The Art of Food" chefs' competition, and to bring back the Soirees, which were called at that point "Meet the Artist Dinners."

Ben Dunlap, AAH Legal Counsel, was working at this time to try to establish the AAH Endowment Fund at the Greater Harrisburg Foundation on a firmer footing. However, with operating expenses having to be constantly met, there were little additional funds to put into the endowment.

In June of 1998, Paul Caulfield was re-elected Chair of the Board, with Jot Bennett as Vice Chair, Kevin Shook as Treasurer, and Kendall Marcocci as Secretary. Other Board members were John Carroll, Mary Davis, Ben Dunlap, Scott Jones, Diane McArdle, Dennis Peoples, Scott Rogers, Jeff Roof, David Skerpon, Robin Balaban, Earl Blust, Kevin Brown, Rodger Ceritelli, Sylvia Coslow, Mary Fager, Rick LeBlanc, Linda Luke Pincock, Ted Webber and Keith Yancey.

A highlight of 1999 was the filming of a Japanese TV commercial at AAH by a Los Angeles company—Clockwork 906 Productions—that made $8000 for the organization. Terrie Hosey worked many additional hours to keep the building open for the crew's filming, which involved six days. The commercial, filmed in the third-floor studio, was for Café Latte and starred Winona Ryder, who was in Harrisburg to film "Girl Interrupted" at the time.

At the June 22, 2001, Board meeting David Skerpon was elected as Chair of the Board, with Geoff McDowell as Vice Chair, Gayle Roberts-Howell as Treasurer, and Judy Hepford as Secretary. Other Board members were Renee Lieux (Legal Counsel), Nancy O'Halloran, Linda Rhinehart, Jeanne Schmedlen, Mary Lundeen, David Morrison, Paul Odom, Trudy Olkowski, Desiree Petrus, Tom Potter, Tina Reiley-Phillips, Scott Rogers, Jeff Roof and Jimmy Wood.

A highlight of 2002 was the "Living Art" exhibition/fundraiser, consisting of tattooed models posed throughout the galleries on March 23. Tattoo Jim of The Illustrated Man helped to organize the event with his clients as models. This novel event generated a great deal of interest and attendance, but when we presented it a second year, the only attendees were other people with tattoos, and it was impossible to discern which were the models and which were the attendees!

Unfortunately, the AAH allocation from Allied Arts Fund was docked $8000 in 2002, and Board Chair David Skerpon stated at the August 28 meeting that he "fears Allied Arts does not realize that AAH 'lives our mission' with our tremendous involvement in the Downtown improvements and events, our outreach with our community shows and scholarships, our serving as an unofficial'tourist bureau,' and our being open seven days per week." Despite the cut in AAF funding, the Association continued to persevere, determined to make up the deficit through more strenuous fundraising on our own.

Another interesting occurrence that year was the discovery that the floor of the second-floor men's restroom was seriously deteriorated, necessitating Herre Bros., Inc.,'s complete re-plumbing of the room. The bill of $12,000 was beyond our means, so I contacted Mr. McBride, President of Herre Bros., and offered to give Herre Bros. "naming rights" to the men's room in exchange for knocking $5000 off our bill. Mr. McBride graciously agreed to decrease the amount we owed, but declined the naming rights! We made him a Platinum Life Member of AAH instead.

AAH was voted "Simply the Best" that year by Harrisburg Magazine readers in the categories of "Best Art Organization," "Best Fundraiser Event" (The Bal Masque), Readers' Choice Best Art Gallery, and "Black-Tie Affair."

It was in 2003 that artist and former AAH Curator Charles "Li" Hidley gave AAH his entire body of paintings to continue to sell after his death, saying that the sales will be a continuing legacy from him in years to come. We hired Rick Walker of Walker's Art and Framing to move all the paintings from Hidley's house at 711 Prince Alley to our fourth floor, which was a huge job, there being well over 300 paintings.

At this juncture, Randy Miller III became our webmaster and the AAH website underwent an "extreme makeover." Molly Sun was the very efficient Administrative Assistant, and Kim Bowie remained part-time School Coordinator.

It was in 2003 that the McCormick Family Foundation generously donated $27,000 to cover the cost of Restorations Unlimited completely refurbishing the basement classrooms, installing new lighting, a dropped ceiling, and extensively painting. We renamed the area "The McCormick Studios." The McCormick family has continued its generous support of the organization. Gertrude and Vance McCormick were instrumental in founding in 1926, always a cornerstone of the success of the Art Association.

David Skerpon resigned as the AAH Board Chair in 2003 because he was elected Chair of the Allied Arts Fund board. Steve Courtney was elected Board Chair in his place, with Geoff McDowell as Vice Chair, Judy Hepford as Secretary, and Gayle Roberts-Howell as Treasurer. The state of AAH finances was not good at this point, despite the Bal, Soirees, school revenues, and a line of credit at the bank. Several proposals were made at the June Board meeting to help the situation, with David Morrison suggesting we send out a year-end appeal, and David Skerpon proposing having a "piano bar" for Art for the Holidays instead of an all-day art and craft sale as in previous years. A membership drive was also proposed.

It was in October that Treasurer Gayle Roberts-Howell announced that AAH had received an inheritance of $38,638 from the estate of Marie Leach of Illinois. The only problem was that the monies were intended for "The Will Brown Scholarship Fund for Youth," which was no longer in existence. The Board determined to deposit the monies in the School Account to meet pressing expenses, with the caveat that the amount should be noted in a special Will Brown Scholarship book, and each time a scholarship was granted, that amount would be subtracted. In 2012, the amount remaining on the books for the Scholarship Fund was $16,602.

The Bal in 2004 was a resounding success, with Board Chair Steve Courtney reporting at the February 25 meeting that we had raised $40,588, a higher sum raised by any Bal since 1996! Due to the financial crunch, the Board determined to hold the Bal annually rather than every other year, so the next Bal was scheduled at the Hilton for Friday, January 14, 2005. (No Saturday was available.)

By 2004, Terrie Hosey's official title was "Curator," and she reported regularly at Board meetings about the exhibitions presented in the AAH galleries. I continued to handle all the Community Exhibitions in the outside sites.

A special fundraiser held in 2004 was titled "Kitchen Mania," consisting of an auction of pottery contributed by our potters on Saturday, June 5. Unfortunately, this was not a huge success, partly because it ran head to head with a major horse race aired on TV that same evening! However, it did generate $1011 for AAH.

Another intriguing event that year was an exhibit of artwork created by dogs and cats from PAWS, displayed in the second-floor Michener Gallery. The cats' artwork was actually rather poetic and haiku-like, whereas the dogs' larger paws created less aesthetically pleasing paintings.

PSECU graciously agreed to be the Bal Masque sponsor for 2005, as well as a sponsor of our children's educational programs. As a part of this, AAH was accepted for membership in the credit union, enabling AAH staff and members to join PSECU if they so desired. AAH was approached in early 2005 to co-sponsor the "Red Hot Strawberry Ball" instead of continuing to present the Bal Masque, but this offer was soundly rejected for a number of reasons. David Morrison said very eloquently, at the February 1 , 2005, meeting, that "The Bal Masque supports our old established organization and our historic building." Furthermore, it was determined that the two costume balls would compete with each other for sponsors and attendees.

At the June 22, 2005, Board meeting it was announced that Bryan Molloy, one of our talented artist members originally from Boston, had been hired as evening Gallery Assistant since Randy

Miller, our webmaster, had to cut back his hours after acquiring a full-time job with the State. At this meeting, Steve Courtney was re-elected as Board Chair, with David Morrison as Vice Chair, Gayle Roberts-Howell as Treasurer, Robert Potter as Assistant Treasurer, and Judy Hepford as Secretary. The rest of the Board consisted of Curtis Fenstermacher, Margaret Delmonico, Linda Rhinehart, Rick LeBlanc, Steve Feinour, Earl Blust, Martha Brown, Gary Christie, Kathleen Kramer, Renee Lieux, Desiree Petrus, Jeanne Schmedlen, Jimmy Wood, and Sylvia Coslow.

Once again the McCormick Family Foundation came forward to contribute $10,000 for a capital project consisting of Restorations Unlimited repairing and repainting the buildings upper front and side windows.

At the August 24, 2005, Board meeting the resignation of Steve Courtney from the Board and Chairmanship was announced, and David Morrison was elected to replace him. Curator Terrie Hosey announced that a "Hidley Extravaganza" had netted $9000 in sales of his paintings in the summer.

Rick LeBlanc was now Building Chairman, and began a rigorous effort to assess the state of the building's infrastructure. He explained that the building had sustained major water damage during the summer as the results of both a roof and a sink leak, and that our insurance had covered the interior repairs. The McCormick Family Foundation contributed $5000 to repair the roof. Rick LeBlanc said that he had arranged for three young architects from his firm Crabtree Rohrbaugh to completely survey and map the building, and that they were engaged in taking exact measurements in order to draw blueprints.

At the October 26, 2005, Board meeting Chair David Morrison congratulated everyone for "surviving during a very difficult year for non-profits." I pointed out that despite the horrid water damage in the summer, we never ceased holding classes, nor did we cancel one exhibit or event.

By March of 2006, the Board was discussing how to make up the deficit caused by the drastically reduced Allied Arts Fund allocation. In 2001, our annual allocation had been $48,000, and in 2006 we were informed that AAH would receive less than $20,000. Discussion ensued concerning various avenues to redress the situation, and I announced that I had applied yet again to the generosity of the McCormick Family Foundation for $28,000 with which to repair the back section of the AAH roof. Robert Potter made the welcome announcement that Penn National Insurance, his employer, had just donated $3000 to the AAH scholarship fund.

David Morrison added that the Finance Committee had met to discuss ways to meet our financial challenges, and that efforts were underway to find sponsors for AAH exhibitions, as well as to increase the membership. David, ever eloquent, emphasized, "although our current financial situation is a challenge, AAH has a strong mission and sound activities and projects." He encouraged everyone to keep a positive attitude, with the staff and Board working together to overcome the funding hurdles.

As 2006 was the 80th anniversary year for AAH, the annual meeting on May 25 was determined to be a celebration of that milestone, with an acknowledgement of all those patrons who contributed $80 in commemoration of the occasion. All Board members were strongly urged to become $80 patrons for the occasion. Former AAH Executive Director Charles Schulz offered to bake a special cake for the celebration, and to create a power-point presentation honouring our founders. It was further decided that Spencer Nauman, grandson of Mrs. Gertrude Olmsted McCormick, would be invited to attend the event.

At the May 17 Board meeting, Chair David Morrison read the newly enhanced AAH Mission Statement, which had been developed at the strategic planning session held on April 29. "The Art Association of Harrisburg enriches the cultural vitality of the region by promoting the visual arts through exhibitions and education." The plan's priority areas were stated as Fundraising, Membership Development, Physical Plant, Education, Public Relations/Marketing, and Governance. It was agreed that a "Board Agreement" be developed that clearly stated each Board member's commitment, that each would sign when elected.

It was at this Board meeting that I announced AAH had inherited the art collection of the late Jack Gross, which was wonderful, because the bequest came with "no strings," and we would be able to sell whichever pieces we wished. Our appraiser Noel Marks and I moved all the collection to the AAH building from Jack's TownHouse apartment, and Noel generated a list of values for the estate. He also assisted tremendously in identifying buyers for pieces from the collection.

It was also agreed, as a result of the strategic planning discussions, that a "hipper" image be created for AAH publications. Subsequently, volunteer graphic designer Shauna Powers began working on a new logo and "look" that would be utilized on all show invitations, the newsletter, and other printed materials. It was decided to combine the quarterly school brochure with the bi-monthly newsletter, creating one glossy publication that would be mailed quarterly to both students and members. Shauna Powers also was tapped to design a classy flyer promoting the capital campaign, intended to raise the monies necessary to make the repairs to the building's infrastructure that the Crabtree-Rohrbaugh team had recommended.

During the summer of 2006, Gallery Assistant Bryan Molloy had the brainstorm to hold "hit-and-run" exhibitions in area bars and restaurants. The first one was a huge success, held at Appalachian Brewing Company on Cameron Street in Harrisburg, and generating almost $2000 in art sales and attendance fees. This concept evolved into "One Night Stand" exhibitions that were presented monthly for a year, on Sundays, in venues such as Stock's On Second, Molly Branigan's, and even a hotel in West Fairview. The series finally ran its course, with fewer attendees each Sunday. As so many innovative projects, the publicity buzz was tremendous at first, but waned as the time went on. So we abandoned the concept, with regret.

The Soirees held the summer of 2006 all had creative titles, such as "Black and White on Green," hosted by Jim Cowden; "Apples and Abstracts on Market" hosted by Milissa Barrick; and "Croquet, Hats and Spats," hosted by Tracey Meloni. The Bal Masque that year was co-chaired by Dr. Kathleen Kramer of Temple University and Tracey Meloni, and the Board and I explored moving the Bal from the Hilton to Appalachian Brewing Company in order to attract a younger audience with the more informal ambiance. If it would be possible to book the Bal at ABC on the actual date of Mardi Gras, the theme could simply be "Mardi Gras."

At the November 29, 2006, Board meeting Treasurer Robert Potter described a potentially unfortunate situation that had been resolved. Namely, Allied Arts had been re-structured and re-branded as the Cultural Enrichment Fund, and The Art Association for some reason had been relegated to a second-tier of organizations due to confusion on the part of their task force as to AAH's unique role and mission in the community. After Robert and I wrote a very detailed letter to the Fund outlining the many services to artists provided by the Art Association, the matter was re-considered, and AAH was added to the twelve top-tier organizations as the "thirteenth warrior."

At this time, AAH staff included Terrie Hosey, Curator; Randy Miller, Webmaster (working Sundays); Bryan Molloy, Gallery Assistant (working evenings); Kay McKee, receptionist, and Kim Bowie, School Coordinator (working 3 and 2 days per week). Alexis Hair was our very capable intern in 2007. The Board at that time consisted of Martha Brown, Margaret Delmonico, Nancy

O'Halloran, Earl Blust, Gary Christie, Sylvia Coslow, Myra Toomey, Steve Feinour, Judy Hepford, Kathleen Kramer, Rick LeBlanc, Renee Lieux, David Morrison, Desiree Petrus, Robert Potter, Linda Rhinehart, Gayle Roberts-Howell, Jeanne Schmedlen and Jimmy Wood.

Kay McKee and Kim Bowie subsequently left the staff, and Molly Sun was hired as receptionist, followed by Brook Lauer, Kelly McGee, a former intern, and then by Rachel O'Connor.

As I write this, it's now 2014. The Art Association successfully celebrated our 85th Anniversary two years ago with a reception in the main gallery and The State of the Association power-point presentation by our Board Chair Rick LeBlanc. The evening was made even more memorable by the fact we had a mini-tornado crash through Harrisburg, with the sky over the River becoming a ghastly shade of yellow just as we were serving champagne and cake! All the attendees were trapped in the building until the storm passed, but luckily were well supplied by champagne and cake. The building was undamaged, although everyone had difficulty driving home through streets filled with the debris of downed trees.

As of February, 2013, the Board included Rick LeBlanc (Chair), Jeff Wiles (Vice Chair), Robert Potter (Treasurer), Martha Brown (Secretary), Steve Feinour (Legal Counsel), Joe and Jan Bahret, Anne Davis, Ade Bakare, Nancy Bartolomaei-Olson, Leisa Craver, Kate Earley, Julia Liberatore, Kathy Marley-Dunbar, Tracey Meloni, Alice Anne Schwab, Kevin Sheets, Karen Shughart, Mariella Trosko, David Volkman, and Ellen Warren. We have a great Board and a great staff, partners together in furthering the Art Association's mission.

Now, in the summer of 2014, our Board includes David Volkman, Chair; Dr. Kevin Sheets, Vice Chair; Martha Brown, Secretary; Jay Scarfone, Treasurer; Jan and Joe Bahret, Alison Ballantine, Anne Davis, Jay Delozier, Kate Earley, David Evenhuis, Mark Everest, Barbara Gutekunst, Amy Huck, Shirley McCormick, Tracey Meloni, Thomas Robel, Sue Rothman, Karen Shughart, and Ellen Warren.

The Art Association has pressed on through many vicissitudes during the past 88 years, but continues to thrive, stronger than ever before. Paul Beers, the late *Patriot News* columnist, left the Association a very generous bequest in 2011, enabling us to pay off the line of credit and to get really "caught up" for the first time in several years. Now, there is in place a successful exhibition sponsorship program, with Board members and others contributing monies to sponsor each of the ten annual exhibitions. We have generous patrons who present five or six Soirees each summer, and art continues to sell through exhibitions, the Sales Gallery and the community exhibitions.

I am ceasing my narrative at this point with the hope that someone else will continue the story where I've left off... The history of the Art Association of Harrisburg continues to be written on a daily basis. For me to continue as the story continues to unfold would make this a memoir or a diary, rather than a history of the organization. I leave the rest of the story as the future unfolds to another writer.

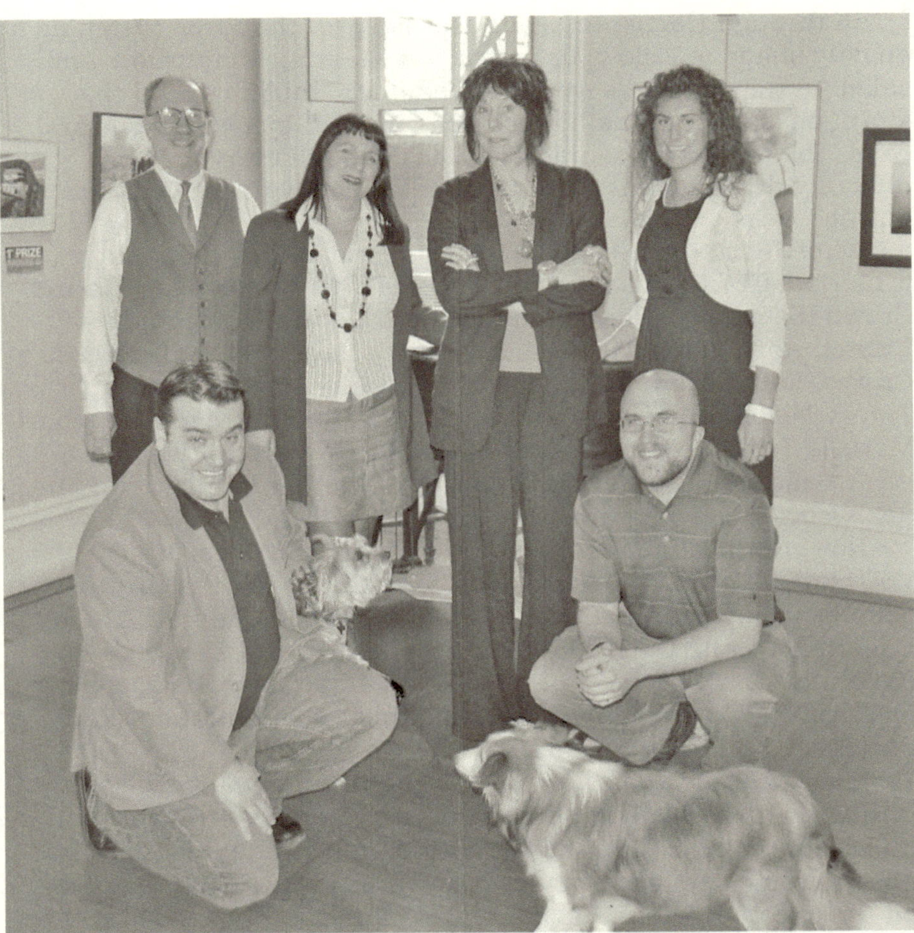

AAH staff in 2013

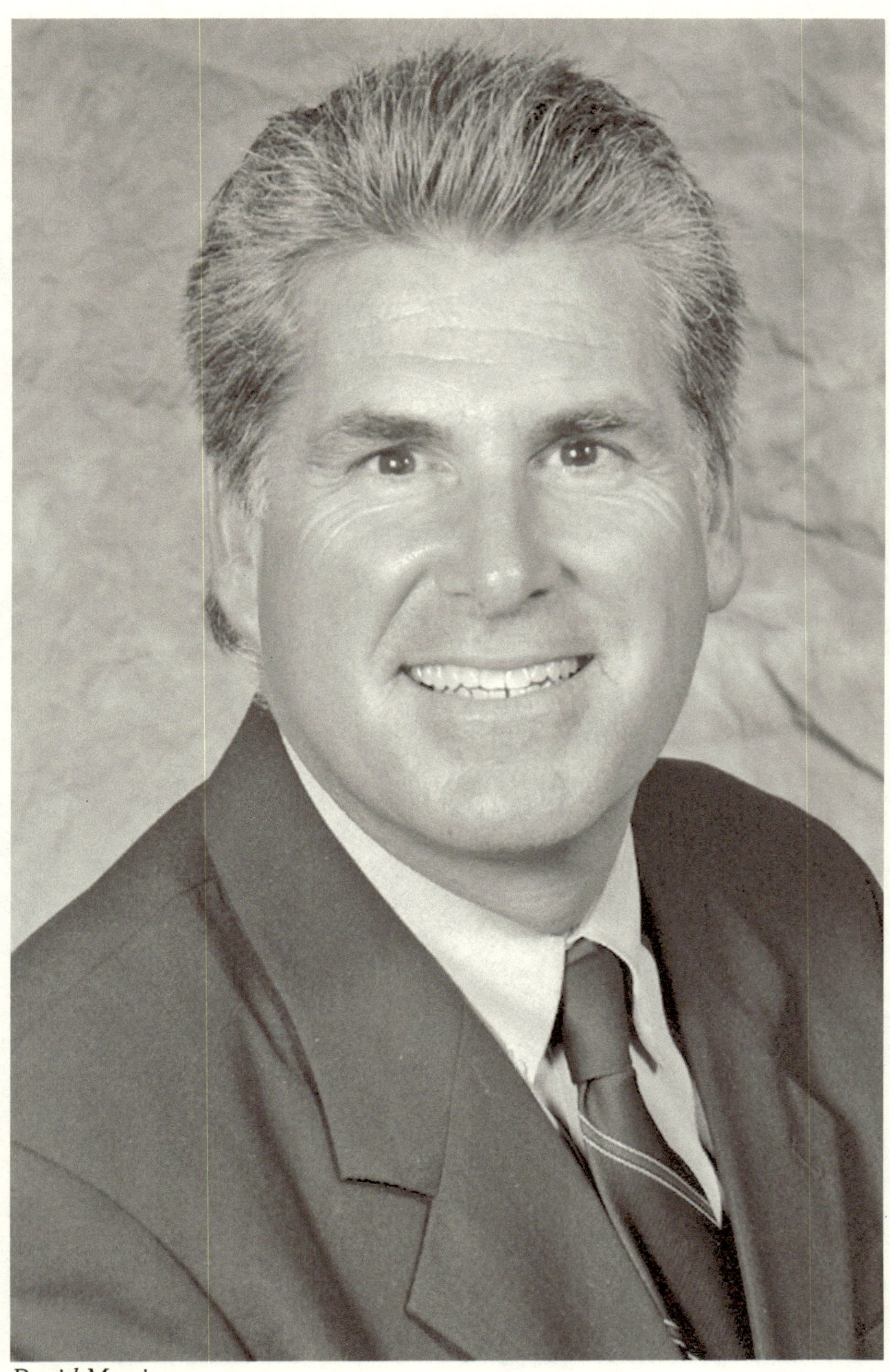

David Morrison

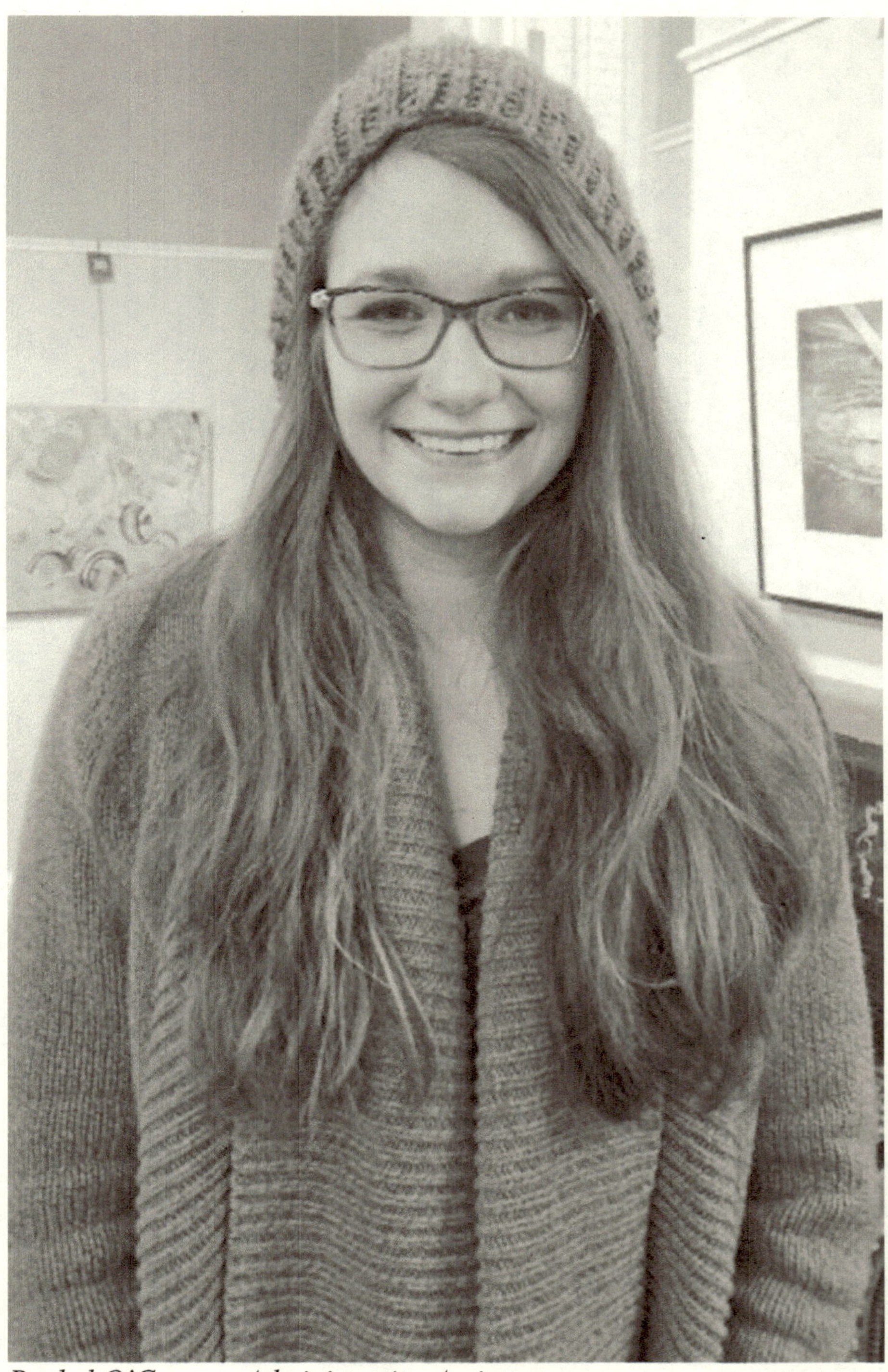

Rachel O'Connor, Administrative Assistant

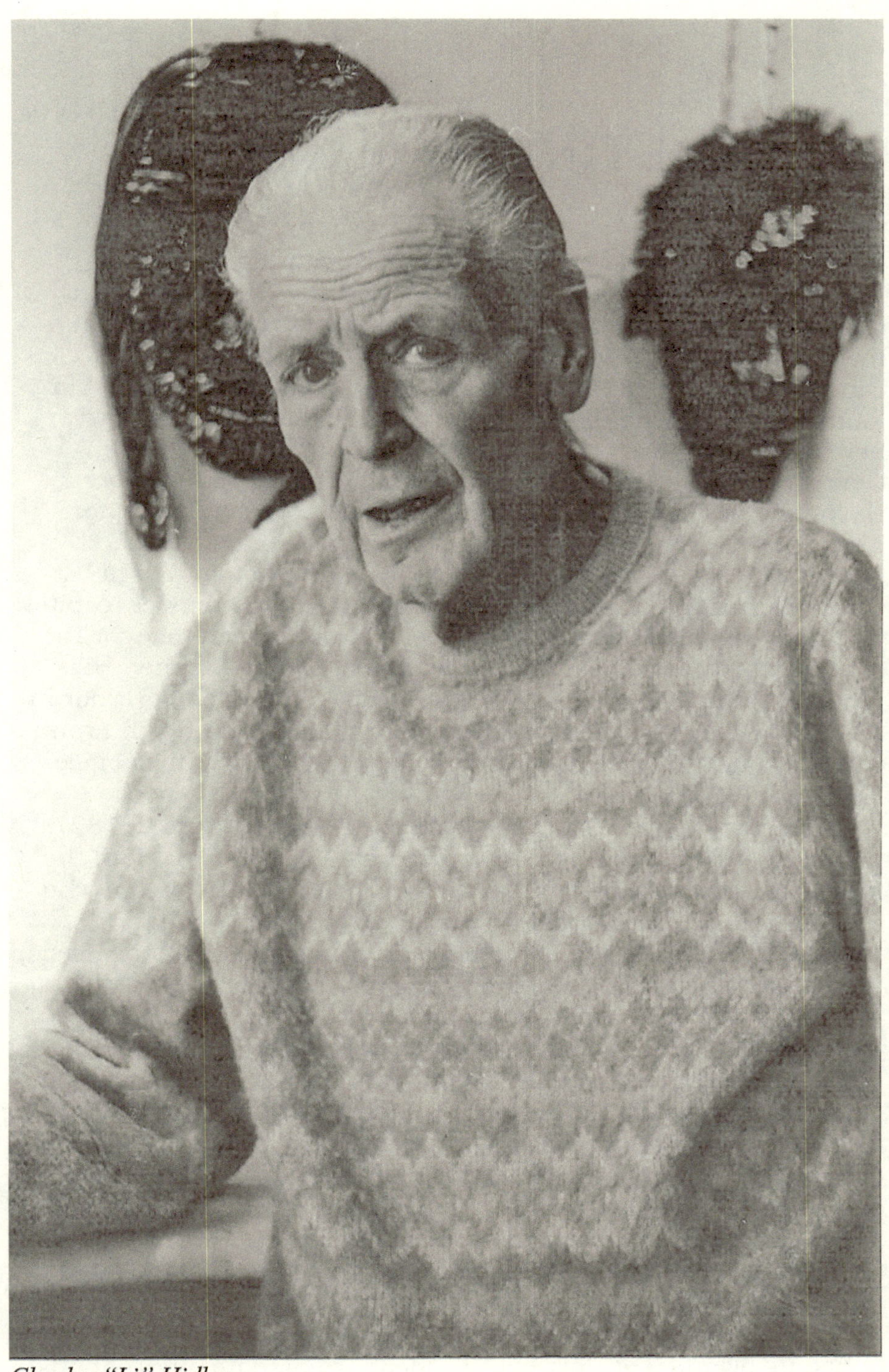

Charles "Li" Hidley

THE FINDLAY MANSION

The Art Association of Harrisburg's current home, the Italianate mansion at 21 North Front Street in Harrisburg, was originally built by architect Stephen A. Hills as one dwelling in a row of two-story, brick, Federal-style townhouses. It was constructed circa 1810 for Robert Harris, grandson of Harrisburg founder John Harris the elder. Governor William Findlay lived here from 1817 to 1821, although he did not own the house. Governor Joseph Heister lived here from 1820 to 1823. Robert Harris either loaned or rented the house to both governors, for neither name appears on the deed. Governor Findlay, the first governor to live in Harrisburg after the capital was moved here, conducted affairs of state from the front parlor, as the new capitol was not yet built. It was Findlay who laid the cornerstone for the capitol, which, like the mansion, was designed by Stephen Hills. Findlay's daughter married Francis R. Shunk, elected governor in 1845, and they resided in the next-door house at 23 North Front, where Findlay lived with them after he retired from public office. He died in 1846.

Robert and Elizabeth Harris sold the house on April 2, 1827, to James and Frances Catherine Peacock. On May 24, 1836, the Peacocks sold the house to Samuel and Sarah A. Patterson, who on February 16, 1850, sold it to Isaac G. McKinley. On April 1, 1857, McKinley sold the home to Henry Buehler. On all the deeds, the house is listed as a two-story brick structure.

Henry Buehler purchased the house for his daughter Mary Wolf Buehler, who had married Thomas Hastings Robinson, the young assistant pastor of the nearby Market Square Presbyterian Church, on May 10, 1856. Henry Buehler died leaving no legally valid will, so the house was inherited by Mary and her brother George Buehler, along with all the rest of Henry Buehler's extensive property and holdings in Harrisburg. On November 20, 1862, George Buehler signed over the house at 21 North Front Street to his sister Mary, as their father had originally intended it for her use.

Thomas H. Robinson became full pastor of his church in 1864, presiding over one of Harrisburg's most prominent congregations, with a new church on Market Square replacing the one that had burned on March 30, 1858. The church had no rectory, nor a study, so Pastor Robinson conducted his ministerial duties (e.g., planning the service, composing sermons, preparing the readings) from his home at 21 North Front. In December 1857, he and wife Mary had a baby son, who died after three days. Subsequently, they had a daughter, Anna Margaretta, born in 1859; a son William Andrew, born in 1861; a daughter Eliza McCormick, born in 1863; and a son Edward Orth, born in May 1865. Due to Pastor Robinson's need for a more spacious study, and because of the increasing size of his young family, the minister and his wife decided in 1865 to enlarge and renovate their 21 North Front home.

The Market Square Presbyterian Church had been designed in 1858 by the prominent Philadelphia architect Joseph C. Hoxie, who had also done the new Harrisburg railroad station about that same time. Hoxie was famous for his Presbyterian churches and his brownstone façade Italianate townhouses. Though no record has been found, it is believed that Hoxie directed the complete renovation of the house at 21 North Front, as he had already designed Pastor Robinson's new church on Market Square.

An insurance policy with The Insurance Company of North America lists the house at 21 North Front as a "new three-story brownstone front dwelling house with two-story brick back building [with] metal roof." The date of the policy is September 12, 1865. Pastor Robinson had been a member of the Christian Commission during the Civil War, directing its work in central Pennsylvania and serving on its behalf for a few months at the Dauphin County Historical Society. He was frequently a speaker at citywide functions, and was mentioned often in the newspapers.

After their fourth child, the Robinsons had two more children while living in their Front Street home. Thomas Hastings Jr. was born in 1871 and Mary Buehler in 1874. However, in 1881, tragedy struck: their eldest daughter, Anna Margaretta, affectionately known as "Annie," died on December 23, probably of "consumption" (tuberculosis). Her obituary, appearing in the Harrisburg *Telegraph*, described her as a talented young lady, "bright and vivacious," with great attraction "among the refined and cultured," and having "great taste for whatever was devoted and pure."

Whether the death of his beloved daughter had any bearing on his decision we do not know, but in 1884 Pastor Robinson announced that he would leave his Market Square church to accept a professorship at the Western Theological Seminary in Pittsburgh. His congregation saddened, Pastor Robinson, his wife Mary, and his children Edward and Thomas moved west. Son William was a professor of Greek at Lehigh by this time, and daughter Eliza was married to George Fleming. We do not know who lived at 21 North Front from 1884 to 1904, when Mary Robinson's heirs sold it to John Hoffer, although we speculate that Eliza and George Fleming resided there.

Pastor Robinson, his wife Mary, their beloved daughter Margaretta, and George and Eliza Fleming are buried in the family plot in a quiet corner of the old Harrisburg Cemetery.

When the Robinson heirs sold the 21 North Front property to John Hoffer in 1904, the selling price was $17,000. The Hoffer and Detweiler families lived there until 1964, when it was sold to the Art Association of Harrisburg. Architect Milford Patterson then supervised the transformation of the dwelling into its new uses as a gallery, studio and art school.

The Art Association had existed in rented quarters ever since its founding in 1926, but now it flourished in its new space. Patterson took great care to preserve as many of the house's Italianate features as possible. The building is a fine example of mid-Victorian architecture, enhanced by its new incarnation rather than diminished by it.

The 21 North Front building is a three-story painted brick house having a brownstone façade originally joined on both sides to two other townhouses (the one on the right now gone and replaced by an alley). The house has a low-pitch gable roof with two attic dormers and a rounded-arch cornice with corbelled stops. Romanesque Revival decorative elements appear on the façade, along with rounded segmented windows on all three floors. Crested 2/2 elongated windows exist on the first and second floors with an elliptical arched window above the front door.

The mansion interior has marble fireplaces on the first and second floors, with original woodwork and plaster molding along the ceilings. Three finished rooms for storage and office space exist in the attic. Massive brick arches are in the basement. All rooms in the front portion of the building have remarkably high ceilings, with those in the back two-story section having lower ceilings. It is likely that the rear two-story part of the building is older than the front part and was not completely rebuilt in 1865.

With the building now used for year-round art exhibitions, featuring a variety of art shown every five weeks by both local and national artists, and with a year-round art school staffed by professional artists, we can imagine that the cultured Anna Margaretta Robinson would be pleased with what has happened to her home.

The AAH is comprised of 800 members from central Pennsylvania and across the country. It is a non-profit cultural organization completely supported by membership dues, contributions by businesses and foundations, yearly grants from the Cultural Enrichment Fund, and fund-raising events. There is also a Sales Gallery where members' works are sold on consignment.

Quality being the watchword of the Art Association of Harrisburg, the building at 21 North Front Street is the perfect setting for its cultural work. The lovely historic townhouse was refurbished again from 1984 to 1987 following an extensive Capital Fund Campaign spearheaded by then President Charles Stoup. In 2007 another major Capital Campaign was begun to upgrade the infrastructure of the building and execute some interior upgrades, under the direction of architect Richard LeBlanc.

This gracious old townhouse at 21 North Front Street is a fitting home for the oldest cultural arts organization in the city, the architecture complementing its art, and its art enhancing the architecture.

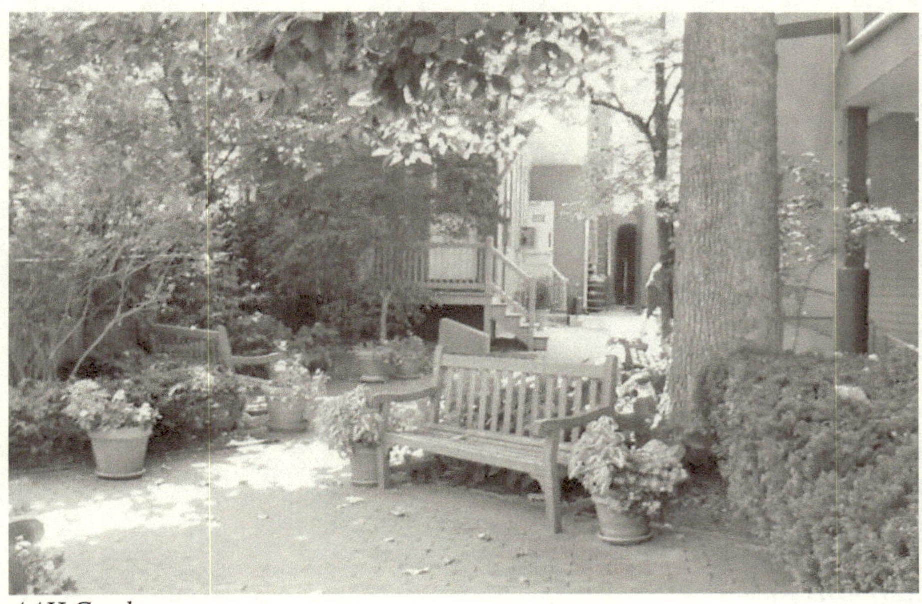

AAH Garden

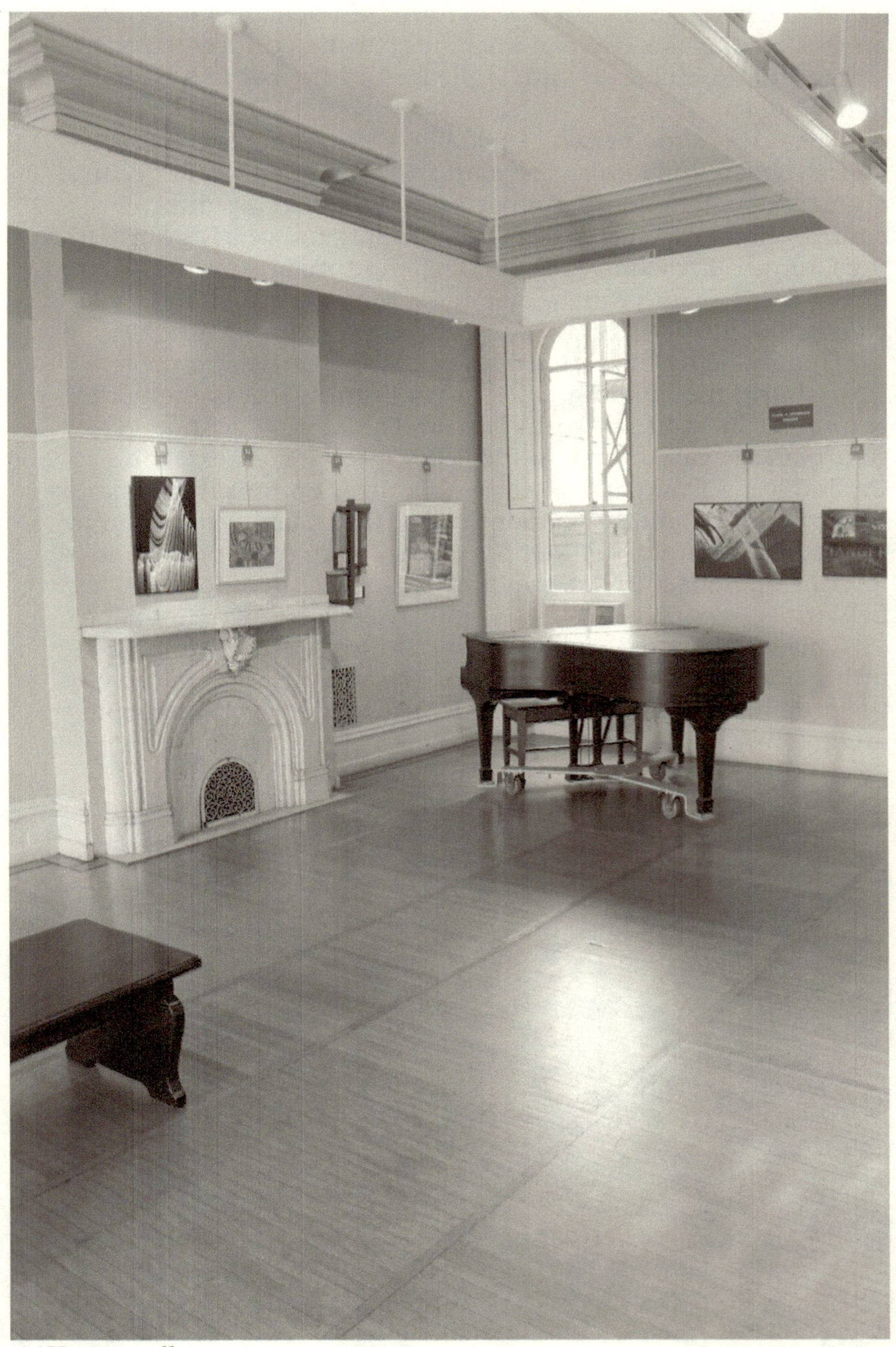

AAH main gallery

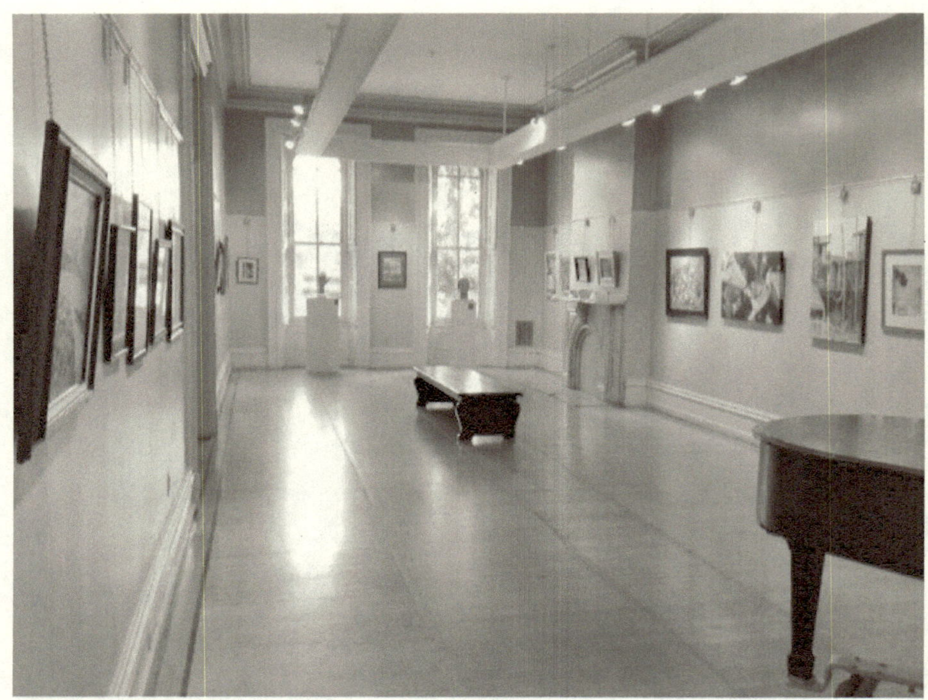

AAH main gallery

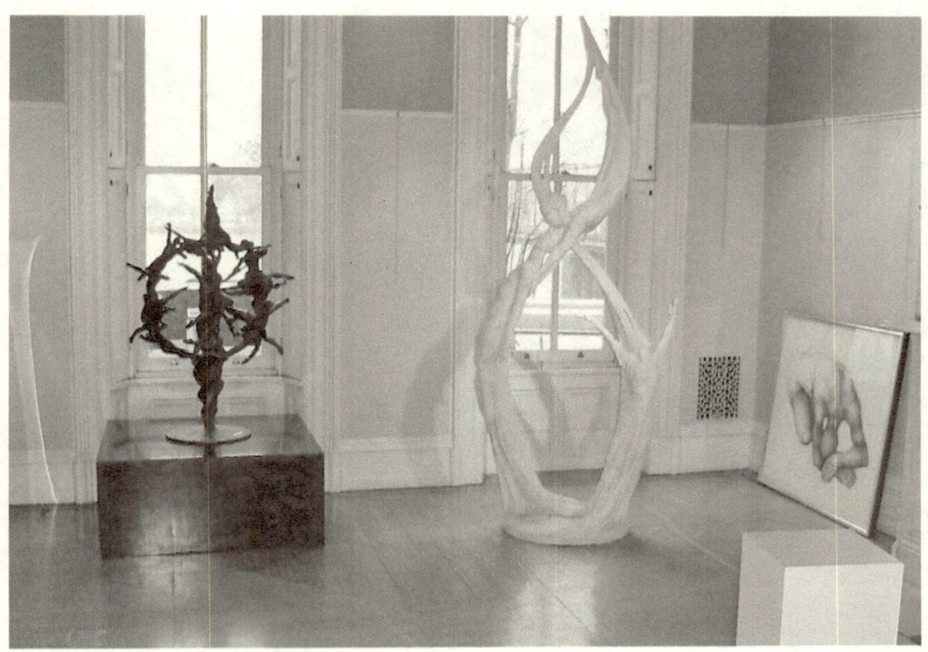

AAH gallery sculptures

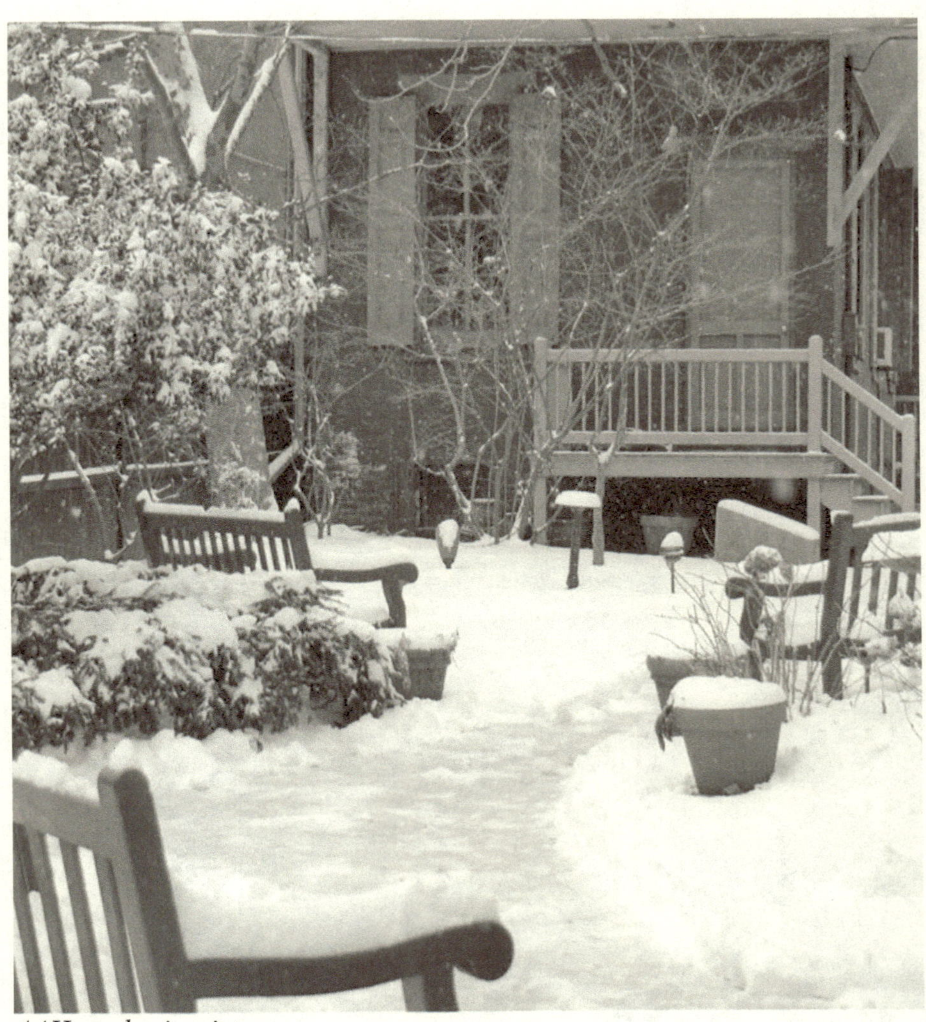

AAH garden in winter

LIFE AND AFTERLIFE BY GENE SUCHMA

When I joined the Life Drawing group at the Art Association in 1972, it had already been existence for about fifteen years. In 1960, illustrator Karl Foster became the moderator of the group. In those days, nude models were scarce, so the group regularly sketched students from a local ballet school in their dance attire. There was one nude model who came regularly, but, after awhile, the members of the drawing group tired of drawing the same model over and over again. Membership shrank. In an effort to revive the drawing group, Karl began advertising for life-drawing models in the newspaper.

In 1964 The Art Association moved into its current location on Front Street. That year, Richard Koontz, who became an important figure in the group's history, joined the life drawing group. Koontz was an industrial designer, who had taught at Syracuse University, he also had designed and built his own home out of steel in the minimalist style of architecture, and he developed and patented his own system of drawing using multiple point perspective. Koontz had been involved in a Jeep accident while on a training mission during the Second World War and for years had lost the use of his arms and legs. Thanks to intense therapy and encouragement by his wife Ruth, Richard finally regained the use of his arms and, to a lesser degree, his legs. Despite his lack of mobility, he was able to walk haltingly, using a cane, up the stairs to the 3rd floor studio and become a regular fixture of the group.

By 1972, Karl was still using classified ads in the papers to get fresh models to draw. At the time, I was living on part-time jobs and freelance artwork and could not afford the tuition to take the life drawing workshop, so I answered one of the ads. On the night of my interview, there was only one other person, a young woman, sitting in the row of chairs set up for job applicants. Neither of us had ever done any modeling before, and we were both nervous about the interview. Since we were the only ones in the room, she asked if I could use a toke on some marijuana. I eagerly accepted.

I suspect the two of us were the first, if not only, persons ever to light up in the main gallery of the Art Association of Harrisburg. Anyway, I went in to the interview feeling very confident. In our discussion about the job I realized that the payment for a modeling session didn't come close to matching the tuition for an entire semester. I made an offer to Karl to allow me to attend the group for that term in exchange for serving as a substitute model any time the assigned didn't show (which happened several times in any given quarter). Karl accepted my offer and I was in.

Life as a life-drawing model

Several weeks passed before a scheduled model cancelled at the last minute. Prior to my arrival, in a situation when the model didn't show, the group would draw each other clothed. However, this time, Karl asked if I was up for the job or if I wanted to continue in the usual practice. I decided to make my debut.

By this time I'd been to enough sessions to know the routine: short poses from one to five minutes, then longer poses, up to one hour, in twenty minute segments. I had been thinking about the sort of poses I liked to draw and decided to pose in those. For the shortest sketches, I'd try to hold a pose as if I were playing basketball, baseball or football. I soon found out that they were easier thought of than done. In less than a minute, my muscles would begin to ache and parts of my body began to shift. The more I modeled, the more I learned how to twist my body in ways that would allow me to be in balance enough for the shorter poses. Because the time frame is short, artists work at a rapid pace and concentrate on the gesture of the pose, not concerning themselves about detail. In poses of fifteen minutes and longer, artists have enough time to refine the sketch in more detail, so shifting of the model become quite irritating. To prevent drifting, I found that I could use the wall for support.

I must have done it too often because Richard Koontz began making fun of me about it. I still would use the wall at least once a class, but began to try other techniques. One of these, I learned from another model, was to pick out a focal point and continue to look at it for the duration of the pose. The next time I was called upon to model, I tried this method. There was a tall good-looking woman with dark curly hair in the group, a regular, who tended to stay in the same spot throughout the session. She always wore pants and a top that offered a peek at her naval which I found to be the perfect spot to fixate on.

I never felt self-conscious about making the transition from being a clothed artist to an unclad model. However not everyone felt the same. There was one class in which I was a substitute model when a good female friend of mine arrived late. She opened the door to the studio when I was nude and already into a pose. "I can't deal with this!" she blurted out as she turned around and left.

I moved out of the area in '74 and I returned in '77. I rejoined the Art Association and life drawing, no longer as a sub but as a one of a small stable of models. In my efforts to contribute to the continued success of the life group, I would try to recruit other people to pose. I asked my pregnant wife to model and encouraged her friend from Florida to pose as well. One week I shared the model's platform with Liz, a friend of mine. We used whatever props we found around the studio, plastic grapes, for example, and created theatrical tableaux to give the artists a chance to draw figure groupings.

Life drawing was a serious but casual class. While the model was posing Karl would hum, Richard would whistle tunes and the rest of us would make brief comments about world or local events. Occasionally someone would express his or her displeasure, which put a stop to the chatter and noise temporarily. I was one of the worst offenders, whether drawing or modeling. Being a cartoonist, I would often think of funny things and share them with the group, which would cause laughter and disrupt the pose. One evening, when I was the model, I waited until almost everyone was present to retreat to the studio's bathroom that doubled as a dressing (or undressing room). It took me about five to ten minutes to disrobe. When I emerged nude, I found an empty room. They all had vanished. I had no problem being nude in a room full of artists, but I didn't know what to make of being naked there all by myself. A short while later they all returned laughing at their joke on me. I think Richard orchestrated the surprise.

Other models, also, experienced unusual situations. One evening a new member joined the group. There was nothing odd about him, he seemed just like the rest of us except that he had no art supplies. When the model assumed her first pose, he got up from his chair, pulled out a camera and began walking around the nude woman taking photographs. The model freaked and began to cover herself. Karl politely and firmly asked the man to leave.

A couple of times, class was interrupted by unexpected visitors. One summer night, the building next door to the Association had been broken into and the police were called to investigate. The third floor drawing studio was extremely hot that evening and the window to the fire escape was open for ventilation. One of the artists chose to set up his easel near the open window. He was working intently when he was distracted by a rhythmic panting behind his ear. He turned and saw a police dog peering in the window and behind the dog, a policeman on the fire escape platform. It is unclear if the dog had ever seen a nude model before but the patrolman was stunned. Apparently he was given the wrong address of the break-in. The mistake discovered, the policeman and dog retreated and class resumed.

On another evening, the ground floor door of the Association had been inadvertently left open, unbeknownst to the drawing group on floor number three. The session was well under way, when suddenly the door next to the model's platform swung open and a policeman, gun drawn, came inside. When he looked around and saw the artists and the nude woman to his immediate left, he quickly shut the door and exited. After what seemed like a count of three, the door opened again and the man in blue came in with his female partner to survey the situation again. Apparently on their usual patrol, the two saw the open outside door and decided to investigate. When they were reassured that everything was all right, the pair left the building and class resumed.

One of Karl's regular models, a belly dancer, was also a member of a naturist group who met on land off Fishing Creek Valley Road, which land is now a part of Felicita Resort. The dancer, Lorna, arranged for the life drawing group to come on designated weekends and sketch the nudists. Clothing was optional for the artists who would set up their easels and sketch books while individuals and small groups, including families, would take time out of their afternoon to model. I attended one of the weekend sessions and opted to draw while fully clothed, thank you.

Afterlife

When I began attending the life drawing sessions, I quickly learned that class didn't end when the model went home. The tradition started years earlier when Karl and artist Tom Ross would meet after class at a downtown doughnut shop. When Richard Koontz joined the group, he eventually convinced the artists to meet at places with more on the menu than doughnuts and coffee. His criteria: the place had to be close to the Art Association, had to serve food and beer and had to be quiet enough to allow for interesting conversation. Abe's Tavern on 3rd street, Harry's Tavern on Allison Hill and Der Maennerchor Club in downtown were some of the venues for the after-class meet, eat, and greet sessions.

By the time I became a member in the mid-seventies, the watering hole of choice was The Iron Kettle, on Simpson Ferry Road in Camp Hill, which was only a few minutes from Richard's home. Each week, a convoy of artists and models would leave Front and Walnut and drive to the pub. The Iron Kettle would reserve a couple of tables for the group. Not only would the class members come, but also Richard's friend Dean Minick. Conversation would be about art, politics and life in general. Wisdom poured forth from Richard's mouth as he would share his life experiences, telling stories like the one about how Thomas Hart Benton stole a model from him to use in his famous painting, Susanna and the Elders. He also narrated tales other famous artists he had the privilege of knowing. Whatever the story, he'd end it with the phrase "but I digress."

Richard, who had once been a liberal, became conservative politically in his later years. He and Dean would discuss politics and social issues with me and the other younger members of the group, some of who tended toward 70's radicalism. I was a freelance cartoonist at the time working for left wing groups and publications. Dean, who served in World War II, and I would argue about the morality of the bombings at Hiroshima and Nagasaki. Sometimes the argument became so intense that Dean would leave the bar. He always came back the next week. Despite our disagreements, he remained my friend. Dean said that I was a great cartoonist but needed to be more objective, something that has stuck with me since.

The conversations and the humor at the Iron Kettle were so interesting that, if I couldn't get to Life Drawing Class, I'd make sure to get to afterlife with Karl and Richard.

When I got a full time teaching job, I had neither the time nor the energy to continue going to draw or to stay up late at the Iron Kettle to talk. Years later, Karl and Richard eventually retired from the group, but it is still going strong.

THE ART ASSOCIATION OF HARRISBURG SCHOOL

According to the minutes of the Art Association's Board meeting on November 11, 1928, the first mention regarding the support of a studio or school was a suggestion by the President that AAH join with others "interested in artistic matters" to identify a place to "provide proper studio facilities for local artists." The space suggested was a building formerly owned by a Lutheran Church at the corner of 15th and Shoop Streets. Apparently a committee was formed at this meeting to do research into this.

The Art Association did align itself with some sort of studio soon afterwards, because in the January 12, 1931, minutes the Exhibition Committee was authorized to make arrangements for "Mrs. Colt's studio... also for the purchase of models up to $100.00 worth." The Mrs. Colt in question was a Mrs. Guy A. Colt, an art instructor in charge of an establishment known as "The Harrisburg Art School." This school was financially supported, though not officially affiliated with, the Association throughout the 1930's. The Association's endorsement of this school was discussed at a March, 1932, meeting:

"It is the belief of the committee established on this subject, that the Harrisburg Art Association cannot better carry on its objects in the city than to support the Harrisburg Art School."

At this time, Mrs. Colt's school offered four-year courses in drawing, painting, sculpture, fashion illustration, design, teacher training, commercial art, and special classes in etching and wood-block printing. The Association was then supporting the school's operations with annual contributions of $500. The school's first location was at Front and Washington Streets, later moving to 414 Spring Street. The school's classes were actually conducted by both Guy Colt and his wife Martha Cox Colt, both professional artists.

According to Edward C. Michener's 1997 booklet "Personal Recollections of the Art Association of Harrisburg," there were reports that the school was not managed well, and it became a financial drain on the Association. This resulted in the abandonment of the school by AAH, and Michener reported that it was out of existence for several years prior to the establishment of the AAH Studio.

Michener goes on to say, "Also prior to the establishment of The Studio, a small group of professional artists pooled their resources to rent space in which to work together. It was located on the second floor above Johnny Kobler's Saloon at Walnut and Court Streets. The group called themselves 'The Independent Artists' Studio,' a name selected presumably to show no connection with the Association. In the beginning years of the Association, there was some feeling of resentment on the part of the artists, since the founders and the trustees were all 'society ' types and there was no artist representation on the Board.

"There were five principal members of the group—Alden Turner, Walt Huber, Nick Ruggieri, Tom Keil, and Earl Johnston. There may have been others but I have never heard them mentioned. Turner and Ruggieri worked in the art department of the Telegraph Press, along with Joe Wolf (Hain's father) and Ray Snow, who was head of the department. Walt Huber was Art Director of McFarland Press. Earl Johnston was the cartoonist of the 'Evening News.' At that time, Tom Keil did not make his living from art, but when he left Harrisburg later, he became successful as an art director in Cleveland and New York.

"Undaunted by the failure of The Harrisburg School of Art, the Association's Trustees revived the idea of a 'working place for artists and students' in 1937, and with the leadership of Dr. C. Valentine Kirby, the head of Art Education in the State Department of Public Instruction, the project was undertaken. A meeting was held to which 40 or more artists were invited and the idea was presented. It was received enthusiastically.

"Catherine Grant, a Vassar graduate with further studies at the Pennsylvania Academy of Fine Arts, was named the first Director. Miss Grant found a splendid location near Front and Paxton Streets, which was not far from central city and easily accessible by bus. The rent at 500 Race Street, as well as Catherine Grant's salary, was underwritten by the Association. All others who agreed to teach did so without pay. Among them were Alden Turner, Walt Huber, Thomas Keil, Betty Troup, Peg Roessing (Mrs. George), Edwin Sponsler, Helen Manahan, Howard Worner and me."

Ed Michener's recollections continue:

"The Studio at 500 Race Street was in effect a loft—one large room about50x75 feet, with windows at the North and East sides.

It had high ceilings and was reached by a wide and long flight of steps on the West side. The remaining half of the second floor was occupied by the Community Theatre, which used it for rehearsals and for building scenery.

"The original volunteers, plus others who joined in the effort after it began, pitched in and cleaned and painted the room so it presented a bright and cheerful ambience. Electricians installed enough bright lights so it became a pleasant and rewarding place to paint by day or night. And it was utilized both day and night, with Catherine Grant, Betty Troup, Mary Scurlock and Peg Roessing teaching in the daytime and Turner, Huber, Sponsler, Worner and Michener taking their turns at nighttime classes.

"Enthusiasm was high on the part of both artists and students. A newspaper story at the time indicated an initial enrollment of 224 students in September 1938. This probably was an exaggeration and may have included both professional artists AND students.

"Among the early members of the Studio who had active roles as students or volunteers, and many proved to be long time supporters were Wilbur and Pauline Nisley (he was a landscape architect and partner in Walter, Nisley and Walter. He also served as President of AAH in 1956), Richard and Edith Heilman (Richard was later to become Chairman and CEO of the Insurance Company of North America), Elsa Beamish, Mrs. Farley Gannett (Janet) and her husband, who was the founder of Gannett, Fleming Corddrey and Carpenter, an international engineering firm,, William Rohrbeck, prominent in the Harrisburg art scene for well over 50 years, Betty Snow, an accomplished painter and portraitist, who was later to become Studio Director, Lucille Wallower, author and illustrator of children's books, and also a Studio Director, Estelle Earnest, Nick Ruggieri, Mary Mowry, Renata Kauffman, Tom Haas, Mrs. John Cowden (Nan), Betsy Baker, Walter Gallagher, Julia Comstock Smith, Jim Spence, Hain Wolf (a later AAH President), Ivan Lenker, John Wright, Roland Walli8s, J. Wesley Gable, Charlie Krone, Richard and Louise (Eaton) Walker, and many others who, unfortunately, faded from memory."

Ed Michener's memories of this formative time for the AAH School are amazing! He continued to say that when Catherine Grant moved elsewhere, the Association Board appointed him as Director. At this time a number of physical changes were implemented at The Studio, including the construction of movable wooden panels that allowed the division of the large space into several smaller studios, so that two or more classes could be conducted simultaneously. He said that some windows on the Studio's East side were blocked off to "permit North light to dominate."

"In addition to the serious side of Studio activities," Ed wrote, "it also provided an opportunity for social relaxation for the members. From time to time, simple meals were prepared outside and brought in to be shared by all. A typical such meal was spaghetti by the 'dishpanful,' with a large salad and Italian bread, all catered by a local Italian Bistro just a few doors away."

The signature event of The Art Association—The Bal Masque—was created as a fundraiser in support of The Studio in 1940. With Studio income at the low level of $12 per semester, making ends meet was obviously a serious problem. Betty Troup apparently arranged to rent the Harrisburg Country Club as the first Bal's locale, with the theme "Ten Nights in an Art Gallery." Ed reported that he, Alden Turner and Howard Worner painted the decorative panels to illustrate the theme. The first Bal was a big success, generating a great deal of publicity. So, another Bal was held the next year at the West Shore Country Club, with "Americana" as the patriotic theme.

Ed continued his narrative by saying, because of the imminent entry of the U.S. into World War II, no plans were made for further Bal Masques, and membership in the Studio was adversely affected. With limited resources, he said it became difficult to pay the rent at 500 Race Street. Ed spoke with Mabel Bitner, Assistant Director of the State Museum where the Studio had been holding exhibitions, and she gave the group permission to use the gallery for their classes, which were reduced to only one or two evenings per week. At the same time, he said, through a friendship with Margaret Wister Meigs, who owned Fort Hunter Museum, the Studio held summer classes there on the grounds and in a studio he and Howard Worner had renovated in an old stone barn. The artists also held outdoor exhibits each weekend, weather permitting.

Ed Michener said that "the long arm of Uncle Sam reached out for me in 1943 and I entered the U.S. Corps of Engineers. Lucille Wallower took over as Director of The Studio and continued classes at the Museum until a change in political power 'changed the rules' and we were no longer permitted to use the Museum. Lucille found a temporary home for The Studio in St. Paul's Episcopal Parish House, on North Second Street, and classes were held there for several years."

After World War II ended, increased interest in art led the Studio to acquiring rental space at 201 Chestnut Street, downtown. Lucille Wallower then left to pursue her writing and illustrating career, and she was followed by a succession of Studio Directors, including: Louise Eaton Walker, Jeanette Boyd, Dora Addams, Laura Pragnell and Betty Snow. Around 1952, Ed remembered, under Betty Snow's Directorship, The Studio moved to 414 Spring Street, ironically once the location of the defunct Harrisburg School of Art!

An interesting footnote of my own is the conversation that I once had with Betty Snow, soon after I became Executive Director of AAH in 1986. She told me that she, as Studio Director, had as part of her responsibility the cleaning of the facility! Fortunately that was not part of my job description!

It was at this juncture that a pivotal occurrence took place. Ed Michener became influential in merging the Studio and The Art Association of Harrisburg parent organization. He explained, "After returning from military service in 1945, I continued to be active in the affairs of The Studio while also serving on the Board of the Art Association. Some years before, knowing the tendency for artists in general to be somewhat disorganized, we made a serious effort to create a more formal organization for The Studio and also to get more involvement from the community at large. We recruited a number of successful business and professional people to take part. Among them were William Lynch Murray (architect), David Shotwell (architect), Russell Charles (General Manager of Bowman's Store), Dr. David Johnston, Howard Newhouse (*The Patriot News*), and John Stapf (President of the John Stapf Companies).

The result of this formalization resulted in a situation in which there were two organizations set up in essentially the same way, trying to achieve the same objectives. I sensed that the Association Board members were by now becoming somewhat weary of their responsibilities, while still being wholly committed to the ideals that inspired them to start the Art Association movement in the first place.

In 1953, I proposed to the Board of the Association that we merge the two entities into one and eliminate the Studio as a separate organization. As expected, the proposal was enthusiastically received, and I was assigned the task of bringing it about.

As President Pro-Tem, I held several meetings, at which all the pros and cons were thoroughly discussed. Attorney Richard Walker was assigned to draw up a new set of By-Laws, which followed to a large extent those of the parent and surviving entity.

A new Board was selected and the previous Board members were designated as advisory and Honorary Trustees. In 1954, an organizing meeting was held, in which the Board was officially elected. Nick Ruggieri was elected President. Other officers were: Richard Walker, Vice President; Mrs. Walker, Secretary; and Mrs. William Addams, Treasurer.

My interest continued through the years, culminating in the Fund Drive for the new building. Will Brown, as President, was the driving force behind the building project and deserves 90% of the credit. Dottie Shaffer and I were co-chairs of the fund drive and Nick Ruggieri was the vigorous chairman of the committee that located the building.

After much rehabilitation, largely under the supervision of Milford Patterson, the building was finally and proudly dedicated on November 9, 1964, beginning an entirely new era in the Arts in Harrisburg."

The building identified and renovated was The Governor Findlay Mansion at 21 North Front Street. With fourteen rooms for studios and galleries... A miraculous find!

According to an article in *The Patriot News*, the Art Association's merger with the Studio occurred at the same time as the move to the 414 Spring Street facilities. This is a bit of a wrinkle in the time frame described by Ed Michener. The article stated, "Reorganization of Harrisburg Art Association was announced today with plans to move headquarters and studio into spacious quarters at 414 Spring St.by April 1. Merger of the Association and the Art Studio, which formerly operated under two official bodies, into one Association was made to extend the culture of the community through rewritten by-laws. Under a newly elected Board, with Nick Ruggieri as President, plans to revitalize the art movement will include augmenting of workshop activities in larger and better lighted quarters."

The article went on to state, "Art classes, now offered to the public five times weekly at 201 Chestnut St., will be established in the new studio covering the entire second floor of the Spring Street building. Downstairs rooms will afford a permanent place for art exhibits, film studies and lectures. The public will be able to enjoy more exhibits by local artists as well as permanent collections." The article concluded by saying, "In 1936-37 the association sponsored an art studio to provide instruction for Harrisburg citizens in all walks of life who were interested in art, as well as a workshop for artists. These quarters have long since been outgrown by the number of children, housewives and businessmen who utilize them in pursuit of art."

The brochure "Your Harrisburg Art Association" must have been printed at this same time, as the first page states, "The first home of the Studio was 500 Race Street. From this, successive moves carried it from the State Museum to the St. Paul's Episcopal Church, to 201 Chestnut Street, and finally, today, 414 Spring Street—by far the most adequate facilities ever obtained!" The ultimate goal of the Art Association, the brochure maintained, is "a permanent gallery-studio... built to accommodate many students and large enough to house weekly gallery exhibitions."

In that late 1950's brochure, the classes listed were Monday Evening Teenagers' Drawing; Tuesday Evening Adult Drawing, Painting; Wednesday Afternoon—Housewives' Oil Painting; Thursday Evening—Adult Portraiture, Drawing; Thursday Evening —Businessmen's Drawing, Painting; Saturday Morning—Children's Painting. The tuition was $8 per semester for the teenagers and $6 for children. The adult classes were all $12 per semester.

After the move in 1964 to the Governor Findlay Mansion, classes were offered in the third-floor studio, the Michener Studio on the second floor, and two studios in the basement. When I joined the Art Association in 1972, eight years later, the class I joined was the Life Class with Karl Foster as Monitor. This was a class for professional artist members, in which we drew from live nude models on Thursday evenings in the third-floor studio with Karl calling the shots with the models—We started off with about five three-minute poses, then working from ½ hour poses, and usually ending with hour-long poses. It was in those early Life Classes that I first met Karl himself, Gene Suchma, Leo Gilroy, and many other artists who became close friends.

Other AAH instructors when I first joined included Vid Petrasic, who taught watercolour in the basement... "Petrasic green" was famous, a highly recognizable grey green that appeared in all his and his students' paintings: Lauren Welker, Bill Rohrbeck, and Peg Brown, children's teacher. Nick Ruggieri had been a tremendously popular watercolour instructor at AAH for years, but I believe by the time I became involved, he had moved his class to the basement of a downtown church, no longer part of the Art Association.

May Voight was the Studio Director for several years during the 1960's, with Mae Johnson following her, and then in 1976, Lauren Emerich Welker was hired. In the Middletown Press & Journal on January 14, 1976, her employment as Studio Director was announced in an article titled "Harrisburg Art Association Marks 50th Anniversary; It Tries to Make Art-Culture Interesting and Fun." Lauren is quoted in the article about the upcoming classes:

"Thirteen new classes are being organized by the school chairman Doris Dunlap. This includes a new class in a suburban area in drawing and pastels taught by Vid Petrasic at the Colonial Park Methodist Church, 430 Colonial Road. It will meet on Tuesday afternoons from 12:30 to 3, beginning February 2. We're trying to decentralize, especially for our daytime activities. Parking is so difficult here in the daytime. In the evenings and on weekends, we can use the parking lot of the Dauphin County Family Services next door. But as I said, the daytimes are bad. And bus service isn't all that good. So we're experimenting with taking classes to areas outside Harrisburg. Colonial Park is the first place we've tried this approach. The idea is to try to get people who are home during the day out of their homes, away from the 'soaps' and doing something interesting."

The range of classes offered in 1976 included watercolours, pastels, oil painting, drawing, wood carving, silk screen printing, motion picture production, and photography. There also were classes for children. The article stated that for the fall term classes, enrollment had totaled 136 adults and 50 children. Tuition that year was $25 for adults and $20 for children, except for the motion picture and photography classes. Life class in those days had no tuition, but students were required to be AAH members and contribute to the model fee.

Then in 1979, Charles Schulz was hired as the Association's first full-time Executive Director under Dave Lenker's Presidency, my Vice-Presidency. When I became AAH President in 1980, Charles and I worked to bring tighter organization to the School, and four school semesters were established with stated tuitions for all the classes. To bring the Life Class into conformity with the others, besides requiring the students to be AAH members, they were also asked to pay tuition, albeit lower than for the other classes, to cover the model fee. The Life Class was always a world unto itself, with the students perennially complaining about having to register in advance and pay tuition, but we felt that paying the models with AAH checks was more professional than having them paid with cash by the students.

It was under Charles' auspices that the Expressionist Artist Charles "Li" Hidley, expatriate from New York City, was engaged as an AAH painting from the figure instructor. This was another pivotal event for the Association, because Hidley opened the floodgates of Expressionism to the Harrisburg art scene. When I first joined AAH in 1972, gallery visitors were known to view the watercolour landscapes and sigh loudly, "You can always tell a student of Nick Ruggieri's!" Now Nick's works and those of his students were lovely, no question, but when Hidley's students began exhibiting Expressionist nudes painted in vivid colours and distorted forms, everything paled in comparison!

We acquired two studios at University Centre in Uptown Harrisburg for Hidley's class, and for my Basic Oil class. "Hidley Hall," as we called it, was in the basement of Richards Hall, and it had a cistern in one corner! Hidley's own huge paint-coated tabouret and palette were at one end, and a mammoth heap of still-life items and cloths were along another wall, including a human skull he maintained had been unearthed in his half-sister's Dillsburg garden. (A University Centre janitor saw it once and accused Hidley of voodoo worship, but I explained the skull was fake and all was well...) In that cluttered and wonderful studio were nurtured top-notch painters, such as Charley Ann Rhoads, Maaike Heitkonig, Charlie Hickok, Bob Bissett, Re' DeSabres', Martin Plaut, Brian Rogers, Steve Barber, Dee Keily, Terrie Hosey (now AAH Curator), and I was delighted to be part of the group. Hidley's models for that Painting from the Model class were drawn from belly dancers, nudists from the nearby colony, body-builders, and friends and relatives of students who posed in costumes. Hidley himself often posed in some costume or other when no models were available, and all of us captured him as a Spanish hidalgo, a homeless person, or an Edgar Allen Poe figure.

Those were heady days. "Hidley's People" began to garner all the prizes in local art shows, and his influence was everywhere. My Basic Oil class on Thursday evenings in North Hall was popular as well, and one of my early students was Steve Wetzel, now AAH landscape instructor. Our favourite story involves the still-life I set up for the class to paint, with a turnip. The beginners in the class took WEEKS to paint that still-life, and the turnip sprouted and put out a very long twining vine, which Steve, an experienced painter, incorporated all around the border of his canvas as it grew and grew like Jack's beanstalk. We still laugh about that!

When the University Centre began a massive renovation and rebuilding project, we had to move out of the two studios there. Historic Harrisburg Association had been given the former bank building at 1230 North Third Street by then, and we rented a mezzanine-level area as the new "Hidley Hall." The main problem we encountered there was the fact that the nude models tended to shock visitors to the HHA Resource Centre whenever they wandered upstairs looking for the meeting rooms! We finally moved Hidley and all his studio accoutrements back to the AAH third-floor studio, since the tuition we collected didn't cover the rental fees to HHA.

Other great teachers in the 1980's were Leo Gilroy, Portraiture, and David Lenker, Watercolour. Both attracted huge followings. Leo, with Charles' permission, offered free classes to a curmudgeonly chap named Fred Leffler, in exchange for his overseeing (I speak the word lightly) the parking lot next to the building where students parked in the evenings. Fred's car was old and huge, and he was a horrible driver, always denting students' cars. However, Leo felt sorry for the chap. Unfortunately, one evening Fred collapsed on the stairs going up to the third-floor studio, and Leo and another student offered to take him to the emergency room. He refused, insisting they take him home to his second-floor apartment catty-corner from the Governor's Residence on North Second Street. Leo and Robin reluctantly took him home and left him. Poor Fred was discovered dead in his apartment several weeks later... a very sad tale.

Later my own son Dylan took Leo's Portraiture class, starting at age 12 and continuing until his graduation from high school. Leo was a fine chap, and his students loved him dearly. He died in the late 1990's and Tina Reily, Paul Gallo, and finally Kimberly Krammes Stone taught his class.

Dave Lenker was another beloved instructor, teaching here from the early 1980's until just a few years before his death in 2009 at age 92. Dave ironically died just a few months after his idol Andrew Wyeth, whose work he strove to emulate and whose Brandywine technique he imparted to his many students. "With every painting you learn something," was one of his favourite phrases. Dave had been an Army Air Force pilot in World War II and worked in counter-intelligence at the Pentagon after the war. He married his lovely wife Nancy when he was forty and they raised two fine daughters and a son. Besides his painting, Dave owned a frame shop and gallery in Hummelstown for many years. His former student Dick Michaelian now teaches the watercolour class, continuing Dave's tradition.

After Charles Schulz left as AAH Executive Director in 1985, I was hired as Director in 1986, having finished my term as Board President in 1984. As Executive Director, I also managed the School. In 1990, I read an article in *The Patriot News* stating that Harrisburg Mayor Stephen R. Reed envisioned building four artist studios in Reservoir Park. We had just had a strategic planning session with the AAH Board, wherein I was admonished to "double the size of the AAH School"! Thinking, how in the world can that be accomplished when the building at 21 North Front Street has limited space, I immediately made an appointment with the Mayor. I told Mayor Reed of the Board's hope to double the size of our school, and inquired as to whether the artists' studios he envisioned in the Park could be built large enough for AAH to hold classes there. Visionary that he was, Mayor Reed agreed!

The Mayor put me in touch with the architect who was designing the studios—Rick LeBlanc, who went on to become an AAH Board Chair. Rick, of Crabtree Rohrbaugh, asked me what needs the various classes had who would be meeting in the Reservoir Park Studios, and I explained the requirements of a painting studio, a sculpture studio, a multi-purpose studio and a pottery studio. He subsequently created racks for painting storage in one studio, counters and storage units in the others. I wrote grant applications to the Wells Foundation, the Kline Foundation, and CCNB and Fulton Banks and received sufficient monies with which to purchase all the equipment needed to outfit the studios, including a kiln, wheels, slab-roller, sculpture stands, easels, and tables. There was a dicey time just before the equipment was to be delivered from Chaselle Company in Baltimore, when our Board Chair was extremely reluctant to allow me to accept delivery before the final version of our rental contract with the City was signed, but all worked out in the end.

Pottery instructor Micheal Starner and I received the equipment and oversaw the placement of everything in the four studios, and classes commenced in 1991. There were a number of challenges in that the Park is located near a "bad" area of the City, and several women dropped out of classes, stating their "husbands would not allow them to take classes in Reservoir Park." Then there were the problems with the mud! From the beginning, every time it rained hard, mud and water flowed under the studio doors and across the floor. The Parks and Recreation Department insisted that the problem would be solved as the landscaping took hold... but unfortunately, the problem persists through the present time.

Then the painters found that they liked the Front Street studios better, so the potters gradually took over the Painting Studio. By this time Erik Harmon was pottery instructor, and his apprentice potter Jerald Phoenix assisted him in tearing out the painting racks and installing wedging tables. I wrote another grant application and with monies from the Kline Foundation, we acquired more wheels and another kiln. Jerald Phoenix is now our wheel pottery instructor and extremely popular, with his classes filling months before the start of each semester. The studios are well liked, even with the ongoing muddy water problems, but the size has always been a problem. The studios are only large enough for five wheel students per class, which does cramp the style a bit.

For several years, AAH had a School Coordinator in the person of Kimberly Bowie, a talented artist who held an Associate Degree from York Academy of Fine Art. She worked with me to oversee the classes, and worked hard to manage our Art in the Park program for children in the Reservoir studios from 1991 through about 2004, when we discontinued the program due to lack of participation. Kim left the Art Association in 2008 to return to her teaching career. I again took over the management of the School.

Martin Plaut taught the first sculpture classes in the Park studio, with Louis Gatling teaching for a while as well. Then, in 2011, Hildegard Becker, a talented German artist, taught the Clay Sculpture Class for several years before moving back to Europe.

In 2014, AAH instructors include Gabriel Middleton, Fantasy Art; Diane Zinn, Junior Drawing and Painting; Cassie LaPorta, Art for Kids and Art for Mommy & Me; Emmanuelle Wambach, Clay for Kids and Hand-Built Pottery; Guy Freeman, Digital Photography; Michael Reed, Jewelry; Matthew LaVier, Mixed Media; Steve Wetzel, Paul Gallo, Paul Flury, Landscape; Jonathan Frazier, Basic Oil; Dick Michaelian, Watercolour; Chad Caldwell, Acrylics; Seward Ryan, Clay Sculpture; Kim Stone, Pastels and Portraiture; Philip Colgan, Old Master's Painting Techniques; Robert Dale Williams, Intermediate Painting; Maaike Heitkonig, Basic Drawing; Barbara Passeri-Warfel, Figure Drawing; Bradley Gebhart, Caricature; Martin Velez, Fantasy Figure Painting.

The enrollment in the AAH classes is similar to that in that 1976 article, with about 120 to 150 adults and 50 children. With the parking still an issue for the Front Street classes in the daytime, all classes are held evenings and weekends, when the lot next door is available, now owned by developer Ralph Vartan. But even more than enrollment for any given semester is the fact that the AAH School has served thousands upon thousands of students throughout all the decades from the Studio's creation until the current era. The School continues to offer top-quality art instruction by professional artists to all who seek it, with scholarships available to individuals with financial need. (The Will Brown Scholarship Fund ensures that.) The School is the second pillar of the AAH mission: The Art Association of Harrisburg enriches the cultural vitality of the region through art education and exhibitions. The School continues to transcend the challenges of the economy and the vicissitudes of popular culture, a light to students of the visual arts from across the region!

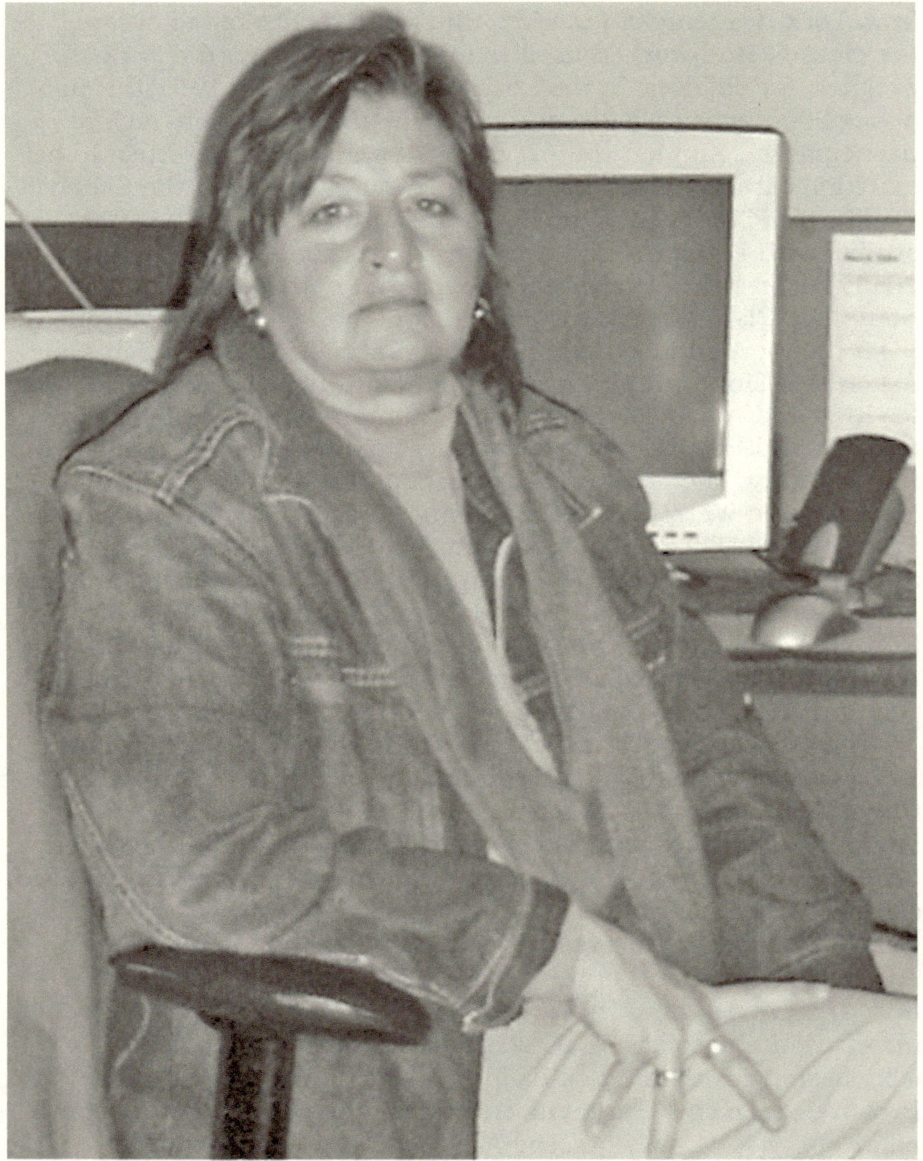

Kim Bowie, School Coordinator

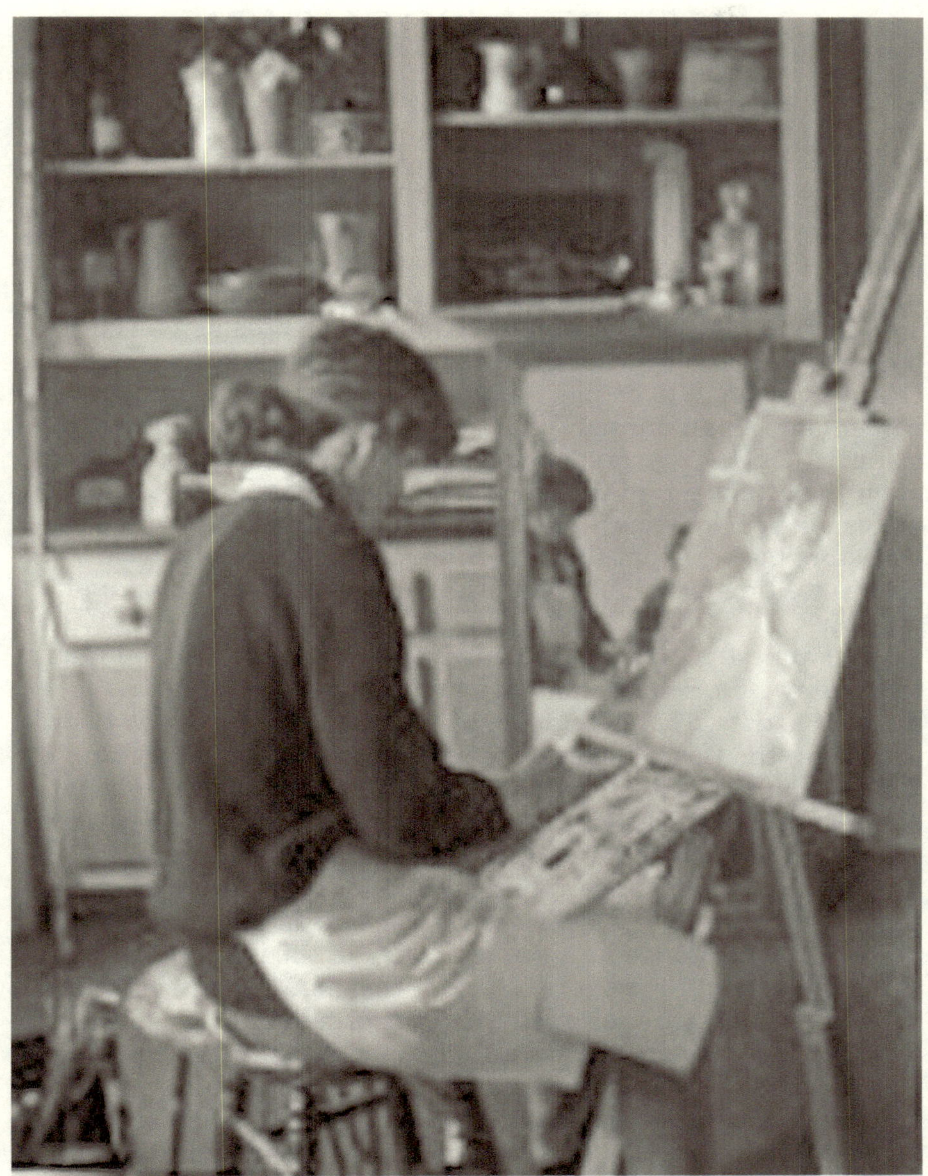

Student in Kim's classroom

THE ART ASSOCIATION SALES GALLERY

Prior to 1984, The Art Association had been presenting an annual art auction, in which members' works were sold to highest bidders. The auction was a bear to organize annually, with handling intake of the artwork, preparing a catalogue, attracting an audience, and then keeping scrupulous records as to who bought what, and at what price. After the event, the artists' commissions had to be paid, with the Association retaining a percentage. As an annual fundraiser, the auction was rather "hit-or-miss." One never could count on the revenues raised, and too often the artists found that their works were sold at abysmally low prices, often barely meeting the set minimum bids. Too often collectors boasted that they never bought art during the year, always waiting for the bargain prices to be found at the annual auction.

The annual art auction definitely had its drawbacks, both as a reliable revenue source, and as a professional way to treat member artists. Therefore, in 1984, during my last year as Board President, the Board determined to create a "Sales Gallery" in which members' works would be offered for sale all year long, at set prices, with the artists treated as the professionals they were. The plan was to offer varied works for sale to individuals and businesses, with no one waiting around for bargain prices at an annual auction. Board members Elsie Swenson, Morrie Schwab, and Dr. David Bronstein were very active in the planning process, with advice from Harrisburg interior designer Mary Knackstedt.

Mary Knackstedt designed the transformation of the former Mrs. Maurice Shaffer Library into the new Sales Gallery, installing custom-made painting bins under a large black formica surface, and having a three-tiered painting storage bin installed in the kitchen. A small white table with two chairs for meeting with art clients, and a new wall-to-wall carpet completed the new look for the space.

After I left as Board President at the end of 1984, the Board hired Shari Brandt as part-time Sales Gallery Manager, working solely on commissions on sales of artwork. Charles Schulz was still Executive Director at this point. I must admit that initially I was very dubious about the whole concept of a "sales gallery," fearing it would be too "commercial" for the nonprofit Art Association. After I became Executive Director/Sales Gallery Manager in April 1986, however, I quickly began to change my opinion dramatically.

I found that selling artwork in a professional manner was a joy, and matching up customers with just the right artwork was a wondrous thing. Even more of a thrill was the selling of a LOT of art to businesses for their new offices! Since I took over in 1986, I have kept scrupulous records of all the sales of art conducted by The Association, with five journals filled with dates, buyers' and artists' names, titles of artwork, sale prices, and sales tax amounts.

Going through these journals is a historical jaunt. The first major sale was in August of 1986, when several executives from PHICO Insurance of Mechanicsburg stopped in to select sculptures for their handsome new building. At the time, sculptures by Janet Veiner of Philadelphia were on view, and they selected four pieces to purchase, at the total price of $11,700. The four sculptures were titled "Sakura," "Hero," "Troubador," and "Cat's Cradle," all of handsome exotic wood in sensuous, organic shapes. The PHICO management team were pleased with the transaction, and in December they asked if I would serve as their artistic advisor, providing art for their entire building. I agreed most readily, and PHICO purchased eight photo-realistic paintings by Barbara Buer, four David Lenker prints, two watercolours by Barbara Piscioneri, an oil by Kathleen Piunti, and an Erna Tunno watercolour, totaling $8190.

In January 1987, I sold $1855 worth of art to Central PA AAA for their offices, and all the while, we were selling art to individuals steadily as well. In February 1989, we sold six oil landscapes by Carol Herr to Hershey Creamery, as well as 13 prints and two watercolours by David Lenker. In April 1989, we sold five Don Lenker watercolours, and two paintings by Wanda Macomber to Pennsylvania Blue Shield for $4670. We also made substantial sales during that time to Susquehanna Centre and the Jewish Home for their nursing facilities.

Gross sales for 1989/90 were $51,497, and for 1991/92, gross sales were $42,135. The artists received 2/3 of all sales, with AAH retaining a donated commission of 1/3. The Sales Gallery was definitely proving to be a dependable funding stream for the organization.

In the spring of 1990, Dauphin Deposit Bank was constructing a new building on Market Square, and Walt Lowery contacted me about artwork from The Art Association. I enjoyed taking a tour of the building under construction with Walt, wearing a hard-hat... One of my happiest times is touring construction sites, visualizing where art will be placed. The bank bought several architectural abstract paintings by Wanda Macomber, and commissioned two large wood sculptures by Janet Veiner to flank the entrance to the investment banking area.

Then came the biggest job of all. I read in the *Patriot News* that Mayor Reed was planning, with Harristown Development, to have a major hotel built on Market Square. I made an appointment with the Mayor, and strongly suggested that the new hotel, the "jewel in the crown" of the city, should be decorated by original art by local artists. The Mayor agreed, and put me in touch with the interior designers for the project. The decorator sent me swatches of fabrics and designs for each public area of the planned hotel, and asked me to pull together samples of artwork for each area.

I subsequently asked about 20 of our top artists to bring in artwork to show the decorator, and I spent a day showing the samples to her team. She eventually selected eight artists to create forty works of art for the various spaces of the new Hilton Harrisburg. Artists selected were:

(1) Barbara Buer—photo-realistic acrylic still-lifes for the Golden Sheaf formal restaurant.

(2) Erna Tunno—seven watercolour scenes of the Susquehanna River and Harrisburg Skyline for The Lobby Bar.

(3) Kathryn Pittinos—two watercolour landscapes for the entrance lobby.

(4) Carol Herr—two oil Impressionist landscapes for the area behind the registration desk, and four more landscapes for two second-floor conference rooms.

(5) Charles Hickok—two abstracts based on the Susquehanna River for the second-floor pre-function area.

(6) Linda LeFevre—two abstract paintings for the third-floor pre-function area.

(7) Fred Haag—six colourful studio interior scenes in oil for The Market Square Café.

(8) Rose Boegli—the 60' mural on the mezzanine-level wall above the main lobby, an "enhanced-realism" Harrisburg Skyline.

The total cost for the artwork came to just under $60,000, with the Hilton also purchasing David Lenker "Star Barn" prints for all the guest rooms. The Harristown and Hilton representatives were wonderful clients to work with. I'd prepared contracts for each artist, with the artist, a Harristown rep, and me signing each one. Harristown paid in three installments, with the first when the artists commenced their work, the second halfway through, and the final payment in October when the artwork was delivered to the framer. The hotel also paid for the creation of brass plaques to be mounted under each painting, stating the title, artist, and the Art Association name. When the hotel opened its doors, it was a very proud moment indeed.

Probably the most fascinating element of the Hilton project was Rose Boegli's painting of the huge mural over the lobby. She had to work from a scaffold placed across the abyss, with another movable scaffold on top of that she that she could reach to top of the wall. She first painted the entire wall a deep maroon, and then transferred her design from her drawing onto the wall with white chalk. She then began painting the top of the sky, working her way down, painting the Front Street skyline, and then the River last. (As a grace-note, she painted her own tiny face in one of the building's windows at the left of the skyline!)

Rose parked in the AAH lot each day when she was working on the mural, habitually wearing her scruffy painting clothes and hauling her buckets with brushes and paints across Market Square. She laughingly tells the story about the well-dressed businessman who offered her money one morning, assuming she was a homeless person! She also still tells the tale of the construction chaps working on the hotel as she was painting, who came over to watch her and offer "helpful suggestions" on her perspective from time to time. She finally began to get off her scaffold and go over to where they were building walls, commenting on their drywall seams, and they ceased their comments! Rose put together a slide show of the entire project, which she presented at the AAH Annual Meeting the next spring.

AAH sold a great many pieces of artwork to the downtown banks during the early 1990's, many of which are no longer in existence due to corporate mergers and name changes. We sold art to First Federal, Hamilton Bank, and Pennsylvania National Bank, as well as to Dauphin Deposit as previously noted. We sold art to Polyclinic Hospital, and attempted to sell original artwork to the new Harrisburg Hotel in 1995, but their decorator selected prints instead, which totaled only $1365.

An interesting challenge presented itself in 1992 when Nationwide Insurance, off Progress Avenue just outside Harrisburg, contacted me to ask if I could procure art for their offices from each of the cities where they had a presence in Pennsylvania. This included Harrisburg, Lancaster, Philadelphia,

Erie, Butler and Pittsburgh. Since this was before the Internet, I had to make phone calls to Chambers of Commerce in Butler, Pittsburg and Erie, to discover artists who could potentially provide the artwork representative of their cities. I was able to identify artists in Erie, Pittsburgh and Butler who then sent me photographs to show the client, and of course I already had artists in Harrisburg and Lancaster. I sent Erna Tunno to Philadelphia to paint watercolours of Boat-House Row, which worked beautifully. All in all, the project worked out very well, with the appropriate artwork shipped in and framed, and then installed in the conference rooms named for each city.

In 1994, The Greater Harrisburg Foundation purchased several prints and watercolours from AAH, totaling $1045, for their conference room. In December of 1994, Fulton Bank bought prints by David Lenker and Linda Luke, totaling $940. In July, 1996, thanks to Dr. David Bronstein, we sold thirty prints to Community General Hospital, totaling $3260.

My modus operandi had always been to arrange to take a large portfolio filled with shrink-wrapped prints to a client after I was contacted about an art need. In August 1996, my visit to PNC Bank in New Cumberland resulted in their purchase on the spot of ten prints by Joann Hensel, Barbara Buer and David Lenker, totaling $1075. I drove back from that appointment very well satisfied.

In October of 1996, I sold 25 prints to the PNC main offices totaling $3715. These included works by William Falkler, Erna Tunno, Carol Herr, Joann Hensel, Charles Krone, and David Lenker. It has always amazed me that the most architecturally contemporary office buildings are always furnished with "traditional" artwork, almost always scenes of the area.

Then in early 1997, S. Geoffrey McDowell contacted me from Penn National Insurance concerning their building under construction on Market Square. He asked me to come to their old office building on Derry Street to view their "corporate collection" of artwork, inviting suggestions on what to do with it. As the pieces in the old PNI collection were largely faded, outdated prints, I suggested that they be offered to sale to the employees, which was what happened. Geoff subsequently took me on a tour of the new building under construction, wearing hard hats again, and we discussed original art for the top-floor executive offices, and prints for the "elevator core" areas on each floor.

Six original paintings were selected for the executive offices, including landscapes by Carol Herr, Earl Blust, Kirby Heltebridle and Mimi Conrey. Twenty-five prints were selected for the elevator areas on the other floors. As was my wont in those days, I took everything to Framer's Workshop in New Cumberland to be framed, and then the framer and I installed all the artwork in a day. I remember how confusing it was, taking the elevator from floor to floor because each area looked so similar. That entire purchase came to $7330, which was splendid.

What was even better was the fact that PNI had arranged to have tracks installed in the handsome lobby in order for AAH to mount ongoing Community Exhibitions. AAH had been installing exhibitions in various businesses in the area from the days before the main organization and the Studio had merged, but in 1986, a formal AAH Community Exhibition Program was formulated. John Guarnera, then AAH Exhibition Chairman, had created a program whereby businesses paid an exhibition fee of $75 per month, and these monies would be utilized in the purchase of art from the rotating shows held in their facilities. Official agreements were signed by AAH and the businesses stipulating all the formalities of this arrangement.

This system continued until 2004, when it was supplanted with a simple exhibition fee of $75 per month paid by the Community site, with no purchase of artwork included. This made the AAH accounting system much more acceptable to the auditors.

The Community Exhibition program has included a wide variety of office and institutions from 1986 through 2012, with Highmark/Blue Shield the first site to enroll in the program. Highmark has always been a plum location for our artists, with a spacious area between Buildings 1 and 2, now with picture rail and excellent lighting. Other former Community Sites were Shumaker Williams, The Jewish Home, Susquehanna Centre, The Central PA Blood Bank (certainly one of our more unusual sites), Penn State Downtown Centre, Penn State Harrisburg in Middletown, Temple Harrisburg, The Pennsylvania Chamber of Commerce, Hilton Harrisburg, Reservoir Mansion, The DID Visitors Centre, and Hershey Medical Centre's Simulation Centre.

Dauphin County Courthouse's Register of Wills/Recorder of Deeds Offices were on board early on, and continue through the current time. (The County always provided parking for AAH students in their former parking lot, so AAH shows have always been on a "trade" basis, ditto with Reservoir Mansion and the City.) Besides Highmark, the other Community Sites in 2014 include Martin M. Sacks & Associates, Homeland Centre, Harrisburg Magazine, Penn National Insurance, Capital Medical Centre, Schein Ernst Eye Associates, Varano Spong Financial

Group, Questmont, Belco Credit Union, Penn State Harrisburg, Widener Law School, and the Atrium of Harrisburg City Government Centre. Once a year, AAH presents an exhibition in Whitaker Centre for Science and Arts. The other exhibitions are two or three months in duration, and consist of solo shows by member artists.

In recent years, there have been fewer big sales to businesses, due to the economy and to the fact fewer large office buildings have been constructed in Harrisburg. However, sales to individual collectors have remained steady and businesspeople continue to purchase artwork for their offices, and often as gifts to retiring colleagues as mementoes of their stay in Harrisburg. The Sales Gallery usually grosses approximately $50,000 annually, with a revenue stream to the Association of about $16,666. Not bad at all.

Even more than the revenue the Sales Gallery provides, however, is the goodwill it establishes with artists. Through the Sales Gallery, artists are treated with respect and professionalism. They aren't subjected to the humiliation of having their work put on the auction block and knocked off all too cheaply to the highest bidder. AAH artists know that the staff represent their work well to the public, and they know that our selling their art is one of the many services AAH provides to our members.

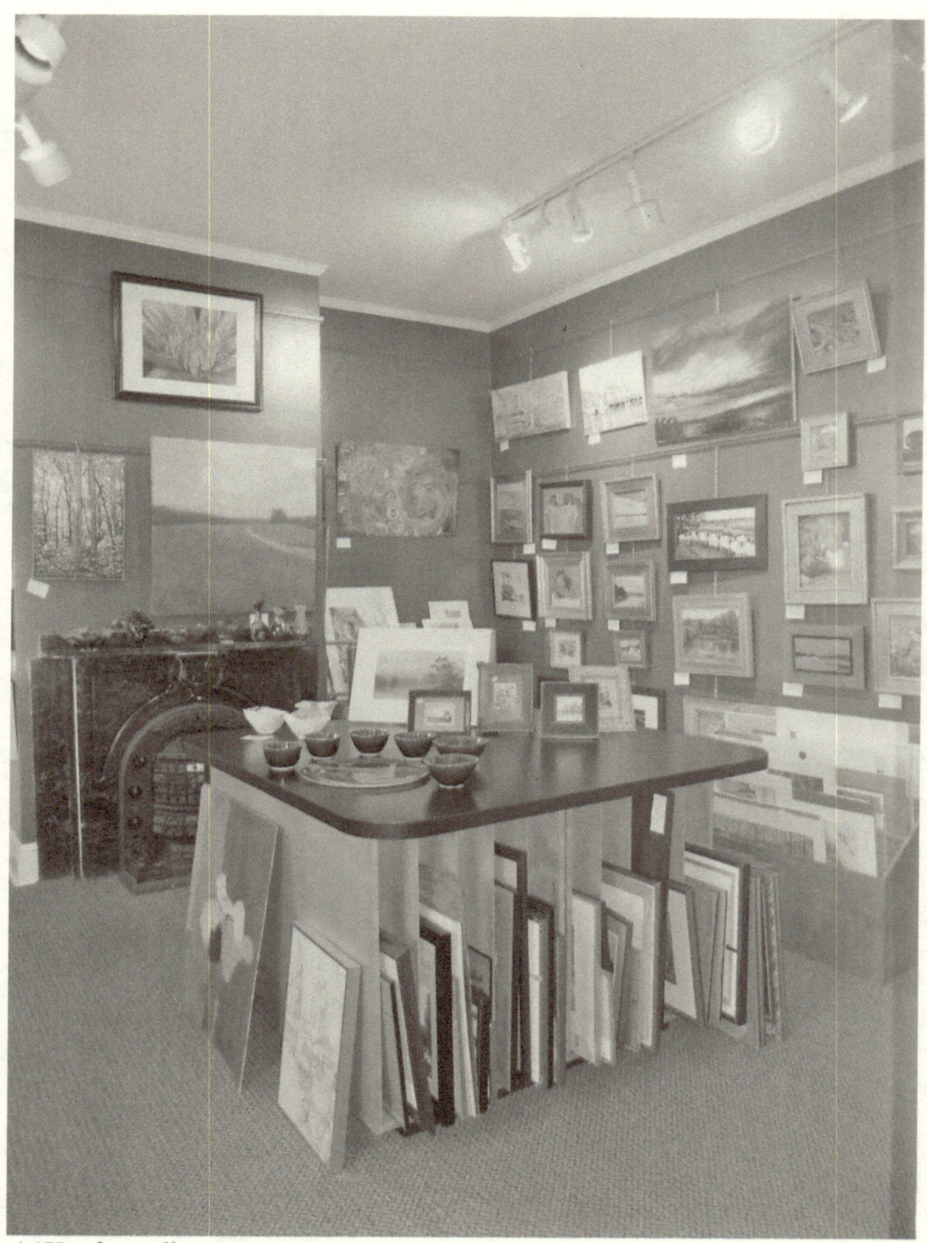

AAH sales gallery

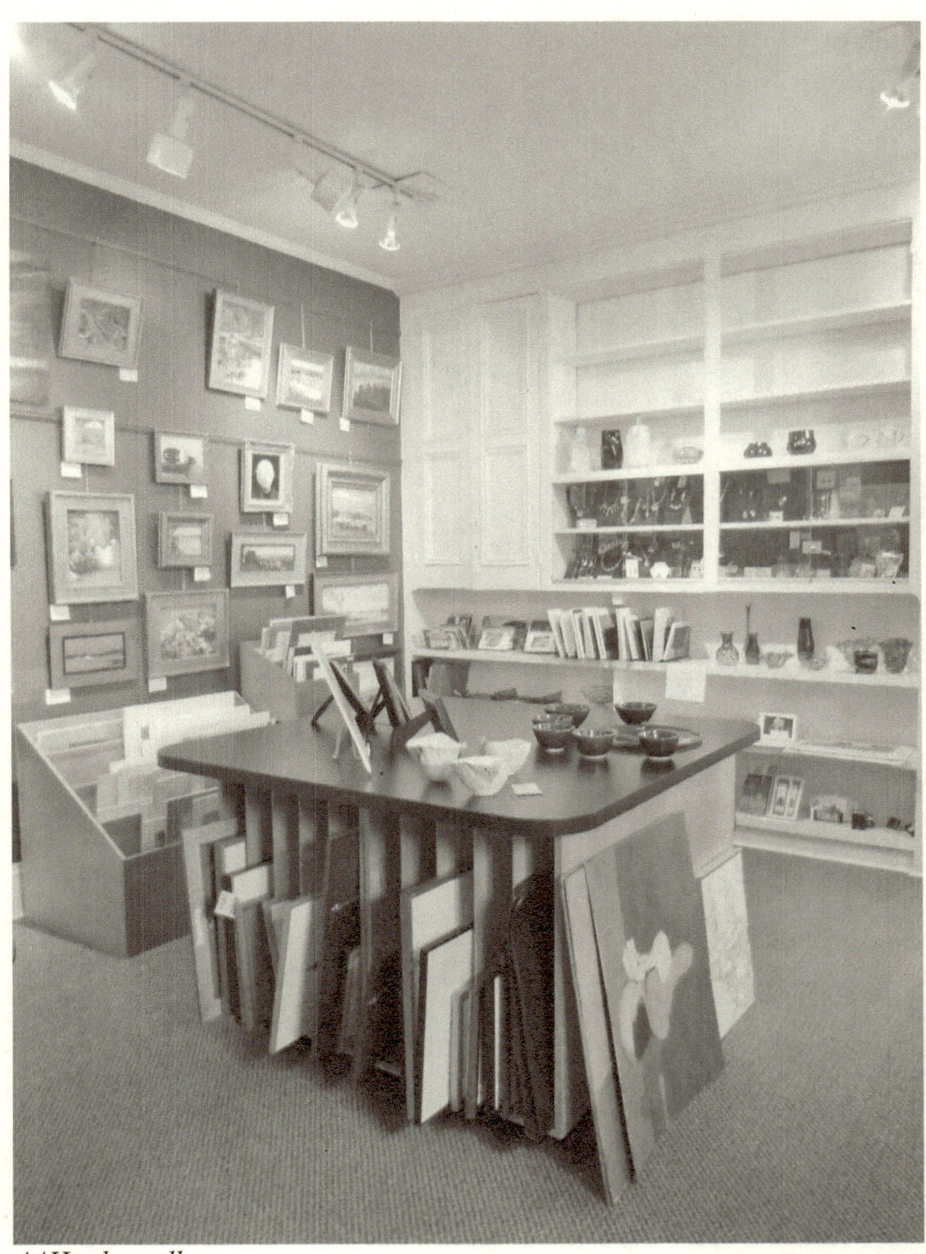

AAH sales gallery

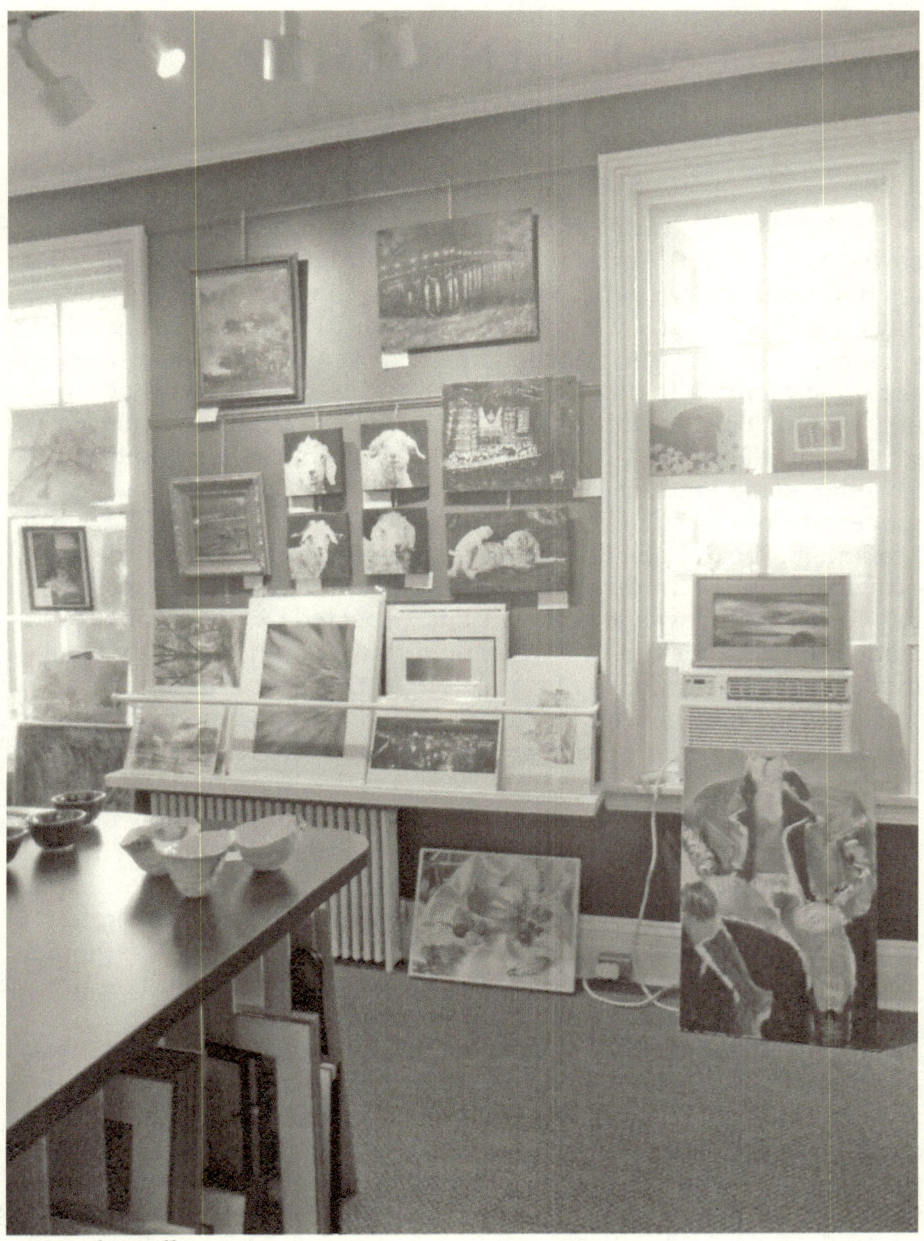

AAH sales gallery

AAH Censorship by Gene Suchma

In 1974 I was living off my freelance art, predominantly cartooning for the *Harrisburg Independent Press*, or HIP. HIP was a small weekly newspaper started during the Harrisburg 8 trial days. I had a few other temporary jobs, but I was also living off my savings. I joined the Art Association that year to take advantage of the opportunities to display my work and to interact with other artists. I saw a want ad in *The Patriot News*. The Art Association was looking for a life-drawing model. I'd never modeled before, but I needed some extra cash. So I decided to try. I met with the moderator of the Life Group, local illustrator Karl Foster. Karl and I talked about the position and the rate of pay. I liked the idea of drawing from the nude but I couldn't afford the tuition and the pay for modeling was less than I had expected. So asked if I could trade modeling for tuition. We agreed that I could be a substitute model in exchange for my attendance in the group. In other words, if the planned model didn't show (as happened fairly often) I would fill in. There were also times when I would be the planned model.

That year I decided to enter a juried membership show at the Association. At the time I was painting friends and people I'd meet in their ordinary settings. I'd take a Polaroid photo and work up a painting. Often I'd give the subject of the piece a working sketch in payment. I've always been interested in realism that was honest and not a glamorization of the subject. I thought I could use the same approach with myself: Paint a frank self-portrait in a mundane situation. So I decided to portray myself, nude, as a way to reveal the real me. It never occurred to me that this would be controversial since I was already being sketched and painted by the life group—from all angles without a stitch of clothing. (Karl had told me I was the first male model at the Association to pose without wearing an athletic supporter.) I asked a close friend to take some Polaroids of me standing nude in the doorway to my kitchen. I chose one from which to paint that was cropped just above my knees. There was nothing sexual about the pose. It was just a slice of life. I finished the piece and took it to the Art Association and thought nothing more about it.

The next time I went to Life Drawing, I found that my piece had been rejected. Karl told me that that wasn't exactly the whole story. At the time Karl was the exhibit chairman on the AAH board and, for the juried show, had arranged for three outside artists to judge the entrants: William Smith, a renowned illustrator; a female artist from the Easton-Scranton area; and a watercolorist from Philadelphia. Although the nude self-portrait wasn't picked to win a prize, in Karl's presence, by a 2-to-1 vote they chose it for the show.

After the jurying, Karl went to an Art Association Board meeting and learned that the painting had been removed from the gallery and placed in the office. At the meeting, the painting was discussed.

According to the *Independent*, who covered the affair, several years previously a painting of a prostitute won a first prize in an Association juried show. Appalled by the selection, the Board of Directors inserted in the exhibit rules that the Board would have the final say about what was suitable for gallery display. That rule was not implemented until the 1974 show. Chair of the Board, Mary Sheffer, and most of the twenty other voting members, thought the painting was inappropriate for public display. Board member Nick Ruggieri didn't think the painting was good enough. Karl Foster objected to the Board's decision because he felt that the artwork in the show had been selected by an unbiased group of outside jurors. His view didn't sway the Board, and the decision stood. Karl subsequently resigned his position on the Board, although he stayed as an active member and continued to monitor the Life Drawing group for many years.

In the *Harrisburg Independent Press*, in its May 10-17, 1974, issue, Karl Foster commented, "I would say the entire thing was blown out of proportion. I think probably if the painting had been hung there would be very little controversy." Another of the dissenters, Maya Schock, the founder and proprietor of the Doshi Center for Contemporary Art since 1972, withdrew her membership from the Art Association entirely. Shock told the Press, "I stayed in the Harrisburg Art Association in the hope that I could change some things. So after twelve years I gave up."

Later in '74 I was living on Second Street, across from the Doshi. I went to her gallery and thanked Maya for supporting me.

She said, " I did it for the principle of the thing. I didn't think it was a very good painting."

NOTABLES OF THE AAH

Nick Ruggieri, Watercolourist Extraordinaire

Nick Ruggieri did not found the Art Association of Harrisburg. That misconception has been floating around for decades, but is not true. Nick was not on the committee of community leaders formed by Mrs. Gertrude Howard Olmsted in 1924 that went on to found the Art Association in 1926. Rather, Nick was one of the five artists who established "The Independent Artists Studio" on the second floor above Johnny Kobler's Saloon at Walnut and Court Streets ("Personal Recollections of The Art Association of Harrisburg" by Edward C. Michener). Nick, along with Alden Turner, Walt Huber, Tom Keil and Earl Johnston, created their Studio in resentment that the AAH founders and trustees were all "society" types and not artists, according to Ed Michener.

Nick Ruggieri and Alden Turner worked in the Art Department of the Telegraph Press at this time. He went on to teach for the Art Association Studio when it was located at 500 Race Street, however, and became intrinsically involved in the school aspect of The Art Association. Then in 1953, with Ed Michener's efforts in merging the Studio with the parent AAH organization, Nick Ruggieri was elected President of the Board of the combined groups. The reorganization of The Art Association was announced in a *Patriot* article, along with the news of the group's move to 414 Spring Street by April 1. "Merger of the Association and the Art Studio, which formerly operated under two official bodies, into one Association was made to extend the culture of the Community through rewritten by-laws." This article accurately went on to state, "The Art Association of Harrisburg was chartered in 1926 by a civic minded group including the late Mr. and Mrs. Vance C. McCormick, Mrs. Lyman D. Gilbert, C. Valentine Kirby and J. Horace McFarland. The founders foresaw the need to 'add art to the cultural influences of the community' by encouraging talent, providing instruction and presenting exhibits with the ultimate hope of acquiring permanent art headquarters."

This 1953 article went on to say, "in 1936-37 the association sponsored an art studio to provide instruction for Harrisburg citizens in all walks of life who were interested in art, as well as a workshop for artists." Nick Ruggieri was an integral part of this studio, but he was NOT a founder of The Art Association of Harrisburg itself.

Nonetheless, the myth persisted, and in an *Evening News* article on March 3, 1969, AAH President Mrs. Chester M. Sheffer was noted to have announced the re-naming of The Founders Room after Ruggieri—"the last of the founders to be living." The front second-floor gallery was named "The Nick Ruggieri Gallery." The honour was well deserved, although the rationale was erroneous.

Nick had been chosen a fellow of The Royal Society for the Arts in London in 1963, which honour columnist Paul Beers had acknowledged with a lengthy article. Beers explained that membership in the Royal Society comes only after a "long career in the arts that can be documented with works and testimonials." He noted that Ruggieri's career had been carefully investigated before the invitation to join the exclusive group was extended. Paul Beers quoted Ruggieri as saying of his art, "I've never thought of doing anything else." Ruggieri had enrolled in art classes at Camp Curtin Junior High, and went on to study at the Art Students' League in New York City, later continuing his studies in Europe. Beers said that Ruggieri was "on the first refugee ship out of France when the war broke out." Apparently he was very active in the Harrisburg Camera Club as well as with The Art Association, and served as President of both organizations. Some of his photography was even shown in the Royal Photographic Society's exhibits in Europe.

Nick Ruggieri was quoted as saying, "Painting is always an experiment. A painting can have all the abstract forces at work within it, all the precious qualities of pigment and surface, all the personal calligraphic lines of strength—and at the same time tell a story or make a statement." His own artistic taste ran the gamut from the old masters to the modern Expressionists, Paul Beers wrote, but he apparently did not appreciate "mere splattering of paint on a canvas."

When Paul Beers wrote this column, The Art Association still hadn't procured the 21 North Front Street building. In the *Evening News* article in 1969, of course, the building had been acquired, and the Founders Gallery was renamed in Ruggieri's honour. In the same article, Ruggieri, the *Patriot's* Art Director for more than 28 years, was also honoured with a very popular exhibition of his paintings. It was said that out of 51 paintings in the show, 45 were sold! He was praised for his "unselfish and dedicated efforts in causes ranging from the West Shore YMCA to the Pennsylvania National Horse Show." Donald von Volffradt, president of the Harrisburg Camera Club, presented Ruggieri with a plaque in recognition of "his outstanding contributions to the art and for being a founder of the organization." Representing Ruggieri's watercolour class at AAH, David L. Musselman presented him with a silver refreshment cooling set.

The article went on to say, "A high point in Saturday's awards came when John H.Baum, publisher of *The Patriot*, gave Ruggieri a framed full-page reproduction of the Monday, Feb. 17, 1941, edition front page, the day the artist started his 28-year *Patriot News* career."

In 1971, Ruggieri began his gigantic project of painting all the 67 Pennsylvania counties in anticipation of the upcoming national Bi-Centennial celebration. Ruggieri's boss at the *Patriot News* liked the concept, and gave his blessing for the artist to conduct the project. He is said to have drawn nearly 200 preliminary sketches and painted 125 watercolours. From these, he chose 80 to actually exhibit. According to an article by Maureen Acquino about the project published in "In Central Pennsylvania," *The Patriot News magazine* in May/June 2010, Ruggieri's only setback during the project was caused by Tropical Storm Agnes and the great Harrisburg Flood of 1972. The flood destroyed much of the completed work that was being stored in the Market Street basement of the newspaper, and he had to start many of the paintings again.

After completion of the series, entitled "Spirit of '76," in 1975 the paintings were exhibited at the future State Museum of Pennsylvania on North Street, Harrisburg. According to the newspaper's coverage, over 6000 people viewed the exhibition, and on September 21, 1975, Governor Shapp declared the day "Nick Ruggieri Day" in Pennsylvania. A travelling exhibition followed, with the paintings touring the state in a specially designed tractor-trailer for sixteen months. According to the "In Central PA" article, tour guides from *The Patriot News* even rode along to serve as hostesses whenever the trailer made its stops at shopping malls, high schools and colleges.

After the tour, the paintings were displayed in *The Patriot News* building at 812 Market Street in Harrisburg until 2010, when the newspaper moved across the River to Hampden Township and the paintings went into storage until in 2011 they were presented to The State Museum of Pennsylvania to form part of their permanent collection.

In 1996, one month after he was feted by the Christopher Columbus 1492 Society, Nick Ruggier died. His influence on several generations of artists was immeasurable, and his artwork is still on view in many area homes and offices.

Charles "Li" Hidley, Expressionist

Charles Billings Hidley was born on March 13, 1921, in Troy, New York, to Charles Billings Hidley and his wife Myrtle. His father lay dying in the next room as Hidley was being born, he always said. He and his widowed mother lived with well-to-do relatives in Troy until the family lost their wealth in the 1929 stock-market crash. He often related stories from his childhood, especially one concerning his and his mother's attending the races at Saratoga, where he consumed too much "sarsaparilla" and became nauseated on the way home in the fancy roadster driven by his flapper cousin Peggy. The traffic was very heavy, and they couldn't stop the car... so his mother told him to "throw up" into his beret, which he proceeded to do... whereupon his mother shouted, "Step on it!" to his cousin as she flung the offending beret out of the roadster, directly onto the windshield of the car behind them! That story was always a favourite one... Hidley was a great storyteller, with a very cultivated accent, and he pronounced beret beautifully!

Hidley's friend Barry Cohen's eulogy stated that his favourite aunt Nini "was a self-styled clairvoyant who impressed in Li a lifelong fascination for the mysteries of the mind and the supernatural; his cousin Peggy was a 'flapper' whose joie de vivre and sense of independence undoubtedly made a big impression on Li as a child." Barry Cohen's eulogy of Hidley went on to state that he "started his life in painting after taking some classes run by two maiden lady friends of his."

After the stock market crash, Hidley and his mother moved to New York City, where she worked "in the hotel trade," and he began to call himself "Li." He told me once that "Li" seemed a timeless name for him, one he'd had during all his existence... he was truly "an old soul." Hidley's childhood in New York was lonely, with his mother working long hours, and he became intrigued by science fiction. He eventually began to submit his stories to a science fiction organization, composed of adult writers. After his work was published, Hidley attended a meeting and revealed his true age. He said that the adult writers were all amazed at the teenager's talent. (Later, when he lived in Harrisburg, friends jokingly called Hidley "The Father of Science Fiction.")

During World War II, Li served as a Staff Sergeant in the US Army stationed in Panama, from 1942 through 1945. Upon his return to civilian life, Hidley began attending classes at The Art Students League in New York on the GI Bill, as did many ex-GI's at that point. At the League, the young artist studied with John Ferren, Byron Brown, and Theodoros Stamos. Robert Rauschenberg was also Hidley's fellow student. Hidley was influenced tremendously in his figurative work by Brown, his colour by Ferren, and his abstraction by Stamos. He said that in Stamos' absence, he even served as the class monitor.

Taking further advantage of the GI Bill, Hidley travelled to Mexico where he said that he "lived like a prince on $25 a month"! There, he attended Escuela de Pintura y Escultura de Esmerelda in Mexico City. Friends said that he returned to New York two years later wearing combat boots, fatigues, and sporting a bushy red beard! He told me that his mother detested the beard, so one morning he shaved it off, and put the clippings into a juice glass on her breakfast table...

After his return to New York, Hidley enrolled in classes at the Brooklyn Museum of Art, studying with Rufino Tamayo and Xavier Gonzalez. Tamayo, both a figurative and abstract painter known for his luscious colours, was an inspiration for Hidley's own work. He also attended Charles Seide's class on materials and techniques, where he learned to grind pigments, make brushes, and gesso canvases in the classic way.

During this period of his life, Hidley and his friends spent every weekend visiting all the galleries on 57th Street, as well as attending all the shows and ballets that he could. He absorbed the New York cultural scene of the 1950's and early '60's to the fullest. Sometime during this period, Hidley worked at the Barone Gallery on Madison Avenue, owned by Jill Kornblee, a friend of Leo Cassili. He also worked in the library at Cooper Union, and even as a security guard at the Metropolitan Museum of Art.

In 1966, Hidley moved to Harrisburg with his mother, buying a house in Mt. Pleasant/Allison Hill, then a quiet residential part of the city. Speculation has always been made concerning why Hidley moved to Harrisburg from New York City... Some people feel he moved here because he didn't have a "big break" in the New York art scene, others think he chose Harrisburg because his friend Lawrence Von Barann had moved here, and others believe it was because his older half-sister lived in the Dillsburg area. At any rate, the Harrisburg area's art scene benefitted from his decision... Hidley's bold Expressionism was a far cry from the competent, but quiet, watercolours that predominated here at that time. The William Penn Museum (now the State Museum of

Pennsylvania) recognized his unique talents and granted him a solo exhibition in 1971.

Then in 1979, Executive Director Charles Schulz invited Hidley to teach Expressionist Painting classes for The Art Association of Harrisburg, and immediately a core group of students materialized, eager to study with him. Known to many of the Realists as "Hidley's People," this group of daring Expressionists began exhibiting together and entering regional shows. These Expressionists, including Hidley himself, began capturing top awards in area juried exhibitions. Some of the Realists became quite exercised, and complained in high dudgeon that "Hidley's People" were taking over The Art Association.

During my tenure as President of the AAH Board, 1980-84, Hidley was elected to the Board and served as Exhibitions Chairman. Under his influence, painters of all styles and individual modes of expression began to feel comfortable showing their work in the Association's galleries. Not able to subsist on income from his teaching and his own art, Hidley around this time joined the Federally-funded Senior Employment Program. He first was assigned work at the Historical Society of Dauphin County, and then came to The Art Association as one of our receptionists. We eventually took him on as a part-time AAH employee. Hidley was NOT a good receptionist. He was easily annoyed by phone callers and NOT gracious to artists entering membership shows whose work he found less than creative. He did like "naïve," and "outsider art," finding work by untaught artists fresh and appealing. But he detested pretentious artists with long credentials and little talent. When I became Executive Director myself in 1986, I often found myself defending Hidley to Board members. Finding his lack of "receptionist's skills" unfortunate myself, I nonetheless continued to keep him on the staff because he needed the paycheck. I changed his title to "Curator" and gave him an office on the fourth floor so that he no longer fielded calls at the front desk.

Eventually, Hidley's health became too precarious to continue working steadily. I attempted to schedule weekly critique sessions for him to conduct, but the fear of his all-too-often acerbic comments to artists made these unfeasible.

At this time, Hidley was living in a small townhouse on Prince Alley in Midtown Harrisburg. He had moved out of the house in Allison Hill in the 1980's because the area had fallen into a bad state. Elderly residents moved out and absentee landlords broke up single-family homes into low-rent apartments. After his house had been broken-into several times, Hidley moved into an apartment with a glorious view in the high-rise City Towers. His good friends Brian Rogers and his father Paul were invaluable in the move.

Unfortunately, Hidley was forced to leave City Towers when in 1996, a horrific ice storm caused a power outage there, and an evacuation. Brian Rogers drove downtown and rescued Hidley that night, taking him to stay for several months with him and his wife in their apartment on North Second Street. Brian and I helped Hidley to locate his house on Prince Alley, and helped him move in. When Hidley had first moved to Harrisburg in the late 1960's, he had owned several small antique shops, so his house was filled with not only his own art and that of artists he liked, but also with all types of antiques.

In the last few years of Hidley's life, the Art Association staff and Brian and Kirsten Rogers were his family. We all helped him with groceries, doctor appointments and errands. When it finally became impossible for him to live alone, Brian found a fine nursing facility for him—his last several months were spent in Outlook Pointe outside Harrisburg. One day while I was visiting him there, Hidley said, "I can't afford to leave a monetary legacy to The Art Association, but if I give the Association all my paintings, every time one is sold, it's a legacy from me. Would you accept them?" Overjoyed, I replied, "Of course!" So Brian Rogers undertook the gargantuan task of retrieving all Hidley's paintings from his house basement, and we paid Rick Walker of Walker's Art & Framing to transport the paintings here to the Art Association's fourth floor. Since there were over 300 canvases and panels to be carried up three flights of stairs, this was no mean feat.

Hidley died at Outlook Pointe on June 8, 2003. His memorial service was held here in the main gallery of the Association, with a huge crowd of former students, fellow artists, and friends from all across the country. Speakers at the service were long-time friend and protegee' Barry Cohen, friend from the earliest days in New York Lawrence Von Barann, close and dear friend Barbara Sherman of California, Brian Rogers and me. Hidley's favourite musical selection was "Meditation from Tais," which was performed by young Jambol Leuenberger of The Wednesday Club. Guitar music was performed by Dante Sobrevilla-Gervaci. An exhibition of portraits of Hidley by his friends and students was on view on easels in the gallery, including paintings by Maggie Harris, Pamela Lackey, Joseph Dudding, Charley Ann Rhoads, Terrie Hosey, Brian Rogers, Delores Kiely, Ruth Garonzik, John

Guarnera, Re' DeSabres, Judith Spaeth, Michael O. Roberts, and me.

In the eulogy I gave at Hidley's memorial service, I opened with, "The moral life of man forms part of the subject-matter of the artist, but the morality of art consists in the perfect use of an imperfect medium. No artist desires to prove anything. Even things that are true can be proved. No artist has ethical sympathies. An ethical sympathy in an artist is an unpardonable mannerism of style. No artist is ever morbid. The artist can express everything. Thought and language are to the artist instruments of an art. Vice and virtue are to the artist materials for an art. From the point of view of feeling, the actor's craft is the type. All art is at once surface and symbol. Those who go beneath the surface do so at their peril. Those who read the symbol do so at their peril. It is the spectator, and not life, that art really mirrors. Diversity of opinion about a work of art shows that the work is new, complex, and vital. When critics disagree the artist is in accord with himself. We can forgive a man for making a useful thing as long as he does not admire it. The only excuse for making a useless thing is that one admires it immensely. All art is quite useless." Although that sounds like something Hidley himself would have said, au contraire, it was pronounced by Oscar Wilde in his preface to "The Picture of Dorian Gray."

I always found Hidley to have been a Wildean figure, larger than life and full of opinions and assertions on art and aesthetics. Like Wilde, he created because he was who he was, and never to please anyone but himself. "When critics disagree the artist is in accord with himself," indeed. Hidley, more than anyone else I have ever known, lived and breathed his art. Fortunately, he always seemed to have friends who helped him with life's practical side.

The other eulogies given at Hidley's service were meaningful and heartfelt. Barry Cohen's wife read his eulogy, as he was too emotional to do so. Barry wrote, "although Li was fond of saying that he liked 'things' more than he liked people, he amassed so many of us. Li saw the creative potential in people and made himself available to help them develop their skills, regardless of age, level of education, or life circumstances. But it helped if they wanted to be artists." Barry also wrote, "On the evening of Sunday, June 8, a week before Father's Day was celebrated, the Harrisburg art community lost its Spirit Father. Li Hidley's death was neither sudden nor unexpected, but for the Hidley clan—mostly creative artists, rebellious spirits, and other social outcasts who started or settled in Central Pennsylvania during the past four decades—the loss was stunning, just the same, and we are here today to celebrate his life and unique personhood."

The next Sunday morning, Brian and Kirsten Rogers, Charles Schulz, Gene and Terrie Hosey, and my husband Scott Thomas and I interred Hidley's ashes in an urn in the AAH McCormick Garden. Also in the grave we placed an urn with his mother's ashes, which Brian had discovered stored in the house on Prince Alley. Each of us placed a meaningful token in the grave—a paintbrush, a rose—and Gene Hosey read a poem he'd written. Several months later, we installed a granite plaque on his grave, stating, "Charles 'Li' Hidley" and "Myrtle, Mother of Li."

After Hidley's death, the Art Association presented a large exhibition of many of the paintings he had given us, and the dollars raised through sales were truly a legacy from Li. Since 2003, The Art Association has received well over $30,000 from sales of Hidley's paintings, an on-going legacy indeed.

Hidley's art was influenced by many things in his evolution as an artist. Besides the effects of studying with the lions of The Art Students League, and his two years in Mexico, Hidley's work was enormously influenced by the writings of Carl Jung. Jung's philosophy fused psychology with mysticism, expanding the interpretation of dreams, which always fascinated Hidley. He often spoke about dreams in relationship with his studies of Jungian analysis, and his paintings usually incorporated universal archetypal themes, threads running through all humanity. Mythology also formed a large part of the psyche of his paintings, not to mention providing his esoteric and arcane titles.

Basing the bulk of his work on the human figure, Hidley interpreted the figure unabashedly and keenly, with slashing lines, vivid colours, and a sure knowledge of anatomy, apparent even when the figures were distorted or truncated. When asked "how long did it take to do this painting?" Hidley would reply, like James McNeill Whistler, "My whole life." He painted rapidly, but with the training and sensibilities of a lifetime guiding his brush. Students in his "Painting from the Model" class learned merely by watching him paint.

Students also learned from his insightful critiques, which sometimes left people in tears. But Hidley inspired students to paint, and paint they did. At his memorial service, Barry Cohen's eulogy observed, "Getting praise from Hidley was something to be proud of. But those of us close to him learned quickly that no kind act—if done not in an acceptable to Hidley manner—would go uncriticized."

Hidley's own words are the most eloquently descriptive of his work, as set forth in an article by then *Patriot News* arts writer Sandy Cullen on Sunday, August 2, 1998. Hidley was one of three artists being honoured at the time by AAH with a retrospective titled "Triad Tribute," the other two being the revered watercolourists Edward C. Michener and David F. Lenker. Of Abstract Expressionism, which rose to prominence in the 1950's, Hidley said, "I hate to say, it's passé. It's not being done much anymore." Sandy wrote that "At 77, Hidley continues to take it all in stride. 'I don't care at all. Que sera, sera,' he said in his characteristically pragmatic manner." He went on to say, "I'm willing to go with the flow, to the extent of my ability to do it. I would have loved to have been a surrealist. I would have loved to have been a sculptor. At some point, you just have to fold in your horns and do what you do best, or what it is you think you do best." He added, "It's too late for regrets. If I were 40, I would say, 'Oh God, why are things changing?' The good thing is that the change may make me go in a completely new direction."

Of the 25 paintings in the AAH exhibit, Hidley explained, "I thought these were the product of my old age. Maybe with my older age will be something new." Sandy Cullen wrote that the paintings in the AAH exhibit had all been done in the past ten years, and Hidley described them as "interior landscapes," reflecting the same creative process of "tapping into the archetypal images described by psychologist Carl Jung." Unlike his two fellow artists in the show, both "so meticulous and so technical," Hidley said he did his work "completely unconsciously. It's like automatic drawing or automatic painting. I just let the images come to me, dictated by the colour and forms that appear."

Hidley went on to say of his works in the exhibition, "I'm intrigued by the eroticism in them. I did not inject this element. It just happened. If you open up the portals of the unconscious, these elements come forth, which aren't demonstrable in any other aspect of one's life. I haven't been erotic for 10 years. I never was much of a hotshot anyway. It's all stuff that's been suppressed—not repressed, kept in reserve for another venue, which is painting."

The article mentioned the fact that Hidley was planning to teach a class in still-life at the Art Asssociation that fall. He emphasized that, "It's not Draconian. You don't have to do still life. If a painter comes to me and they have an agenda of their own, that's fine by me. I don't mean to have the stuff be representational. God forbid! You look at Braque and you look at Picasso and you look at Max Beckman—they all did still life. But they were compositionally inventive, which is what I hope to get across." He was looking forward to working with students again, saying, "I miss the exchange. Also, I can be influenced by their work."

Hidley was adamant that artists should never let concerns about where their work will be shown to restrict their creativity. He stated, "I used to say years ago, 'I'll exhibit my work anywhere, even in a subway men's room.' If you're not going to imbue your work with a personal quality, nobody's going to be interested in your work."

Sandy Cullen wrote that a "friend once asked him if he painted for money or fame." Hidley had incredulously replied, "In Harrisburg?" His friend then inquired, "Why do you do it?" "For me," Hidley had said. "I paint to do it."

The interview concluded with this quote from Hidley: "My walls are covered with artwork by other people. I'm not interested in my work when it's finished. I'm interested in the next one."

Now, the fourth floor "Hidley room" is filled with all his remaining paintings. And eerily, every time I go there to show his work to potential clients, it seems that there are new pieces there.

David F. Lenker, Beloved Watercolourist

David Lenker graduated from Lebanon Valley College in 1940 and began a seven-year stint as a commercial and military aviator, serving in the US Air Force for four years during World War II as a pilot and special agent in counter intelligence. He became involved in his family's dairy business after leaving aviation, and eventually became vice president of Lenkerbrook Farms. Dave married his lovely wife Nancy when he was forty, and they raised two daughters and a son.

After his retirement from the dairy business, Dave turned to painting full-time, and was President of the AAH Board in 1979-1980. Involved in a myriad of varied activities, Dave was also President of the Colonial Park Rotary Club, owned a small gallery/framing shop in Hummelstown for many years, and taught watercolour at The Art Association over 20 years, only retiring in 2005 when his eyesight prevented him from driving at night.

When Dave died at age 92 in 2009, *Patriot News* art columnist David Dunkle wrote a fine tribute to him entitled "A Life in Colour." He wrote that "artists packed David F.Lenker's watercolour classes as much to hear his colourful stories as to draw on his considerable painting skills." "He was famous for his stories," I said in the article. I went on to say, "People came back to his classes again and again, even some who became well-known painters in their own right." Dave Lenker's stories were of his experiences as an Army Air Forces pilot during World War II and working in counter-intelligence at the Pentagon after the war, as well as colourful tales about farming, life during the Great Depression, and the African safari he went on with his wife Nancy, a travel agent.

Nancy Lenker was laughingly quoted as saying about the safari, "He never recovered from that. He talked about it every day from then on."

Richard Michaelian, Dave's student who took over the class after Dave's retirement, quipped, "We still use some 'Lenkerisms' in the class. He'd say things like, 'With every painting, you learn something.' He was 90 years old when he told me that."

At the memorial service held for Dave at St. Andrews in the Valley Episcopal Church, just outside Harrisburg, among the speakers was fellow watercolourist and friend Erna Tunno, who had helped, along with Dave, to found the Pennsylvania Watercolour Society in 1979. "We had a mutual admiration for watercolours," said Erna. "That was our true bond."

David Dunkle went on to write that Nancy Lenker had married the 40-year-old bachelor farmer-painter, and that they'd had a happy life together. "He was such a great guy and a lot of fun," Nancy said. "All the years that the children were growing up, he would paint every day in the basement. He developed his own style."

Dave Lenker took a few art lessons, but was mostly self-taught. He patterned his realistic style after that of his idol, the famed watercolourist Andrew Wyeth, and his Art Association class description stated that he taught "The Brandywine Style." In fact, when Wyeth had died earlier in 2009, *The Patriot News* quoted Dave Lenker as saying, "His paintings make mine look like a piece of junk out in the yard, but he was a real influence on me." Dick Michaelian told David Dunkle that "Lenker was modest and quick with a joke, but had profound insights into painting." That was one of the reasons he continued to attend Lenker's AAH classes long after he was no longer "strictly a student."

Dick Michaelian remembered, "We weren't necessarily there for David to hold our hands, but he would come around and give us advice. And it was always good advice. I think David is up there right now, telling the Lord what colour of blue to paint the sky. I really do."

David Lenker's paintings and limited edition prints continue to delight viewers throughout the area. In 1990, when the Hilton

Harrisburg first opened, the hotel purchased prints of Lenker's "Star Barn" for all the guest rooms, and guests still visit the AAH Sales Gallery to look for prints to take home.

The Seven Lively Artists, A 56-Year-Old Art Institution

The Seven Lively Artists, now a loosely-organized group of nineteen painters, began in the fall of 1956 when Walt Huber, an accomplished landscape painter who also did editorial cartoons for *The Patriot News*, joined Bob Bartlett, owner of the Ad-Art advertising company in Camp Hill, in encouraging five of their friends from the commercial art world to embark on weekly painting expeditions. According to an extensive article by David Dunkle in *The Patriot News,* "In Central Pennsylvania" magazine, Earl Blust, brothers George and Meade Logan, Charles Krone, and Jack Slepicka became part of the fledging group.

David Dunkle wrote that in so doing, "They were following in the footsteps of artistic giants. Perhaps the most famous plein air painters are the French Impressionists, a late 19th-century group that included Claude Monet and Pierre-Auguste Renoir, and later, the Dutch-born painter Vincent van Gogh and Frenchman Paul Gaugin." In America, the landscape had been a favourite subject for artists throughout the 19th-century, with the famous Hudson River School in mid-century, followed by the American Impressionists, such as William Merritt Chase and Childe Hassam. But in the mid-20th century, landscape painting was being over-shadowed by new schools of painting, such as abstract expressionism, surrealism, and pop art. David Dunkle wrote that, "Into this miasma walked the Seven Lively Artists, eager to breathe new life into the time-tested art of painting landscapes. Group members had no delusions they were going to reverse the tide of art history, but they shared a commitment to plein air painting that continues today."

Earl Blust, the only surviving member of the original 1956 group, told David Dunkle for the article, "We never expected any fame, if that's what we got. We just loved to paint."

When Dunkle asked Blust where the name "The Seven Lively Artists" originated, he told him that Walt Huber may have been inspired by "The Seven Lively Arts," the title of a well-known book by Gilbert Seldes, a public television program, or even a Cole Porter musical. "No one seems quite sure, but the name stuck, and members continue to wear it with pride," Dunkle wrote.

Over the intervening years, many more artists joined the original seven, and the original chaps passed away. As of 2011, the Seven Lively Artists consisted of Bill Anderson, Earl Blust,

Dominick Brandt, Joseph John Dudding, Brian Eppley, Karl Foster, Jonathan Frazier, Paul Gallo, Barry Ginder, David Henry, Ralph Hocker, Robert Hughes, William T.Kerman, Don Lenker, John McNulty, Edward Webber, Steve Wetzel, John David Wissler, and Robert Zimmerman.

All the past and present Seven Livelies had or have connections to The Art Association of Harrisburg. Earl Blust has been on the AAH Board numerous times over the decades, and Karl Foster served as Life Study Workshop monitor from 1964 until 2009. Ted Webber was on the AAH Board for a time, and J. D. Wissler taught the popular Saturday Landscape Class for several years, to be followed by current instructor Steve Wetzel. Jonathan Frazier, a musician as well as an artist, performs for many AAH receptions, and has taught both Basic Oil Painting and Basic Drawing classes. Robert Hughes taught a figure drawing class at AAH for a time, and Paul Gallo, who taught Portraiture for a semester or two, now teaches Landscape.

The Seven Lively Artists have exhibited often at the Art Association throughout the years, both as a group and as individual artists. The group continues to meet for weekly Friday lunches, and paint together annually on Cape Cod, as well as other picturesque destinations. When jobs and weather cooperate, the Friday lunches end with the artists going out to paint afterwards.

Veteran artist Earl Blust sums it up by saying, “Painting together with this group of men is not only enjoyable, it is a tremendous learning experience. This group has been my inspiration.”

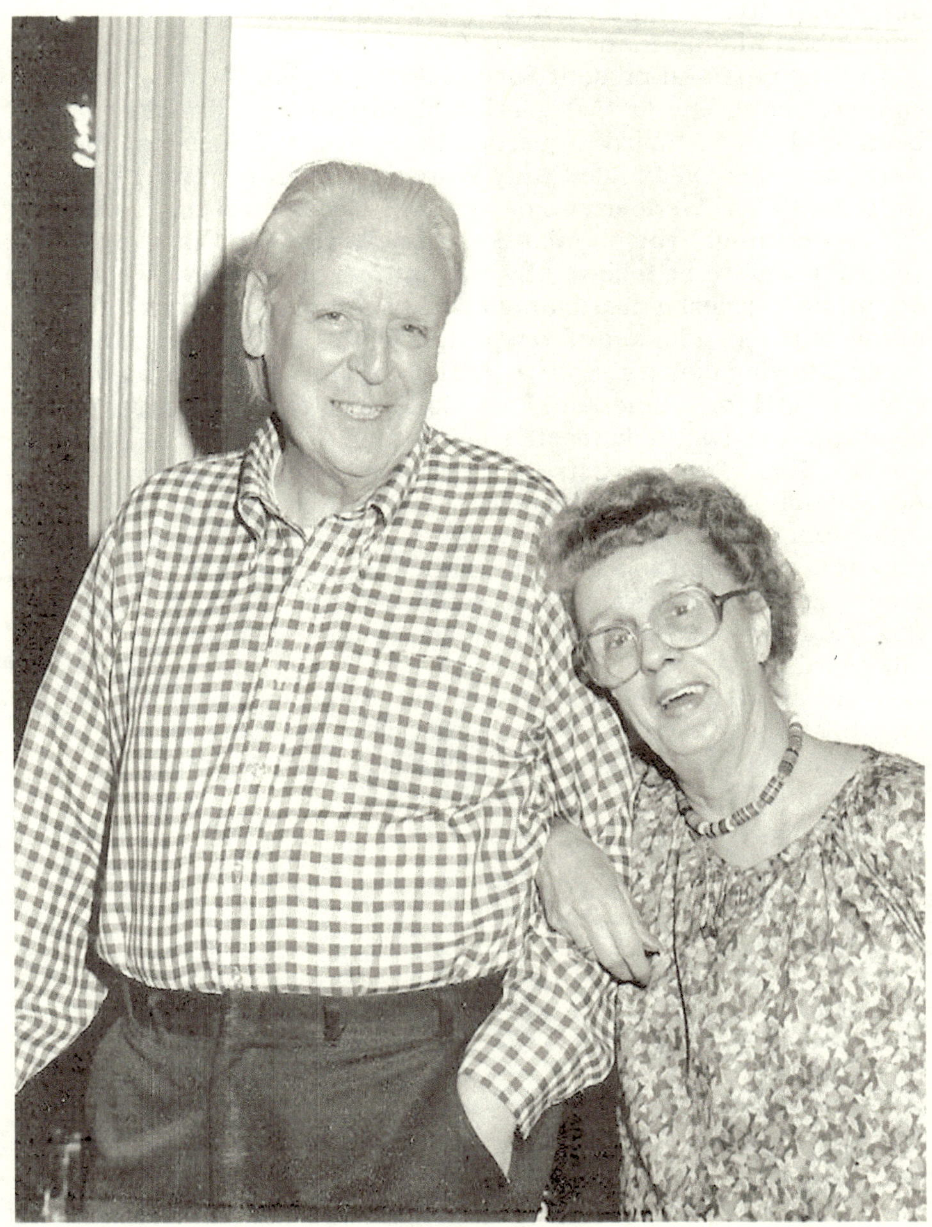

Hidley and Viola

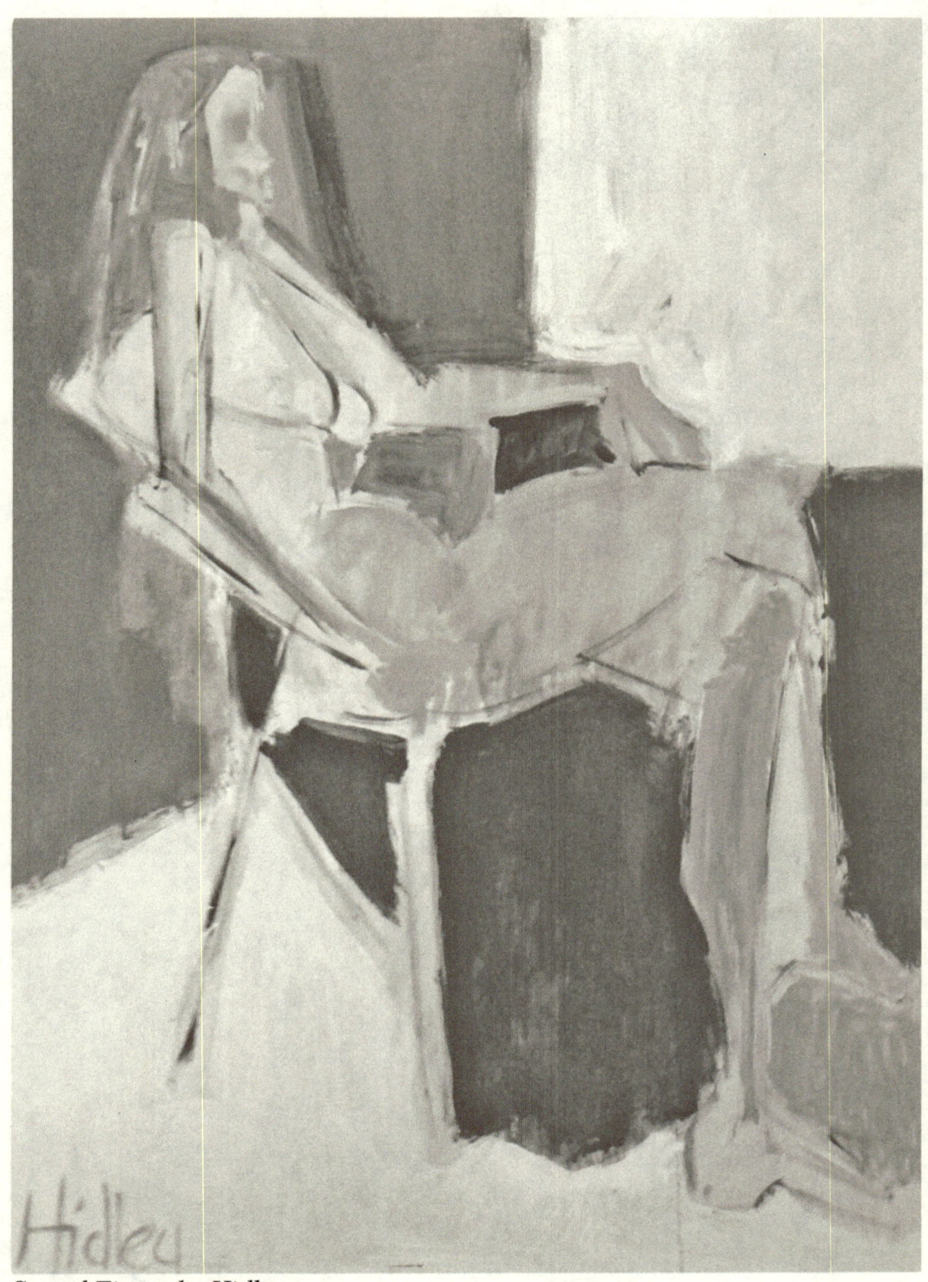

Seated Figure by Hidley

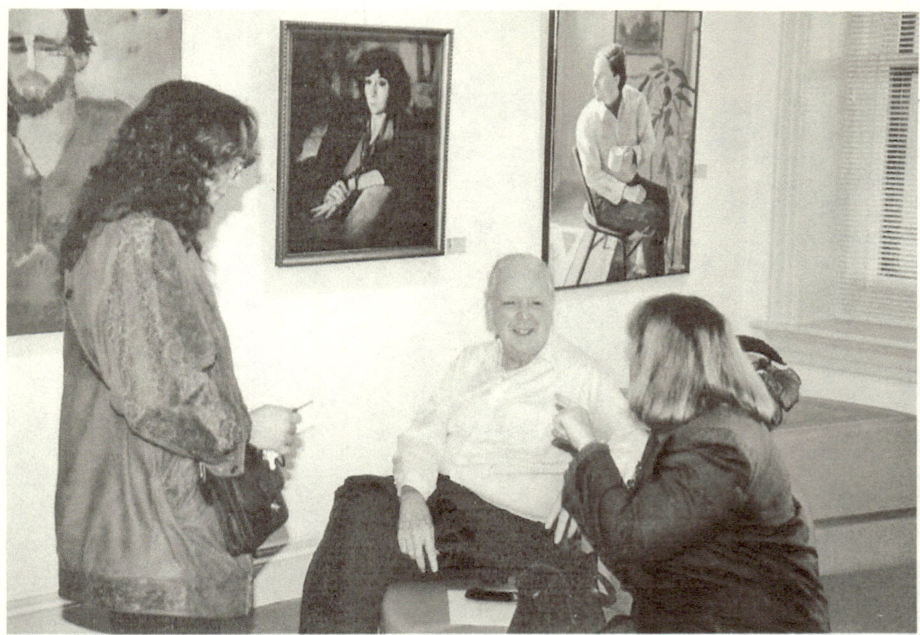

Hidley holding forth

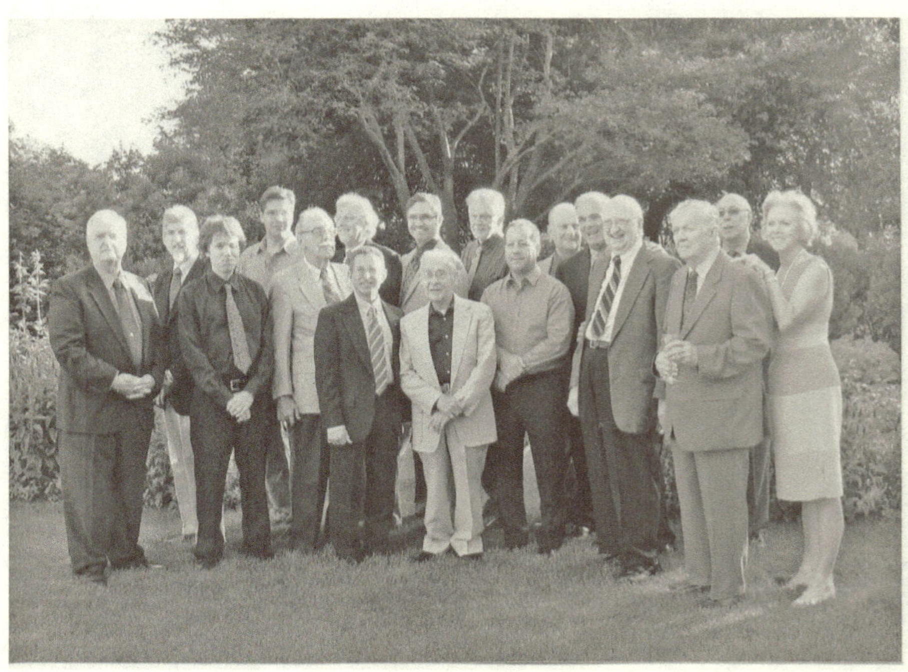

The Seven Lively Artists

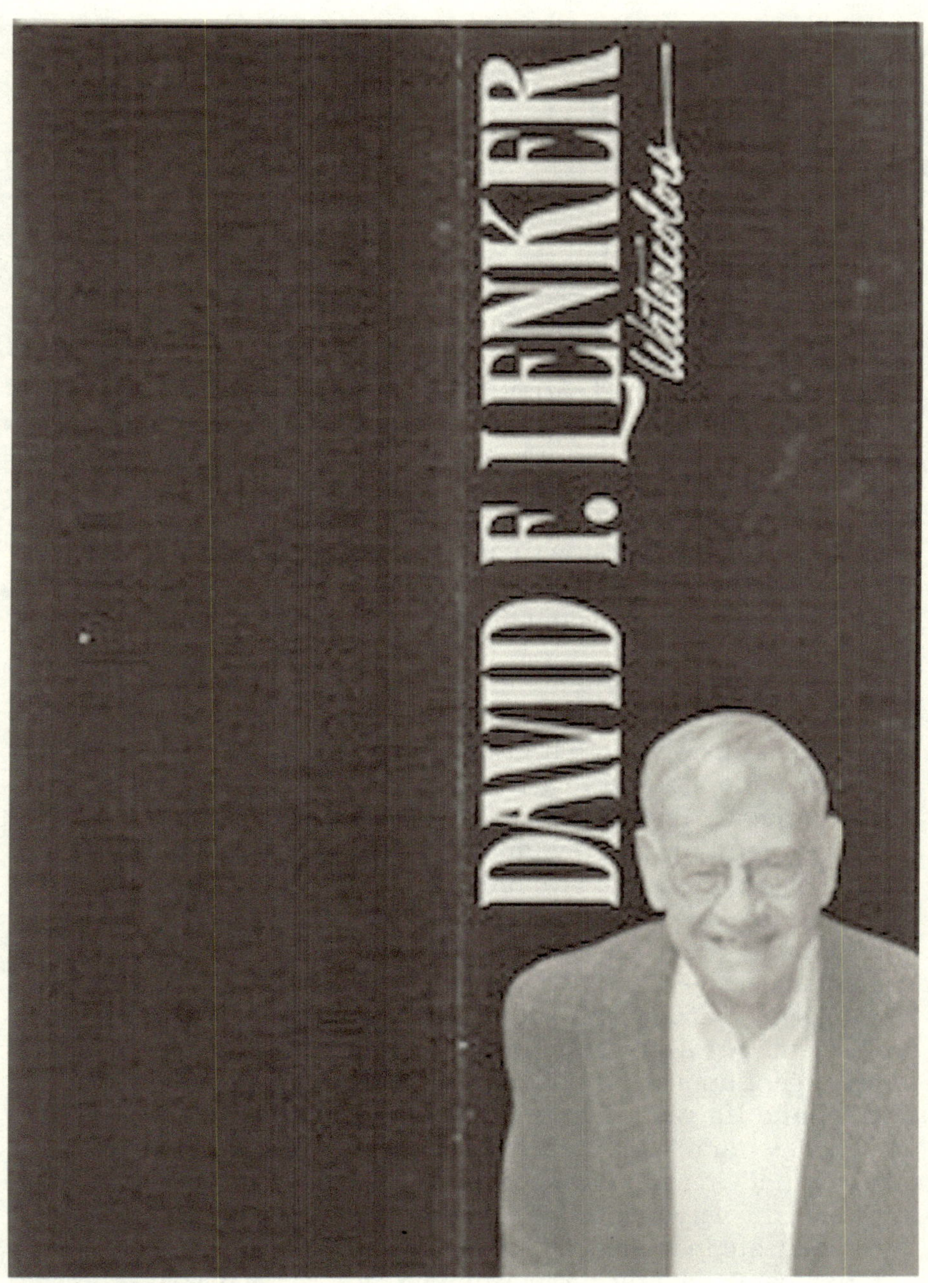

David F. Lenker

MY ASSOCIATION WITH AAH
TRACEY MELONI

I can honestly say that the Art Association saved, if not my life, then certainly my art-loving heart and soul. It also nourished my need for like-minded friends. And, ultimately, those friends have become like family.

As a diplomat's child, Army brat and Navy wife, “moving" is my middle name. In total I've moved 39 times. But the last one, a voluntary move to Harrisburg from the Washington, DC area, was both the best and the most difficult of moving decisions.

“Most difficult” because, unlike DC with its transient population eager to bond with other newcomers from elsewhere, all the Harrisburgers I met seemed to have full dance cards. They grew up here, making lifelong friends in church, school and neighborhood.

I am a free-lance writer who, in 2000 when I arrived here, was the sole arts correspondent in central PA for AOL’s online CityGuide and several other outlets. I needed a map to find my own way home, but it was exciting to set off in pursuit of art exhibits, theatre openings and festivals around the area.

More often than not my Philadelphia editor would ask for last-minute pieces (“can you give me this by tomorrow?")—and that meant finding a Reliable Source. Because she *was* the most reliable of art-event sources, I discovered and exploited—selfishly and shamelessly—Carrie Wissler-Thomas.

Burdened with looming deadlines and clueless that the very professional Art Association did not have a staff of twelve to cater to my urgent appeals, I relied upon Carrie not only for information on AAH and Harrisburg art events, but also those as far and wide as Lancaster and York. Nobody knew the art scene better.

Eventually reason dawned: I joined the Art Association mostly to receive the very helpful newsletter, and to give back something to compensate in some small way for all the help Carrie gave me.

Then came my first Bal Masque (“Secrets") I was sold—this had to be the best event of its kind I had attended since leaving Washington!

Summer Soirees came next—I enjoyed attending them so much that it was hard to resist the idea of hosting one—which became two, then three.

With each event—exhibit openings, soirees, Gallery Walk, Bal Masque—I met more people I was pleased to call friends. They were committed to the arts, to the community, to each other—the best kind of new friends. I am now in the first year of my third term on the Board, perhaps my proudest accomplishment.

Unfortunately, circumstances of late have made me a lax board member, but again the Art Association has given me support and friendship. The best evidence of that is my writing this alone, with affection for all I know at AAH.

I moved here in 2000 with my husband, Dr. C. Robert Meloni —Bob to his friends—who loved the Art Association and its efforts as much as I did. When I first joined the board, he was affectionately known as a cheerleading "Board In-law," one who encouraged art acquisitions, contributions, and other sponsorships. A jazz pianist by avocation, he loved his AAH gigs when asked.

When he died in August, my Art Association friends were again there with me, and perhaps the most memorable eulogy was given not by family members, but by my first friend at AAH and in Harrisburg, the woman I so imposed upon a decade ago: Carrie Wissler-Thomas.

I will never be able to thank the Art Association enough for welcoming a stranger to town, for adding me to the Board, and encouraging my love of art, for forgiving my often-absence, and for helping to make me whole again.

There can be no better definition of committed community friend.

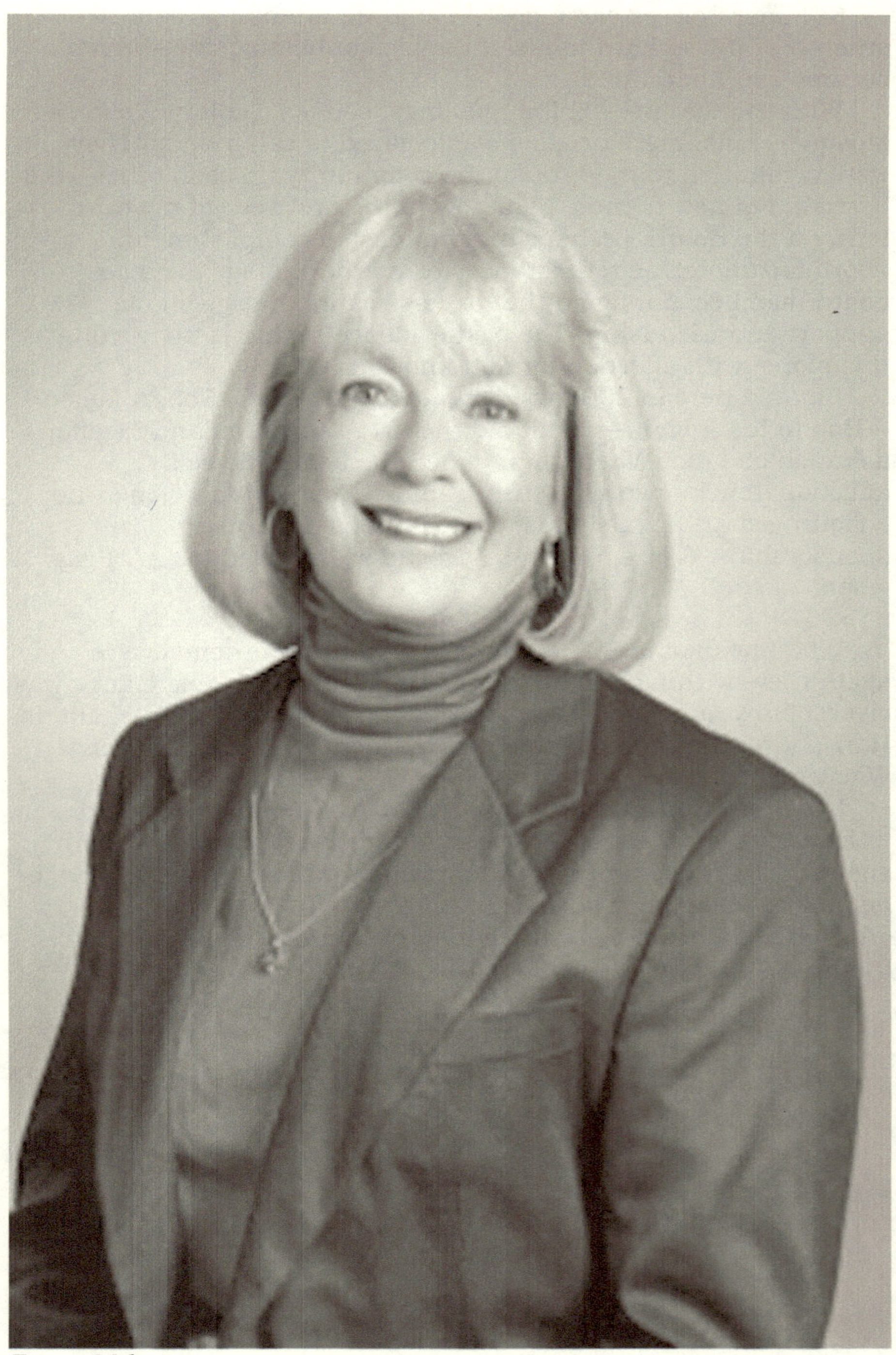

Tracey Meloni

A Note on Sources and Assistance

The history of The Art Association was relatively easy to research, because most of the source materials were right here in our archives at 21 North Front Street. In the archives are scrapbooks dating from 1926 through the present day, as well as all the organization's Board of Directors meeting minutes from 1926 through today. For the information on the formation of The Art Association, I borrowed the minutes from 1922 through 1925 from The Civic Club of Harrisburg. The scrapbooks are chock full of old newspaper clippings, exhibition catalogues, and other memorabilia. From 1986 through the 2000's are photograph albums that were a source for the illustrations of people and events in the modern era.

Edward C. Michener's booklet entitled "Personal Recollections of The Art Association of Harrisburg," written in 1997, was extremely helpful with the early history of the Art Association Studio, which evolved into the AAH School and then merged with the parent organization in the 1950's.

The AAH Permanent Collection was the source of the images of the artwork in the book. Semontee Mitra, a PhD student in American Studies at Penn State Harrisburg, compiled and digitized those images.

Dr. Michael Barton, known for his work on local history, recruited Semontee for our project. He consulted with me on the book and contributed to the writing and editing.

My own memory was jogged by going through the minutes and records from 1972 on, since I lived through it all. I joined AAH when my husband and I first moved here in 1972, so I have been involved with AAH forty-two years of the organization's eighty-eight years' existence. I feel as though I "channel" our founder Mrs. Gertrude Howard Olmsted McCormick every day, keeping her dream alive. And I even portrayed her in the Open Stage play, "Stories From Home II," in June 2013!

Both the book and my daily work at The Art Association of Harrisburg have been a labour of love.

www.ingramcontent.com/pod-product-compliance
Lightning Source LLC
LaVergne TN
LVHW090943080826
845145LV00003B/866

9781620065006